Advertising and Promotional Culture

P. David Marshall and Joanne Morreale

Advertising and Promotional Culture

Case Histories

 macmillan education palgrave

First published 2018 by
PALGRAVE

Palgrave in the UK is an imprint of Macmillan Publishers Limited, registered in England, company number 785998, of 4 Crinan Street, London, N1 9XW.

Palgrave® and Macmillan® are registered trademarks in the United States, the United Kingdom, Europe and other countries.

ISBN 978–1–137–02624–8 hardback
ISBN 978–1–137–02623–1 paperback

This book is printed on paper suitable for recycling and made from fully managed and sustained forest sources. Logging, pulping and manufacturing processes are expected to conform to the environmental regulations of the country of origin.

A catalogue record for this book is available from the British Library.

A catalog record for this book is available from the Library of Congress.

Contents

List of Figures

Acknowledgments

From its inception, this project has been an incredible collaboration. The value and direction of this book was originally built from our shared experiences of teaching an advertising course at Northeastern University in Boston and then David's experiences of rearticulating that work in a course at Deakin University in Melbourne, Australia. We both saw the need for developed and historically nuanced case studies that helped us better identify the way that advertising works, particularly where it has drawn on its past for its future and for where advertising has genuinely developed new approaches for promotion and communication. We want to thank our institutions, schools, and departments for their support of our thinking, research, and teaching in this area for over more than a decade.

In addition, we would also like to thank the many people who have helped with getting the ideas behind this book into tangible and presentable case histories. Praba Bangaroo, Adriana Szili, and Meylani Yo contributed research assistance to exploring particular companies. Dr Gerti Szili has been a valued editor and reader to ensure we effectively made connections between and among our chapters. Cassondra Dolan has helped find, procure, and display the very important advertising images contained in the text. Without the support of the editorial team at Palgrave Macmillan this final outcome would not have been realized. We want to thank in particular Jenna Steventon and Nicola Cattini for their resolute support for the value of the book, along with Lloyd Langman and Rebecca Barden for their work in the earlier incarnations of the book as a proposal and as a few model chapters.

David: I would also like to thank my family – Paul, Julia, Zak, and Erin – for their very valued support and their insights into the contemporary attention economy. In addition, I would like to thank my wonderful and beautiful wife Sally for all her love, encouragement, listening and invaluable advice that have helped in inestimable ways in the completion of this book and so much more.

Joanne: I'd like to thank Emma and Isabel for their support throughout the various stages of this project. I'm fortunate to have two smart and insightful daughters who love ideas, and I appreciate our many conversations about contemporary culture. And I couldn't have written this book without my husband, Richard, who has managed to keep me amused with his wit, engaged by his intellect, and grateful for his love for more than 30 years.

P. David Marshall
Deakin University,
Melbourne, Australia

Joanne Morreale
Northeastern University,
Boston, MA

The authors and publishers would like to thank the copyright holders for permission to reproduce the following copyrighted material:

Figure 3.1 Wanamaker's trade card, undated, which is courtesy of Historic New England.

Figure 11.1 Adbuster's parody of Obsession advertisement, which is reprinted with permission from Adbusters Media.

1

Introduction: The Strange Cases of Advertising

This book is about advertising. It addresses through rich case histories how advertising has developed and changed over time. Advertising is an interesting phenomenon. It is clearly a form of media and communication, but it also identifies, often in the most creative way, how economic motivations work their way through our media forms. Moreover, perhaps more than any other media and communication form, advertising has had to adjust and insinuate itself into the new spectrum of how media works in the era of online and mobile culture.

In contrast to a great deal of recent scholarship in media and communication which has focused on change and transformation (see for example Merrin 2015; Gauntlett 2015; Turner 2015), our study looks for the longer trajectories of how advertising's varied messages have been incorporated into culture. In the ever-changing media and culture-scape, it is vitally important to identify what has appeared in the past and how that patterning of media helps us understand what is developing in the present. All is not new, and it is important to not allow the overextended discourse of innovation to overwhelm our understanding of what parts of our cultural activity have a longer arc, have occurred in previous eras and have perhaps informed the constellation of newness that we allow to envelope our interpretations.

This book's intention is to look backward in order to make sense of contemporary advertising and consumer culture. Through a series of "case histories", *Advertising and Promotional Culture* explores how advertising has become a twinned discourse to modernity. This twinning to the future-oriented focus of modernity – to notions of progress, change, and transformation – describes how advertising has always been a way of communicating some sort of instability couched in terms of a pathway to a new level of satisfaction and fulfilment. We see this through concepts such as T.J. Jackson Lear's therapeutic ethos, which posits that the quest for self-fulfilment is the motor of consumer culture, or Wolfgang Haug's work on commodity aesthetics, which posits that seductive sensory appeals promise to satisfy unfulfilled aspects of the self.

Although advertising's intentions are simple – at the most basic level advertising is the expansion of sales of good or services – the way that it achieves this objective through its various messages and its connections to the living people of markets is complex and reveals a great deal about the way particular cultures and societies situate value. *Advertising and Promotional Culture: Case Histories* investigates these complexities through what we would call a deep structural analysis of the commodity sign: how a particular commodity form/product is expressed, promulgated, made new, and thereby integrated in some manner into the very fabric of everyday life. Histories of advertising usually point to it rivalling the oldest profession in terms of its ever-presence, but our work here underlines its increased deployment in the last two centuries. So, yes, a town crier advertising the pamphlets of the eighteenth century and the ancient realm of the agora and the bazaar are defined by competing voices connected to an array of products that are desgned to lure the consumer, but there is a qualitative difference in this earlier practice of what could be called forms of promotion and what now is understood as advertising. As much research has explored, the growth of advertising is wedded to the emergence of a consumer culture that some describe as a definable "anthropological type" of society (Leiss et al. 2005). The case histories in this book trace this development from the mid-nineteenth century in order to explore the key transformations from a producer-oriented to a consumer-oriented society. They identify the breakdown in the relation of both the production and distribution of goods and services that defined more traditional societies (a term that in and of itself generalizes to too great a degree the pre-nineteenth century relation to production). They also highlight how cultural meaning and communication become central aspects of consumption by the end of the nineteenth century.

As we discuss in Chapter 2, by the mid-nineteenth century the Industrial Revolution, which facilitated the "democratization" of goods, expanded the realms of choice and consumption available to the middle classes in both Europe and the United States. In this context, advertising developed as a form of communication and became an industry in its own right in order to make goods more appealing in a competitive marketplace. The production of desire became a central principle that guided advertising. While advertising agencies initially arose in order to help advertisers place their ads in newspapers and magazines, they quickly expanded to include copywriters to craft the persuasive language of ads, and then graphic artists to produce alluring images. The centrality of the advertising agency, and the range of functions and services it provides, has continued to grow into the twenty-first century as advertising has become integral to the way goods and services are distributed. The significance of this growth, expansion, and normalization of the advertising industry cannot be underestimated in its importance in understanding contemporary culture.

As advertising developed from the nineteenth to the twentieth century, several functions emerged that are still relevant today. We will see in our discussion of patent medicines, as well as other case histories we explore in the book, that much early advertising focused on the product and offered the consumer a reason for buying. Although advertising was clearly a discourse of persuasion, in a cultural milieu marked by the growing authority of science and medicine, advertising claims were often linked to the rational discourse of science. The re-expression of science through advertising often produced bizarre and overly bombastic claims that appeared in cigarette advertising as much as cereal promotions, drawing on the original puffery of patent medicine advertisements.

Beyond the seemingly rational reason for buying, advertising also communicated some aspect of the future via its persuasive tenor. Throughout its more than 150-year-old history, advertising has operated as an affirming discourse of the near future, a way of incrementally changing the status of the individual for some form of improvement. Because advertising's fundamental work is on transforming a potential consumer into a purchaser of a product or service, individual advertisements often herald what the individual can achieve through possession, whether the literal health benefits of a patent medicine or the symbolic attributes associated with a brand image. As we explore advertising's transformative discouse of the self throughout the book, one of our central themes concerns how advertising both creates and promises to fulfil desire for self-transformation through some form of consumption. As we move from brands as material symbols of production to brands as configurations of aesthetic, emotional, and social qualities, we see how they become resources for the construction of personal and social identity.

While advertising promises individual fulfilment, it simultaneously addresses the desire to belong. Klingman (2006, 56) writes, "a brand is both a personal and social identity, an expression of who we think we are and with whom we want or expect to be compared". Similarly, as Thorstein Veblen's original work in the early twentieth century on the "leisure class" and the cultural game of emulation first analysed (Veblen 1970), the desire for recognition and status, displayed through commodities, was essential to the formation of consumer culture. Advertisers' techniques were designed to draw on the cultural codes of reputation and prestige and somehow insinuate their product into how those codes were maintained or replicated. Reputation and prestige, however, are transformable codes. By the latter half of the twentieth century, rather than differentiating consumers by hierarchies of class, advertisers began to segment markets into increasingly niche groups of consumers defined by taste and "lifestyle". Prestige became associated with an array of goods for youth subcultures that bore no relation to the styles of the economic and cultural elites. For example, hipster style established a wholly different repertoire of prestige, from the choice of dress to the patterns of cosmetics that helped define what was significant and valued. While jeans were once a durable working-class staple, frayed, shredded, or torn jeans became hipster fashion statements that could cost hundreds of dollars. What is key here is how prestige, status, and value become determined by structures of emulative belonging.

In contemporary consumer culture almost every activity becomes a signifier of one's lifestyle and identity, so that consumers both express their desire for belonging and achieve recognition and social status through their shared affinities for products and brands. We refer to these as brand tribes: groups of consumers who share interests and tastes based around a product. In a global economy, consumers become members of a clan who are linked by brands rather than nation state. Members of a brand tribe do not buy products as much as they buy signifiers of a lifestyle or identity in order to increase social recognition and prestige. This new tribalism is another of the central themes that motivates our work.

Further, advertising from the nineteenth to twenty-first century has increasingly worked to engage consumers through participatory experiences. In the early stages of industrialization and mass production, consumers would seek out products and advertising would provide information about their attributes and benefits. But in a marketplace of competing, often similar, products, advertisers recognize the need to foster brand loyalty and connection through some kind of investment of the self. Testimonials and endorsements provide one kind of participatory experience, while trade cards for cigarettes and department stores, or box tops from cereal packages, also encouraged consumers to actively engage with a product. Similarly, it is a truism that consumers who build their own IKEA products feel more atttached to them than if they had been purchased already assembled. We examine the different forms of participation in early advertisements as they move towards the co-creation of meaning and the eventual blurring of the lines between consumer and producer, so that we end with the prosumer who is simultaneously a producer and consumer of meaning. Members of tribes express their identities through brands, but simultaneously help to produce and amplify the brand's meaning by participating in brand experiences – whether purchasing a branded piece of apparel, posting a message on a brand's website, liking a brand on Facebook, or even sending a viral video on to a friend. Consumers and brands mutually constitute one another, though we note in Chapter 12 that practices of brand management channel the production of value in the service of the brand. Throughout the book, we return to this theme of participatory engagement as it has evolved from the nineteenth century to the present.

Finally, advertising functions in all of its diversity as an attention-shifting form of communication, an element that perhaps is its most enduring characteristic. A billboard on the side of the road is designed to draw your attention. Similarly, a television commercial, if it is cleverly constructed, pulls you away from the programme you are viewing into the 30- or 60-second narrative orbit of its advertised product. An attractive model in a fashion magazine likewise draws your eye into a closer study of the hair product or cosmetics being depicted.

Online culture with its pre-content ads and its pop-ups serves as a remarkably similar form of distraction and attraction to these earlier forms. Because advertising is by design and focus all about attention, its past forms of attracting our eyes not only define contemporary advertising in many ways, they also help us understand other dimensions of the attention economy (see Goldhaber 2006). For example, even the presentation of news, which has traditionally been considered a discourse whose primary aim is to inform rather than persuade, is increasingly similar to the discourse of advertising. Major online news sites currently focus on producing "click-bait", which are small, attractive, image-rich, and alluring stories to pull the online reader into further stories. Similarly, information moves in what are now called "listicles", where "facts" are organized into top-10, best and worst lists for any type of content. Social media serves as a further passage to the news as Instragrammers, Pinteresters, Facebook wall and feed climbers, and Twitter users attempt to attract attention with phrases such as "if you are only going to read one story today, read this", or "you are not going to believe this story". Like advertising, these rely on techniques designed to attract the attention of "friends" and "followers" who, when interlinked, define the new audience and the new market of online culture. Both advertising and promotion inform this new culture of attraction and provide the basic interlinked communicative techniques of both distraction and attention. We explore this final theme by examining how advertising seeks to capture attention by blurring the categories of advertising, news, art, education, or entertainment. In so doing, advertising, to borrow from the infamous words of Guy deBord (1967), "has attained the total occupation of social life".

Organization of Chapters

This book makes the past of advertising and promotion legible in the contemporary moment through a comprehensive reading of its forms of communication. *Advertising and Promotional Culture: Case Histories* takes 11 case histories of advertising and promotion and explores in-depth the way that they form the meaning of the product itself – its sign value – and have informed the organization of advertising as a nineteenth to twenty-first century privileged discourse.

Each of our cases positions the significance and importance of various approaches to advertising differently: collectively, the case histories allow us to address many theoretical positions and weigh their value in making sense of advertising in contemporary culture. Our case histories provide parallel and overlapping maps of how advertising and the advertising industry works. Thus, you will find that our case histories are not contained by a single campaign. For instance, our study of cigarettes in Chapter 4 maps the advertising industry's relationship to selling tobacco over more than a century and then isolates one of its most provocative campaigns in the 1990s. We have also made very direct choices about our case histories so that they are designed specifically to explain the position of advertising in the larger fields and operations of promotion and marketing. These various promotional pathways appear in our case history of Annoying Orange in Chapter 12, but also in the ambient approaches to advertising privileged in selling cereal to families in Chapter 5, a case that studies 70 years of presenting a range of products. Similarly, our study in Chapter 11 of Dove's efforts at social activism also points to how advertising campaigns are rarely contained within the text, images, and graphics of display ads and commercials.

Each of our case histories is structured for two related purposes. First, through individual case histories we have tried to stitch together a valuable reading of advertising from the nineteenth century to the twenty-first century. Thus, you will see that in general, the case histories at the beginning of the book – the development of patent medicines and the birth of the department store, the marketing of Camel cigarettes, and the ambient advertising of children's cereals – have origins in the nineteenth century and then move into the twentieth century. The case histories of Volkswagen, IKEA, and Nike that follow describe the rise of multinational corporations in the mid-twentieth century, though they also have precursors and have continued to advance well into the twenty-first century. The final group of case histories – which explore presidential politics, self-branding, commodity activism, and the YouTube prosumer – are analytically focused on the contemporary as advertising has become inextricably related to identity.

Our second objective was to use the best case histories to explain a particular, peculiar but important, aspect of advertising. One of the most interesting elements of advertising is its very ubiquitousness. However, in its very particular dimensions of cultural and social activity, we see some very specific and innovative developments emerge in advertising. There is no question that one of the fascinating elements of patent medicine advertising and promotion, for example – which we explore in-depth in Chapter 2 – is that the practices helped define the emergence of consumer culture itself. In a similar vein, our case history in Chapter 3 on department stores further identifies the naturalization of the experience and pleasure of shopping as these megastores attempted to produce a sensorium of attractions to lure the individual into the possibilities of transformation through buying and consumption.

Because our study in Chapter 4 focuses on cigarettes through the long history of Camel, conceptually it has two objectives. First, cigarette manufacturers happened to be one of the earliest adopters of advertising agencies to make their products move nationally and, ultimately, internationally. This case history allows us to focus on the industrial organization of advertising with all its various creative and research subsidiaries. Second, the case history of Camel cigarettes points to techniques of innovation that have been used more broadly in advertising. Cigarettes are a product with a very tainted history – after all, from its earliest incarnation, smoking was seen to be unhealthy; yet cigarettes have consistently circumvented waves of negative publicity and regulation through clever marketing and advertising. This case history explores those techniques with its focus on the Camel brand over many decades.

Chapter 5 uses the complex relationship between children and advertising to build a case history of understanding what we are calling "ambient advertising". Ambient advertising refers to techniques of promotion that surround a product with activities that enrich the experience of the product itself. Through the example of children's cereal advertising and promotion, the case history explores the way that products become part of popular culture. In addition, from the first decades of the twentieth century to the present, cereals have been linked to children's health and betterment. Paralleling this form of promotion was the effort to make cereals a form of play for children through the creation of promotional products and toys, the development of characters and shows, and the incredible focus on children themselves as the primary market for the family's food-buying practices.

Chapter 6's case history involves the car manufacturer Volkswagen. The case history is a study of how advertising in the middle decades of the twentieth century became self-reflexive of its own industry and outwardly linked to new trends in popular and political culture. The selling of the VW Beetle is a beautiful case history in how difference in a product is linked to differences in a culture and generates potential attractions in a segmented mass market.

Via the case history of IKEA, Chapter 7 focuses on the relationship between design and advertising from the mid-twentieth century to the present. IKEA, the Swedish furniture company, has developed a sophisticated conceptual understanding of its wide array of products as distinctive from all other furniture products because of their design features and IKEA's business practices. IKEA is notable for designing a unified corporate image and product. It has developed both a look and a sensibility about the superiority of their product through the inherent culture and ethics of their designs.

Behind the case history of Nike, Chapter 8 considers the relationship advertising has to globalization. Expanding markets is one of the essential motivations of capitalism, and the discourse of advertising is essential for the transnational movement of goods and services as advertising works to construct its allures through these new markets. As a sport shoe and clothing manufacturer, Nike has used the transnational nature of sport to move products more and more widely. Interestingly, Nike has also recognized that globalization can mean that the design and advertising message of a given product can be divorced from its manufacturing source. The case history demonstrates how advertising has helped situate brands in cultural spaces that express the ultimate ethical sense of sporting objectives as the other possible ethical messages, for example, how Nike products are manufactured, become minimized.

Chapter 9 works to identify how advertising has become a naturalized partner of politics. With political elections, in some way or another a form of promotional campaign, politics has represented one of the most innovative spaces in advertising as a form of communication. The case history maps how advertising has been both limited and structured into international politics and then focuses on the advertising history of American President Barack Obama's two presidential campaigns. What this case history underlines are two developments that are endemic to advertising: the massive amount of effort that has focused on market research and the considerable transformation of political advertising in its integration of online forms of promotion in concert with other media campaigns.

Chapter 10 investigates the expanding world of brands and branding. Via its case history of perfume promotion, the chapter reveals how branding works in contemporary culture, how it constructs a new system of value beyond other forms of financial value, and ultimately how it has led to the adoption of self-branding as one way to promote the self in the contemporary world. Perfume manufacturing has been increasingly focused on personalizing fragrances through attaching them to celebrities and their partially pre-constructed personas. This model of self-branding that the perfume industry has drawn from the wider entertainment industry has now been expanded to the way that much of online culture is currently constructed. Many individuals engage with the world by self-branding; it is an accepted form of identity, as promotional culture normalizes what might have in the past been seen as an inappropriate presentation of self.

Our last two chapters deal with more current developments in advertising. In the latter two decades of the twentieth century, an anti-consumer movement that targeted specifically advertising emerged, generating protests from the well-known Adbusters magazine to the graffiti-like interventions on advertising billboards throughout the world, both of which aggressively tried to alter the meaning of ad campaigns and challenge consumers to think of the other political and cultural ramifications of consumer culture. Advertising is an incredibly adaptable discourse and, in the early part of the twenty-first century, products increasingly appropriate resistance to consumption and define themselves in terms of "commodity activism": through the purchase and support of particular products such as fair trade coffee or the hybrid electric car, consumers feel that they have made ethical and responsible purchases that contribute to social change. Chapter 11 looks at how Dove, a brand deeply connected to the beauty industry, repositioned itself as a socially responsible company whose array of products reflected a new "anti-beauty" beauty campaign that tied purchasing a product to female empowerment.

Our last case history in Chapter 12 identifies the new level in which products and consumers establish some sort of close and affective bond in the era of online culture. One of the interesting developments in the twenty-first century has been the encouragement of consumer-generated online content. The array of videos on YouTube reflect this self-generation; but they also identify how products and services have insinuated themselves into the forms of communication and exchange that are part of Web 2.0. This new variation of advertising, promotion, and consumer culture has fostered a culture of prosumption, where consumers are simultaneously producers of media content. Our case history of the YouTube webseries *Annoying Orange* explores both the monetization and activation of online "prosumer" structures to demonstrate how advertising has adapted to our shifting attention economy in the digital age in ways that work in the service of brands.

Through these 11 case histories that span from the mid-nineteenth century to the present, *Advertising and Promotional Culture: Case Histories* illuminates how advertising has adapted to changing cultural, political, economic, and technological environments. Advertising simultaneously represents constancy (in terms of how an enduring attention economy has defined consumer culture since the nineteenth century) and change (in terms of how advertising obsessively provides a discourse of the new and innovative). Each case history can stand on its own in terms of how it helps reveal some major aspect of advertising. Nonetheless, there is a strength in reading these case histories in a connected way to help identify the recurring patterns and directions in advertising. Whatever way you engage with the subsequent chapters, these case histories will develop our understanding of how contemporary consumer culture has functioned and flourished in a codependent way with advertising's sometimes bizarre, distracting, attracting, powerful, innocuous, and alluring discourse.

To extend our work even further, we have made a concerted effort to pull all of these various exemplifications, strands, and theories together in our book's Conclusion, as it ambitiously and perhaps provocatively identifies how the particular and peculiar advertising and promotional pathways these case histories have privileged now operate in contemporary culture. Here we reinforce the four main themes that animated our case studies and provided a link from past to present. We describe how individual chapters address each of the following: how advertising imagines the future through the promise of transformation, how tribalism/market segmentation creates a sense of collective identity organized around a product, how advertising builds engagement through participation/prosumption, and how the blurring of advertising, news, art, education, and entertainment characterizes the attention economy. All of these themes can be traced back to the origins of consumer culture, and while they have adapted to accord with new technologies, they remain central foci for understanding the contemporary milieu and future directions for advertising. For both the advertising practitioner and the scholar of advertising, we are hoping our case histories provide insight into the often overlooked links between our past forms of advertising and promotion and what is often perceived as our inchoate present moment.

2

From Production to Consumption:
The Rise of Patent Medicines

We begin our study of advertising by relating the emergence of consumer culture to the Industrial Revolution, which emerged in the period from 1750 to 1850. While multiple factors contributed to the rise of consumption, with the groundwork laid long before the Industrial Revolution, there is little dispute that the late eighteenth century marked an explosion of new production and marketing techniques and led to a revolution in consumption patterns. Concomitantly, more people than in any other time in history had access to consumer goods (McKendrick et al. 1982). As we explore the shift from a production-based to consumption-based society, we relate the formation and development of consumer culture to T.J. Jackson Lears concept of the therapeutic ethos and Karl Marx's formulation of commodity fetishism. These illuminate two core principles that are foundational to our work: advertising promises that products will fulfil the self, and products create sign values through which people construct their identities. We selected our case study of patent medicines, which became prominent in the nineteenth century, because they are emblematic of the interplay of advertising, the therapeutic ethos, and commodity fetishism that came to characterize consumer culture in the United States.

Origins of Consumer Culture

The Industrial Revolution signified a radical change in social, economic, and cultural conditions in Europe and the United States. According to most accounts, it originated in Great Britain and then spread to the rest of Europe and North America. Trade expansion, made possible by the building of canals and railways, innovations in the cotton industry, the use of steam engines and coal as power sources, iron making, and the creation of the machine tool industry fundamentally altered everyday life. As populations began to amass in urban centres, there were new levels of prosperity and opportunities for social mobility. While even as far back as the sixteenth century, many people in European societies purchased goods rather than producing their own (Mukerji 1983, cited in Sassatelli 2007, 33), living standards improved as mass production made a wider array of goods available for purchase. The mass manufacture and advertising of new goods produced an unprecedented propensity to consume. Indeed, McKendrick et al. (1982) note that the ability for the middle classes to purchase different types of clothing and the consequent emphasis on fashion were fundamental markers of the emergence of consumer society in Britain.

Throughout the nineteenth century, both Europe and the United States shifted away from an agriculture-based society to an industrial one, with huge influxes of the population moving to towns and cities. In the United States, urban centres grew rapidly; for example, by 1880, over half of the population of New England, New York, New Jersey, and Pennsylvania lived in cities, while New York City alone had over a million inhabitants (Benson 1979, 199). Overall, the proportion of Americans living in towns of 2500 or more increased from just 6% in 1800 to 46% by 1910 (Starr 1982, 69). In Europe, a similar pattern of urbanization took hold: according to Trentman, "in 1800, 12% of Europeans lived in towns. By 1910, it was 41%" (2015, 174).

By around 1850 in the United States, often referred to as the beginning of the Second Industrial Revolution, there was a massive increase in the production of goods due to the rise of factories, while better transportation meant products could be moved across the country. Large quantities of standardized products became available for the first time, which necessitated advertising to build awareness and desire. As Ackerman (1997, 115) notes, advertising was the handmaiden of industrialization that allowed producers to foster demand. Business growth allowed, and indeed depended on, the creation of new commercial institutions, new advertising strategies, and new ways of life centred on modern consumption.

In the United States, national advertising began in the period just before the Civil War, when there was a steady stream of new inventions and more goods and services available to advertise. While the early American household was largely self-sufficient, with families making their own food, clothes, furniture, household utensils, farm implements, and building materials, by 1830 the transition to factory-made goods was nearly accomplished, and by 1860 the factory, aided by improved transportation, supplied manufactured goods (Starr 1982, 66). By the 1880s, a national network of railroads, an industrialized system of mass production, westward expansion, and a large population in urban centres made a national marketplace for advertised goods and services possible.

While consumption has always been part of material culture, consumer society, where goods have become the principal aspiration, source of identity, and leisure activity for great numbers of people, emerged in the nineteenth century (Ackerman 1997, 108). As Sturken and Cartwright (2001, 193) assert, "It has been argued that in consumer societies people derive their sense of their place in the world and their self-image at least in part through their purchase and use of commodities, which seems to give meaning to their lives in the absence of the meaning derived from a closer-knit community." As people moved into cities and away from agrarian lifestyles, the distance between public sphere of work and the domestic sphere of home increased, and concepts of self and identity became constituted outside of the family. Gagnier (2000) writes about the shift from a society oriented towards production to a consumer society, and the idea of Economic Man as productive pursuer of gain to a consumer who ranked his preferences and chose among scarce resources. She asserts that in the shift to a consumer society, modern man became known by the insatiability of his desires. Accordingly, she writes, "His nature, insatiability, was henceforth human nature itself. His mode, consumer society, was no longer one stage of human progress but its culmination and end, the end of history" (Gagnier 2000, 4).

Lears (1983), in his classic essay, "From Salvation to Self-Realization: Advertising and the Therapeutic Roots of Consumer Culture 1880–1930", argues that shifts in economic structures, from a production-based to consumption-based society, occurred concurrently with a shift in values in the late nineteenth and early twentieth century. Advertising, whose role in promoting a consumer culture occurred within a nexus of institutional, religious, and psychological changes, both influenced and reflected this shift. The character structure of the nineteenth century was shaped by the Protestant ethic, where dominant cultural values were thrift, saving, perpetual work, civic responsibility, and the morality of self-denial (characterized by the belief that you would be rewarded in the next life). In the United States, most of the population consisted of Puritans, and thus much has been written about the influence of Protestantism on the American character and value system. According to sociologist Daniel Bell (1976, 55), who draws very different conclusions than Lears (1983, 55), "The Protestant ethic and the Puritan temper emphasized work, sobriety, frugality, sexual restraint, and a forbidding attitude toward life. They defined the nature of moral conduct and social responsibility." For Lears, the decline of the Protestant ethic correlated with the decline of religious authority, while for Bell it signalled a new, debilitating cultural permissiveness. From another vantage, Max Weber's *The Protestant Ethic and the Spirit of Capitalism*, written in 1904, also argued that there was a relationship between the Protestant mentality and the development of capitalism, a relationship that influenced much of Europe and North America. Weber presented the thesis that the values of hard work and asceticism at the core of the Protestant ethic made it possible for capitalism to flourish. This ethic was the world view of an agrarian, small-town, mercantile, and artisan way of life; its key, according to Bell (1976, 56), was that it provided meaning and justification for work and restraint in subsistence economies.

For both Lears and Bell, the early twentieth century marked the transformation to modern consumer culture in the United States. By the turn of the century, business and industry were expanding at a remarkable pace, with their new power undermining the traditional potency of family, church, and community. Lears (1983) suggests that as Americans became increasingly urbanized, along with having more leisure time and discretionary income, they also became more alienated as they found themselves unmoored in a sea of technological changes. In the transition from farms to factories, they became disconnected from work and production as a source of satisfaction, and so sought fulfilment through consumption. As Gagnier (2000) observes, the nineteenth century may be characterized by the pursuit of material well-being, scientific knowledge, and political emancipation. But by the end of the nineteenth century, there was for the first time surplus and excess, as production and leisure time increased. Material well-being and the labour that produced it became less significant (so much so, Gagnier notes, that Lyotard dropped material well-being from his account of the master narratives of the twentieth century). Instead, she asserts that the dominant narrative of the twentieth century may well be "reducible to a single dominant narrative about the total actualization of individual pleasure" (Gagnier 2000, 1). The promise of future betterment that is central to advertising took root as insatiable wants and desires replaced needs, which are finite.

Consumer Culture and the Therapeutic Ethos

Lears (1983, 4) articulates the shift to the insatiability of wants through the concept of the therapeutic ethos, broadly characterized as "an almost obsessive concern with mental and physical health", as a dominant cultural value. The therapeutic ethos emerged in the late nineteenth century as communal, ethical, and religious frameworks were eroding. These societal changes thus help explain the shift from a production to consumer society. In contrast to the Protestant ethos that emphasized self-restraint and reward in the after-life, the therapeutic ethos stresses the possibility of self-fulfilment in this life. While the values that characterized the Protestant work ethic were necessary in the early stages of the market society, consumer society depended upon people who would indulge freely. As the therapeutic ethos emerged in psychology, social science, religion, and popular magazines in the twentieth century, "abundance therapy" replaced themes of control, self-restraint, and conserving energy: letting oneself go, releasing one's potential, and being spontaneous. Unlike the self-restraint imposed in Protestant culture, people could consume freely and be absolved from guilt or sin, because they were "improving" themselves. The Protestant ethos made sense for a society of scarce resources that required thrift and conservation, while the therapeutic ethos fit a society that offered abundance and encouraged pursuit of pleasure. Daniel Bell (1976, 33) writes, "The glorification of plenty, rather than the bending to niggardly nature, became the justification of the system." Consumer society both val-orized, and depended upon, leisure, spending, immediate gratification, and belief in self-fulfilment through the acquisition of goods. From the nineteenth to the twentieth century, production as source of gratification became super-seded by consumption, and the therapeutic ethos overtook the Protestant ethos as the dominant value system.

As the therapeutic ethos was manifest in cultural practice, its theme became that people can find meaning, whether conceptualized as gratifica-tion, fulfilment, or well-being, through commodities. While all people may be preoccupied with physical and emotional well-being, the therapeutic ethos was unique in its promise to create a sense of self through consump-tion. Lears (1983, 4) suggests that in contrast to earlier times, at the turn of the century, "The quest for health was becoming an entirely secular and self-referential project, rooted in peculiarly modern emotional needs – above all the need to renew a sense of selfhood that had grown fragmented, diffuse, and somehow 'unreal'." He adds, "And the longings behind that ethos – the fretful preoccupation with preserving secular well-being, the anxious concern with regenerating selfhood – these provided fertile ground for the growth of advertising and for the spread of a new way of life" (Lears 1983, 4). In part, the therapeutic ethos was a response to the loss of autonomy as people moved from rural, self-regulating environments to an increasingly urban and cor-porate landscape where they felt isolated. The sense of unreality engendered became a search for self-fulfilment as the way to resolve feelings of aliena-tion and regain a stable sense of identity. Advertising spoke to fundamental anxieties and identity crises and offered harmony, vitality, and the prospect of self-realization. The therapeutic ethos was the foundational principle behind advertising – that products would transform the self by providing physical, psychic, or social well-being (or conversely, it implied that the consumer would suffer if they did not purchase the product).

Advertising became what Raymond Williams (1980, 185) refers to as a "magic system" of inducements and satisfactions akin to magical systems in traditional societies. He writes that advertising is central in modern culture because of its perceived ability to fulfil us, or in his words, of "bringing the good things of life". He laments that while modern culture is often criticized for excessive materialism, in fact it is not material enough. If we were concerned with materiality rather than intangible benefits, he writes, "Beer would be enough for us, without the additional promise that in drinking it we show ourselves to be manly, young in heart, or neighborly" (Williams 1980, 185). Williams is referring to the promise of advertising encapsulated in Lear's notion of the therapeutic ethos: products will transform us.

The Appearance of Commodity Fetishism

As first articulated in Marxist theory, every commodity has a use value that refers to its function, as well as an exchange value that refers to its worth in the marketplace when it is offered in exchange for other goods. Use value expresses a relationship between people and objects, so that, for example, beer quenches thirst. Exchange value, on the other hand, appears to express a relationship between objects, but for Marx, this appearance is the basis of commodity fetishism. Commodity fetishism is the inevitable outcome of mass production and advertising practices in a market society. As the market expands, more and more elements of both the natural environment and human qualities become objectified forms, or commodities, with both use and exchange value, but at the same time, the preponderance of goods masks the social relations involved in their production and consumption. Thus, commodities have an enigmatic or mysterious character; they reveal their capacity to satisfy wants and desires and to communicate social meanings, but they simultaneously mask the context in which they are made and the labour required to produce them. In this way, fundamentally, social relationships appear to be relationships between objects that exist outside the realm of the social. Through advertising and marketing, objects are emptied of the meanings attached to their exchange value and instead acquire a sign value, a set of symbolic meanings or associations. According to (Sennett 1976, 145) they become "social hieroglyphics" that divert attention from the social conditions under which they are made to the objects themselves, which acquire a meaning and set of associations that go beyond their use. Moreover, although Marx saw use value as intrinsically rooted in human needs, in a sophisticated market economy even use value is socially constructed. As Myers (1986, 170) writes, "the construction of use values, and the transformation of those values into meanings identifiable by the consumer, constitutes the central role of advertising practice. The act of producing values and meanings simultaneously provides identities for commodities and consumers." Commodity fetishism thus refers to the "masks" in which goods appear to offer the possibility of fulfilment. Raymond Williams states (1980, 185), "we have a cultural pattern in which the objects are not enough but must be validated, if only in fantasy, by association with social and cultural meanings which in a different cultural pattern might be more directly available." In a statement that evokes Williams's (1980) comment on beer, Burt Manning, CEO of J. Walter Thompson, encapsulates the commodity fetishism at the heart of modern day advertising: "People don't always drink the beer; they drink the advertising. The brand selected by beer drinkers is in some way a badge. People tend to associate certain characteristics with a brand, and that becomes their statement to the world: This is what I believe. This is my badge. When you see me drinking this beer, this is something you know about me" (Wayne 1985). In this cultural pattern, "brand tribes" often emerge that unite consumers through their shared loyalty to a particular brand.

Consumer culture is in this way related to the idea that people construct their identities and form group affinities through products. As Stuart Ewen writes about the "commodity self", subjectivities are mediated through the consumption and use of commodities (Sturken and Cartwright 2001, 198). Advertising creates an abstract world of signs that appear to transform the self, as objects become commodities that promise to fulfil desires. But desires are, of course, endless, and thus fulfilment is always deferred.

Case History: Patent Medicines and Lydia Pinkham's Vegetable Compound

Patent medicines were one of the earliest sources of national advertising in the United States (Goodrum and Dalrymple 1990, 16). They exemplify products that claim to provide well-being, and their growth in popularity parallels the rise of the therapeutic ethos from the nineteenth into the twentieth century.

Patent medicines were pills or nostrums, typically concocted by a layperson rather than a medical doctor, that promised to cure any number of maladies. They first became proprietary medicines in England when King James II granted a "letters patent" to the maker of Anderson's Scots Pills in 1687. The patent was a legal document that offered endorsement by the King and granted exclusivity so that no one could replicate the formula. Patent medicines moved to the American colonies from Britain and were widely used beginning in the eighteenth century. For example, one of the first English patent medicines shipped to the American colonies was Elixir Salutis: The Choise [sic] Drink of Health or Health-bringing Drink, Being a Famous Cordial Drink (see Figure 2.1). It claimed to cure gout, kidney and bladder stones, languishing and melancholy, shortness of breath, tuberculosis, scurvy, dropsy, rickets, pestilence, ague, and the "king's evil", a tubercular infection of the lymph nodes in the throat (Dary 2008, 245). At first, most patent medicines consisted of these cure-alls, though manufacturers soon learned that it was more profitable to market drugs for specific ailments (Applegate 1998).

Until the twentieth century, there were no laws to control what ingredients went into products or what benefits a maker could claim without offering proof, and ingredients did not need to be specified. Most patent medicines were herbal concoctions, and some, such as those that contained quinine or digitalis, had medicinal value. But many were, like some drugs today, prone to medicalize everyday symptoms such as fatigue, nervousness, headaches, or indigestion and to promise an instant cure. According to Young (1960, 656), "Small symptoms were exaggerated and normal physiological phenomena converted to dread signs of incipient pain and death. Thus patent medicine men sought not only to prescribe for the sick. They sought to make men sick so that they might be made well again by the expensive therapy of patent medicines." Moreover, many patent medicines contained harmful or addictive substances. Medicines for infants, such as Mrs. Winslow's Soothing Syrup, or Dr. Winchell's Teething Syrup, contained morphine. Products such as Ayers Cherry Pectoral contained heroin, Birney's Catarrh Powder contained cocaine, Jayne's Expectorant contained opium, and Piso's Cure for Consumption contained cannabis. Others used calomel, a mercury compound that supposedly cleaned out the system but was in fact a poison. One of the most popular medicines during the Civil War was Peruna, given to soldiers for catarrh, which contained up to 28% alcohol. In fact, most patent medicines consisted of 20% to 40% ethyl alcohol, necessary as a solvent and to preserve the herbal components. The alcohol was often mixed with anything from innocuous roots to dangerous narcotics. In this way, patent medicines offered to provide health and vitality while hiding the conditions of their production and misrepresenting their use value.

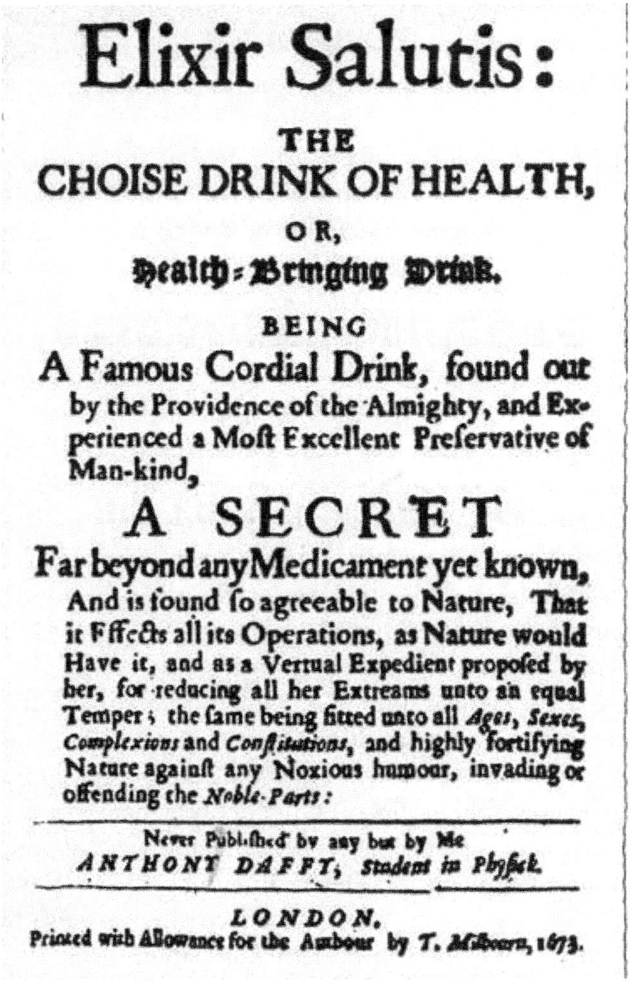

Elixir Salutis:

THE
CHOISE DRINK OF HEALTH,

O R,

𝕳𝖊𝖆𝖑𝖙𝖍-𝖇𝖗𝖎𝖓𝖌𝖎𝖓𝖌 𝖉𝖗𝖎𝖓𝖐.

BEING

A Famous Cordial Drink, found out
by the Providence of the Almighty, and Experienced a Moſt Excellent Preſervative of
Man-kind,

A SECRET

Far beyond any Medicament yet known,
And is found ſo agreeable to Nature, That
it Effects all its Operations, as Nature would
Have it, and as a Vertual Expedient propoſed by
her, for reducing all her Extreams unto an equal
Temper ; the ſame being fitted unto all *Ages, Sexes,
Complexions* and *Conſtitutions*, and highly fortifying
Nature againſt any Noxious humour, invading or
offending the *Noble-Parts* :

Never Publiſhed by any but by Me
ANTHONY DAFFY, Student in Phyſick.

LONDON.
Printed with Allowance for the Authour by *T. Milbourn*, 1673.

Figure 2.1 Daffy's Elixir Salutis was one of the most popular and frequently advertised patent medicines in eighteenth century Britain

Source: Wellcome Library, London. Available under the Attribution 4.0 International (CC BY 4.0)

The post–Civil War population was largely rural, and there were few doctors. For many people, nostrums made at home, sold at the general store, or peddled by itinerant salesmen were the only options available. Moreover, there was a preponderance of little understood diseases, as germ theory was not developed until 1865. People often died from smallpox, yellow fever, and even respiratory and dysenteric infections. Patent medicines offered a promise of a cure; moreover, they were a welcome alternative to the "heroic" medicine practices of the time, such as bleeding, blistering, and leeching. They offered hope in a bottle – the quick fix for both serious illnesses and everyday life problems.

Patent medicines grew in popularity throughout the nineteenth century, and by the 1870s, were a major industry in the United States. While many early patent medicines were locally produced and thus familiar to those who consumed them, with industrialization they were mass-manufactured and sold nationally. According to Laird (1998, 15), growth in population, territory, wealth, and income paralleled the dramatic expansion of the size and character of markets for goods. As the population expanded across the continent, especially westward after the Civil War, and with the establishment of a national railroad, patent medicines could be distributed over long distances. But because their products' benefits were not self-evident and required explanation, patent medicine makers needed to create a market for their products. As a result, patent medicine manufacturers played a pioneering role in marketing and advertising, and became the largest group of advertisers in the nineteenth century (Laird 1998, cited in Young 1961, 40–41). Advertising created familiarity and desire – in other words, it established sign value to distinguish otherwise similar products from one another. In fact, patent medicines were among the first products to achieve a national market under a single brand name (Bingham 1994, 26). Manufacturers developed distinctive symbols as trademarks, sold products in distinctively shaped or designed packages, and advertised in newspapers to entice people to buy products locally that had been made hundreds of miles away (Young 1960). The expansion of the market for patent medicines through advertising was also facilitated by the proliferation of newspapers in the growing nation, from 200 in 1800 to nearly 4000 by 1860 (Dary 2008, 250). A.J. Ayer of Lowell, Massachusetts, for example, developed Ayer's Cherry Pectoral to treat pulmonary troubles in 1843, and by 1870, he was advertising in nearly 2000 periodicals, magazines, and daily and weekly newspapers throughout the country (Dary 2008, 254). By the end of the 1800s, patent medicine advertising provided one-third of the profits made by the American press.

Patent medicine advertisements made use of emotive words and images that promised transformation. They were known for puffery: overblown, exaggerated language that contrasted with the more pedantic language that marked other kinds of advertisements. Young (1960, 42) writes of the patent medicine manufacturer, "While other advertising in the press was drab, his was vivid; while other appeals were straightforward, his were devilishly clever". Ads for generic products functioned more like announcements, but patent medicine manufacturers had to explain what a specific nostrum was, how it worked, and to promote it in the face of competition from other manufacturers. Thus, makers would argue their product's merits and associate those merits with a specific name or trademark (what we now call branding). Although newspapers did not print images until they began using woodcuts in the 1850s, the labels of patent medicines would identify their brand by using reassuring images of angels, children, doctors, or grandmothers, or by depicting exotic places to create positive associations (Laird 1998, 18). With the development of colour lithography in the 1870s, posters and trade cards enabled patent medicine makers to appeal more directly to the emotions through images. Depictions of the flag and or religious symbols were often linked to a medicine; alternatively, patent medicine makers preyed on the fear of illness by stressing their medicines' preventative abilities, often by frightening customers with pictorial images of serpents or the devil. Trade cards were typically distributed free of charge, with a compelling picture on one side and the advertising message on the reverse. Later, these became included in product packaging so that consumers could collect them. While patent medicine makers were among the first to see the potential of trade cards (Twitchell 2000, 30), they were also used by department stores, cigarette manufacturers, and cereal brands, all of which encouraged a participatory form of engagement with products that was a forerunner of the interactive advertising typical of the present day.

Patent medicine advertisers also sold their wares in travelling medicine shows, which were precursors to the mix of advertising and entertainment that characterizes modern advertising. Although medicine shows existed during colonial times, their size and scope increased throughout the nineteenth century. The best known were the Kickapoo Indian or Wild West Shows, with as many as 75 shows that toured the country at one time. An Indian "medicine man", relying on the credibility attributed to Native American remedies, would tout the virtues of a medicine, while a "scout" would interpret his speech (Young 1961, 192–193). On occasion, purported "doctors" or satisfied consumers attested to the benefits of a product. Some salesmen used shills or accomplices, while others managed to produce endorsements from those who genuinely believed they were "cured" by using a nostrum.

Other shows, drawing on promotional techniques pioneered by P.T. Barnum and his Traveling Circus in 1840, would offer a variety of entertainments to draw a crowd – jugglers, magicians, minstrels, vaudeville performers, or exotic women – after which the patent medicine salesmen would pitch the curative properties of their products, which were often touted as "magical". Most important in all the shows, Young writes, was that audiences were made receptive by creating a mood that "beguiled a crowd, drove from their minds extraneous concerns, and focused attention on a novel and entrancing spectacle" (1974, 195). The mood prepared people to believe in the promise of transformation. According to Lears, "The desire for a magical transformation of the self was a key element in the continuing vitality of the carnivalesque advertising tradition, and an essential part of consumer goods appeal in the nineteenth century" (1994, 3).

Lydia Pinkham's Vegetable Compound

One of the most successful patent medicines developed in the nineteenth century was Lydia Pinkham's Vegetable Compound, which pioneered many techniques that became commonplace in later advertising. As with most patent medicines, the medicinal properties of something like Mrs. Pinkham's Vegetable Compound were not immediately obvious, so that use and sign value had to be created to create desire for the product. Typically, patent medicine manufacturers created a steady supply of the product, then generated demand by making vast promises of ailments that it would cure (Anderson 2000, 11)

In 1843, Lydia Pinkham brewed a formula in her basement that treated female ailments. Because medicine was not far advanced in addressing female maladies, women often concocted their own home remedies. She largely relied upon John King's American Dispensary, which listed herbal ingredients beneficial to women, though she added other ingredients. She began selling the product privately as early as 1859, but did not formally establish a company until 1873. Since botanical remedies were popular at the time (largely in response to doctors' use of harsh purgatives and emetics), she named it Lydia Pinkham's Vegetable Compound. The original ingredients were Unicorn Root, Life Root, Black Cohosh, Pleurisy Root, and Fenugreek Seed, all immersed in 18% alcohol (the latter was a preservative, as Pinkham was a temperance supporter). In 1875, the family began more aggressively marketing the product: they printed a four-page "Guide for Women" that her sons distributed in areas around their home in Lynn, Massachusetts, and they asked local druggists to take bottles on consignment. She described her nostrum as "A Positive Cure for all those Complaints and Weaknesses so Common to Our Female Population". The ad copy read: "A sure cure for PROLAPSUS UTERI, or falling of the womb and all FEMALE WEAKNESSES including leucorrhoea, irregular and painful menstruation, inflammation and ulceration of the womb, flooding… for all weaknesses of the generative organs of either sex, it is second to no remedy that has ever been before the public, and for all diseases of the kidneys it is the GREATEST REMEDY IN THE WORLD". Over the years, the specific claims made for the product varied, from indicating that it would increase fertility to relieving menstrual cramps to "brightening" the mood. She also expanded the market for the Vegetable Compound to include men. After Pinkham's son Daniel went to New York to explore opportunities to grow the business, he wrote home that he was hearing men complain about kidney and uterine complaints, and recommended that the product address these ailments too (Stage 1979, 34).

In 1876 Pinkham made her compound into a proprietary medicine and registered it with the patent office in Boston. Her son William placed an advertisement for Lydia Pinkham's Vegetable Compound on the front page of the Boston Herald, a newspaper that then had a circulation of 50,000. After orders began multiplying, Pinkham hired an advertising agent, Harlan Page Hubbard, who placed ads in newspapers across the United States.

By 1879, Pinkham no longer brewed the product herself in her basement, but had workers to manufacture and bottle the product, and she expanded her products to include Liver Pills, a laxative, and a blood purifier (Rosenberg 2007). People who purchased the compound – at $1 per bottle or six bottles for $5, which was quite expensive at the time – were advised that the additional purchase of Pinkham's other products was highly recommended. Pinkham also "branded" the product by offering items such as calendars, manicure sets, perfume vials, tape measures, sewing cards, picture puzzles, and vanity pencils, all with the name of Lydia Pinkham.

Pinkham was, in modern terms, a pioneer in direct-to-consumer advertising whose ads, like advertorials or native advertising today, blurred the line between news and advertising. The newspaper ads were designed to emulate news stories, with "scare" headlines that would catch readers' attention and entice them to read the copy. One sensational headline, for example, capitalized on a murder case: "A FEARFUL TRAGEDY – A Clergyman of Stratford, Conn., KILLED BY HIS OWN WIFE. Insanity brought on by 16 years of Suffering with Female Complaints the Cause. Lydia E. Pinkham's Vegetable Compound, The Sure Cure for These Complaints, Would Have Prevented the Direful Deed" (Stage 1979, 100). The text of the ad made "transformational" promises to both men and women:

> It removes Dyspepsia, Faintness, Flatulency, destroys all cravings for stimulants, and relieves weakness of the stomach. It will cure entirely the worst forms of falling of the Uterus. Leucorrhea, Painful Menstruation, Inflammation or Ulceration, Irregularities, Floodings, etc. For the cure of Kidney complaints of either sex this Compound is unsurpassed.

Stage (1979) writes that in addition to claiming to cure non-specific ailments such as "stomach weakness", there were other subtle claims in this ad. In a context where many people were addicted to opium, the ad offered to reduce cravings, and at a time when many women tried to self-induce abortions, the promise to cure "irregularities" and "floodings" had added weight.

The Pinkham Company used other advertising techniques that linked the product to a symbolic meaning in a manner evocative of modern advertising. In 1879, Pinkham's son suggested that she print trade cards – then an innovative strategy to differentiate products through enticing imagery. The trade cards were the first to use a woman's likeness in advertising, presenting Lydia Pinkham as a reassuring grandmotherly presence (Barnes-Brus 2014) (See Figure 2.2). The copy also used a mode of address that was direct and personal, with her signature on the cards under the words, "Faithfully Yours". Her picture was also put on the label of bottles and in newspaper ads.

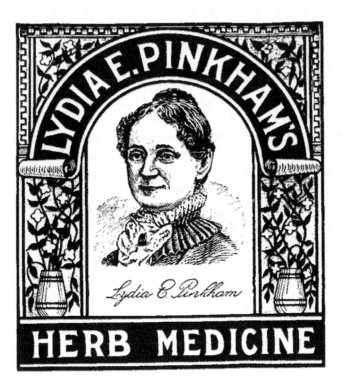

Figure 2.2   Lydia Pinkham trade card

As Lydia Pinkham came to embody the product and to connote authenticity, her picture became one of the best-known female images in print at the time (Stage 1979, 41).

Although Lydia Pinkham died in 1883, the family carried on the business. In 1889, they hired the Pettingill ad agency of Boston to handle the advertising, with James Wetherald in charge of the account. Ad agencies were beginning to expand their services from merely placing ads to developing copy. Wetherald, who left the agency in 1900 to work solely for the Pinkham family, added "nervous disorders" to the list of ailments that the Compound cured. Stage (1979, 117) writes, "By the 1890s George Beard's diagnosis of 'American nervousness' had become a commonplace. Men and women spoke of a 'case of nerves' as they might have spoken earlier of measles or scarlet fever. The symptoms of nervous debility, from sleeplessness to irritability, provided the patent medicine man with a grab bag of specific and non-specific symptoms that could be turned to profit." Some of the symptoms were as vague as having a "don't care" and "want-to-be-left-alone" feeling, and all were attributed to "female weakness" or derangement of the womb. Crucially, Wetherald's ads shifted the emphasis from health as an end to health as a route to beauty – with the promise that Mrs. Pinkham's Vegetable Compound "cleanses, invigorates, and consequently beautifies, the form of woman" (Stage 1979, 118).

The company also issued "Lydia Pinkham's Guide to Health: A Private Textbook" in the 1890s, which not only competed with the medical authority of doctors, but which recommended her product as a palliative. Wetherald's ads also understood the importance of attaching the product to women's aspirations. One series of ads that ran 1890 to 1894 shifted from a blatant description of "prolapsis uteri" to a subtle description of "those peculiar weaknesses and ailments of our best female population" (Stage 1979, 123). The ads played on the prevalent medical belief that all female diseases emanated from the womb, and moreover, that they were most apt to affect upper-class women (in the words of the ad, "our best female population"). Though most of the customers were working women rather than middle-class women (who were more likely to use doctors), Wetherald's ads equated female "weakness" with status, in a sense flattering the working class women most apt to buy the product. In other ads, however, the copy was more invidious. For example, one ad said that any woman was responsible for her own suffering if she did not write to Mrs. Pinkham for advice. In this case, the implication was that sickness was a sign of personal failure. Another ad implied that "good health" was a woman's duty and a woman's duty consisted of making herself attractive to men (by using the product).

The Pinkham ads also attached themselves to social trends, for example, the Suffragette movement in the 1900s. One 1903 booklet was addressed to "The New Woman", and its motto was "Only a woman understands women's ills." Long after Lydia Pinkham's death, women were invited to write to her for counsel on both medical and non-medical troubles after which "Mrs. Pinkham" published booklets filled with their testimonial letters. The company provided these letter writers with fringe benefits, such as a small stipend for stationary or to pay for a photographer so that their pictures could be printed with the testimonials. The company developed an extensive mail organization; women kept writing for advice until finally in 1904 journalist Edwards Bok wrote an article for *The Ladies' Home Journal* in which he published a photograph of her tombstone and informed readers that she had been dead since 1883. He also claimed that for years the letters had been answered by a pool of typists who used form letters that routinely advocated the continued use of the vegetable compound, and that the company sold the names and addresses of letter writers to other companies (Stage 1979, 116).

However, despite Bok's admonition, by 1912 sales exceeded $1 million. By the mid-twenties, the company had 450 employees and at its peak earned $3.8 million in sales. The Pinkham family continued to manufacture the product until 1925, and even into the 1930s they continued to publish advice in booklets that were translated into several different languages and mailed around the world.

Patent Medicines in the Twentieth Century

Towards the end of the nineteenth century and into the twentieth, muckraking journalists and scholars began to expose the spurious claims made by patent medicine makers, including Mrs. Pinkham, and to protest for reform of industries, particularly the food and drug industries. Samuel Hopkins Adams wrote a public exposé of patent medicines for *Colliers Weekly* in 1905, where he detailed the false claims made in many patent medicine advertisements. The writers and editors of both *Colliers* and *The Ladies' Home Journal*, where Bok also wrote his exposé of Mrs. Pinkham, called for federal regulation of patent medicines. Public outcry, muckraking journalists, criticism from the newly formed American Medical Association, and the fact that many patent medicines were dangerous were important factors that led to the passage of Pure Food and Drug Act in 1906. Manufacturers had to disclose specified ingredients, provide truth in labelling, and were subject to government inspection and control of all foods and drugs sold in the United States.

Most importantly, they had to list any dangerous or addictive substances such as alcohol, cocaine, opium morphine, or heroin. Mrs. Pinkham's Vegetable Compound reduced the alcohol content from 18% to 15% in 1914 (and currently is 10% alcohol). It also modified its claims about the product's effectiveness for female complaints to read "Recommended as a Vegetable Tonic in conditions for which the preparation has been adapted" (Starr 1982, 132).

Moreover, by the end of the nineteenth century the false claims and hyperbolic language in patent medicine advertising made other advertisers fear that duplicitous patent medicine manufacturers were giving advertising a bad name. On another front, patent medicines were undermining the authority of the fledgling medical profession. To combat the latter, the American Medical Association set standards for "ethical" drugs in 1906, setting up an agreement that physicians would legitimate "ethical" drugs, and that "ethical" drug manufacturers would be honest about the contents of their medicines, would not knowingly make fraudulent claims, and would not bypass the authority of doctors (Conrad and Leiter 2009, 15). The prohibition against unclear and misleading statements was implemented after the 1912 Sherley Amendment to the Food and Drug Act, after which medicines stopped making claims for a "sure cure" (Bingham 1994, 31). In response, Lydia Pinkham's "Sure Cure for Falling of the Womb" became "Recommended for the treatment of non-surgical cases of weakness and disorders of the female genital organs".

Similarly, advertisers spurred the development of a National Advertising Industry to self-regulate the industry in 1910. By the late nineteenth century, as increased factory production led to the spectre of over-production and under-consumption, advertising began to appropriate the hyperbolic and sensationalist methods of patent medicine advertisers. Yet, while advertisers wanted to use the techniques employed by patent medicine salespeople, they also wanted to dissociate themselves from the perception that they were "snake-oil" salespeople who made deceptive claims to convince people of needs they did not know they had – hence the eventual establishment of a voluntary organization that favoured "responsible" advertising. As Frank Presbey (1929, 289) writes in his history of advertising, "In time the better classes of advertising took possession and crowded out the objectionable."

Conclusion: Patent Medicines from Then to Now

Our case study of patent medicines illustrated the cultural shift from a Protestant ethos that valued thrift, self-restraint, and delayed gratification to one characterized by a therapeutic ethos that posited individual self-fulfilment as not only possible, but desirable. In this way, our case study illustrates how the promise of future transformation is central to advertising as it has developed from the nineteenth century to the present day. Patent medicines, widely popular in nineteenth-century Europe and the United States, offered to cure any number of physical or psychic ailments and thus to improve and "revitalize" the self. With Lydia Pinkham's Vegetable Compound, we saw the development of modern marketing and advertising techniques; as in contemporary advertising, the Lydia Pinkham "brand" did not simply promise to cure female (and as she expanded her market, male) complaints, but worked to orient consumers to an improved version of the self. Her practices also encouraged consumers to participate in the brand, either by collecting trade cards or by writing to Lydia Pinkham for advice. Free promotional materials such as calendars, pencils, or sewing kits fostered goodwill and instilled brand loyalty, as did the iconic image of the grandmotherly Lydia Pinkham. Advertisements disguised as sensational news stories blurred the line between advertising and entertainment, while Mrs. Pinkham's advice column, pamphlets, and medical textbook presaged modern-day practices that disguise advertising as information.

While regulation and the growing influence of the medical profession led many patent medicines to disappear in the early twentieth century, some have remained on the market as alternatives to prescription medicine. Mrs. Pinkham's Vegetable Compound, for example, is still available, though the family-owned company was sold to Cooper Laboratories in 1968, then it was sold to Numark Laboratories in 1987. Today, advertising claims are more modest than in the days of Lydia Pinkham; the compound is promoted as an herbal medicine that provides "nutritional support for women in all stages of life from menstruation to menopause". "Nutritional support", of course, is not the same as a remedy.

Many of today's drugs, vitamin supplements, and herbal remedies are like the patent medicines of yesteryear, albeit with even more inscrutable ingredients and pseudoscientific nomenclature. Instead of Lydia Pinkham we have Dr. Oz, who promotes health-related products (of questionable medical benefit) for weight loss, energy, or a better sex life. Instead of the Cumberland Chemical Company's nostrum called Sextonique, which purported to "restore manhood", we now have Viagra. Instead of Hall's Vegetable Sicilian Hair Renewer, we have Rogaine. Brown's Iron Bitters, a cure for dyspepsia and indigestion, has been replaced by Prilosec.

For much of the twentieth century, the pharmaceutical industry was prohibited from advertising directly to consumers, making physicians the gateway to prescribing drugs. However, deregulation of the industry in 1980 led to the reinstatement of direct-to-consumer advertising and paved the way for a plethora of new drugs that promised to better and revitalize the self. While drug companies were initially slow to test the waters for what was acceptable in prescription drug advertising, by 1985 they began advertising in print publications, and in 1997 they began advertising on television. The industry now spends more than $3 billion a year on direct-to-consumer advertising. Many prescription drugs now have become modern versions of patent medicines, where people are offered a quick fix for their spiritual, emotional, or physical maladies. There are two major concerns regarding pharmaceutical drug advertising that evoke patent medicines and demonstrate the persistence of the therapeutic ethos into the twenty-first century: the medicalization of everyday life, where minor problems are represented as diseases to be cured, and the idea that all life complaints can and should be treated with a pill (Moynihan and Cassels 2005).

An example of the medicalization of ordinary life can be seen in the marketing of the drug Sarafem, a pharmaceutical-based version of Mrs. Pinkham's Vegetable Compound that similarly addresses "female complaints". Sarafem is an antidepressant drug that purports to cure "premenstrual dysphoric distress disorder" (PMDD) rather than the more straightforward "female complaints" of days past. Ely Lilly developed the drug after its patent for the antidepressant Prozac expired in 1990, which meant that Lilly would lose hundreds of millions of dollars when generic competitors came on the market. In 1998, Lilly funded a meeting of researchers, a group of Food and Drug Administration staff, and Lilly representatives. The group concluded that PMDD was a disease and that antidepressants like Prozac could treat it. When they got approval to market its drug for PMDD, they decided to sell it as a lavender pill, renamed it Sarafem, and promoted it with images of sunflowers and attractive women. In fact, the ingredients in Prozac and Sarafem are identical.

Whether PMDD even exists is controversial; critics argue that, much like patent medicines, it is creating an illness by medicalizing the normal emotional ups and downs that many women experience prior to their periods. While some women may indeed experience pain and mood swings, it is less clear that there is a disorder called PMDD. As in the nineteenth century, drug manufacturers entice consumers with promises of self-improvement.

While the false claims and puffery of patent medicines relied upon faith in home remedies, modern pharmaceutical advertising relies on belief in the authority of science and medicine. In both cases, we see the continued dominance of the therapeutic ethos and the quest for individual self-fulfilment achieved through a product. There is a pill for every ill, as instant solutions are dangled before consumers who seek fulfilment in a product. From patent medicines to contemporary drug advertisements, products have come to provide meaning in a culture oriented towards consumption.

3

Building Consumer Culture: The Department Store and Mail Order Catalogue

As we described in Chapter 2, in the late 1800s, Western Europe and the United States shifted from a producer to consumer society. To summarize, Laermans (1993, 80) writes, "The interim results of historical research justify the tentative assertion that modern consumer culture took on its contours during the 2nd half of the nineteenth century. In Western Europe and the US, the years between 1860 and 1914 were probably decisive for the massive breakthrough and the definitive formation of the present-day consumer society." As we saw, several factors linked to industrialization, such as innovations in production, new modes of transportation, and urbanization, made this possible. Mass production meant that consumer items could be standardized and duplicated in great quantities and at low costs. In the United States, transport systems such as railways enabled the movement of goods and facilitated urban migration from farms to factories, while in Europe, horse-drawn carriages and then trams provided access to thriving city centres. In both Europe and the United States, the expansion of newspapers and magazines in which products were advertised and new techniques of visual representation helped to shape consumer culture.

William Leach (1993) describes the development of consumer culture in the late-nineteenth-century United States. As the influences of the Protestant ethic waned, American culture became distinctly secular and market-oriented, with the exchange and circulation of money and goods at the foundation of moral sensibility. This shift in sensibilities had several consequences that informed the emerging consumer culture, particularly in regard to the idea of acquisition and consumption as routes to happiness and the "democratization" of desire. As Leach (1993) explains, the proliferation of mass-produced goods in the post–Civil War period led American businesses to create "a commercial aesthetic of desire" to move goods. This aesthetic relates to Jackson Lear's description of the therapeutic ethos – a conception of the good life available through the purchase of commodities. As wealth became defined more by the accumulation of capital than ownership of property, and people who moved from rural farms to urban centres lost control over their own productivity, it was comfort and prosperity, rather than ownership of land and self-sufficiency, that became the aspirational ideals that defined the American experience. In this milieu, desire became democratized as the right for everyone to want the same goods and aspire to enter the same world of comfort and luxury.

As urban populations grew, the rise of a professional class led to higher incomes and standards of living. Laermans (1993) writes that in the United States where there were no entrenched class systems, urban populations invented new ways of living, new habits, and new forms of interaction. These changes were not confined to urban areas. While in the 1890s the United States still largely consisted of farmers, rising agricultural prices and land values also created a class of consumers with purchasing power in rural areas. In both city and country, commodities promised ease, comfort, and happiness. Whether through advertising, store displays, or mail order catalogues, representations of mass-produced objects whetted desires for some kind of self-betterment attainable through products. Wolfgang Haug (1986, 17) writes about the creation of desire in his work on commodity aesthetics, defined as both the sensual appearance and the (illusory) conception of an object's use value (1986, 17). He describes a "technocracy of sensuality", where domination over people is effected through their fascination with technically produced artificial appearances. Commodity aesthetics creates desire through the "enchantment of the sense of sight", so that attention is not directed to objects, but to their external appearances, or "looks", that become expressions of intangible qualities such as personality, individuality, or social status. Most importantly, he states, "commodities are designed to stimulate in the onlooker the desire to possess and the impulse to buy" (1986, 8).

Drawing on the democratization of desire and Haug's notion of commodity aesthetics, in this chapter we focus on the new sensibilities and relationships to goods that emerged in the United States in the period from 1860 to 1920. Our case study of the rise of department stores and their corollary, the mail order catalogue, is concerned with how advertising and the sumptuous display of goods work to command attention and stimulate desire. We illustrate how department stores and mail order catalogues created desire for products by offering them as a means to create personal and social identities, and thus were crucial factors in the development of modern consumer culture.

Origins of the Department Store and Mail Order Catalogue

The confluence of urbanization, mass transportation, and mass production gave rise to both the department store and the mail order catalogue, which was in many ways "a mall between two covers" (Keller 1995, 157). Benson (1979) asserts that the coming of the department store symbolizes one of the most profound changes in modern history regarding the shift from a production oriented to consumer society, one that according to Perrot (1984, cited in Laermans 1993, 81) brought about the desire for consumption and the socialization of needs. It was certainly one of the most significant markers of the modern consumer society, emerging in the mid-1800s to acquaint people with new products and teach people to desire them, primarily through their aestheticization. As factories produced volumes of machine-made goods that could be sold at low cost, this mass production required a retail system greater than what could be provided by small shopkeepers. Department stores, along with mail order catalogues in rural areas, emerged as distribution outlets.

Until the beginning of the nineteenth century in Europe and the United States, local shops, open markets, and peddlers largely filled daily needs, while specialized luxury-goods stores were primarily located in cities. Most department stores grew out of small dry-goods stores located in city centres; as more goods became available, shopkeepers gradually increased their offerings, and then departmentalized to facilitate shopping. The shift from small shops to department stores also benefitted from the development of railroads to transport manufactured goods across the country and to bring customers from rural areas. In addition, the transportation of people in cities, first by horse-drawn trolleys, then by cable cars, helped make the centrally located department store feasible.

One of the first department stores in the United States was A.J. Stewart's Marble Dry Goods Palace, which opened in New York City in 1846. Like many early department stores, it began as a dry-goods store that primarily sold textiles. As real estate in urban centres became more expensive, many of these small stores expanded upward, particularly in the United States where there were less height restrictions than in Europe. For example, the Marble Dry Goods Palace in 1848 had an Italianate marble front that set the style for the opulent stores that followed. Inside, it had a frescoed interior that was built around a circular staircase and a central rotunda capped with a glass dome. The walls had 13-foot mirrors which were the first such glass seen by Americans, and its plate glass "French windows" became a tourist attraction for visitors to New York (Abelson 1989, 67). The Bon Marché in Paris (1852), however, is widely credited as the world's first department store designed as such, and it became one of the largest volume stores in the world until the end of the nineteenth century (Whitaker 2006). In the United States, other well-known early department stores were Macy's (1858), Jordan Marsh (1861), Marshall Field's (1865), Wanamaker's (1876), and Filene's (1881), while Montgomery Ward (1872) and Sears, Roebuck and Co. (1886) took on the function of department stores by distributing mail order catalogues to rural parts of the United States. The result, as Cross (2013, 13) writes, was that "goods of all kinds became available to most Americans and were seen by almost everyone".

Department stores changed patterns of commerce, and as Trentman points out, around the world they were "self-conscious global institutions not seen before, working in tandem with those other forces of globalization at the time" such as the remarkable displays at world exhibitions (2016, 193). As early as 1850, Bon Marché was one of the first stores to develop a new sales model by setting fixed prices, and it was soon emulated by department stores in the United States and replicated by name at least in Brixton and Liverpool in the United Kingdom (Trentman 2016, 193). In the world of small shopkeepers in both the United States and Europe, prices were negotiable rather than fixed, and goods were rarely advertised or put on display. People who entered shops engaged in an implicit contract to buy, based on the time investment of both shopkeeper and customer involved in negotiating prices. However, the larger, more impersonal department stores gradually changed the culture of buying and selling by setting fixed prices, carrying a high volume of goods with a small mark-up, and most importantly, doing away with an implicit obligation to buy. A high volume of goods required more employees, many of whom did not necessarily have the skills to negotiate prices. Thus, fixed prices removed the salesperson from an active role in selling goods. According to Haug (1986), in small shops, sellers created desire for products through their verbal performances, often using learned strategies to valorize a commodity and flatter the buyer to make a sale. With department stores, sales talk went from being a ritualized social interaction to an impersonal monetary exchange. Similarly, Sennett (1976) writes that the rise of the department store is a paradigm of how the public realm as an active interchange gave way to an experience of publicness more intense and less social. Both buyers and sellers took on a more passive role; shopping became a more impersonal experience of looking, and rather than being a purposeful activity, it became a way to pass leisure time. Anyone could enter a store, browse, and imagine themselves as potential owners of goods.

Department Stores and Advertising

At the same time, stores were meant for profit, and the newly legitimated activity of "looking" had to be linked to "buying". Advertising was one means to create desire for new products. Before the 1880s, newspapers and magazines offered little advertising, and what they did offer was basically informational, with no visual appeal. By 1885, as merchandise flowed out of factories, national manufacturers and retailers began to advertise in newspapers and magazines using visual images, as well as catchy phrases such as slogans and iterations. Posters and postcards were made using techniques such as chromolithography and photogravure not only to catch the eye, but to promise happiness through the purchase of a product. As was the case with patent medicines, trade cards often consisted of colourful and exotic scenes that created desire for mass-manufactured goods sold in department stores, as well as to advertise the stores themselves. Trade cards from Bon Marché in Paris, for example, showed comets, magic carpets, and sultans, implying that the store, too, was a wonder of the world (Whitaker 2006). Similarly, an early Wanamaker's trade card depicted the store with Eastern-style onion domes (see Figure 3.1).

National advertising, made possible by the expansion of newspapers and magazines, enabled widespread recognition of brands and trademarks, which

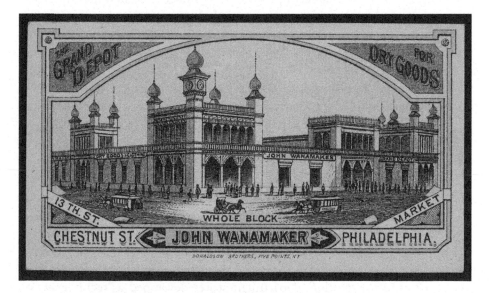

Figure 3.1 Wanamaker's trade card, undated
Source: Courtesy of Historic New England

also emerged in response to mass production. Trademarks, like trade cards, were first employed by patent medicine manufacturers (see also Chapter 2), but by the late nineteenth century were used for most mass-produced goods. Products that had once been sold in bulk, or that had been handmade rather than mass-manufactured, needed to stand out among competing products. Oats, for example, once sold in unmarked bins, became one of the first successes with brand-name packaged goods when they were sold in a cardboard package printed with the reassuring image of a Quaker man. By 1888, oats, which had been considered food for invalids and Scottish immigrants, was a desirable product familiar across the country (Sivulka 1998).

Haug (1986) highlights the importance of branding in relation to commodity aesthetics. When products were nameless and largely indistinguishable from others of the same type, their use value determined their worth, and aesthetic value was tied to the commodity itself. However, when goods became defined in terms of brand name, use value became less important and aesthetic value became elevated. He writes, "With the subordination and control of certain use-values by private enterprise, commodity aesthetics receives not only qualitative new meaning – to codify a new class of information – but it also detaches itself from the body of the commodity, whose styling is heightened by the packaging and widely distributed by advertising" (Haug 1986, 25). Haug (1986) explains that aesthetic, visual, and verbal elements are concentrated into one image that identifies the manufacturers and gives them an air of prestige. Image, in this sense, refers to sign value: "the total impression, the total experience of all objects, services and facilities of a business" (Haug 1986, 30). The image itself, dissociated from any specific use value, becomes a sign of quality. In this context, department stores – such as Wanamaker's, Macy's, or Filene's in the United States – became brands whose names acquired status. Thus, according to Whitaker (2006), department stores did everything in their power to keep their names before the public, and as the department store industry developed, national advertising and large-scale marketing became one of their primary activities. Haug (1986, 25) adds, "the trans-regional brand-names of large companies imposed themselves onto the public's experience and virtually assumed the status of natural phenomena". Department stores, and shopping as a pastime, became ingrained in ordinary life.

Department stores were instrumental in utilizing both national advertising and branding to create a commodity aesthetic that fostered consumer desire. To capture attention, department stores developed a "technocracy of the eye" that ultimately changed mere merchandise into spectacular commodity signs (Laermans 1993, 82). They were instrumental in the process of aesthetic valorization through the presentation, design, and arrangement of commodities within the shopping environment. Strategies within the stores' décor served to attract the shopper who was "just looking".

As Sennett (1976, 144) writes, to stimulate people to buy, they created "a kind of spectacle out of the store, a spectacle which would endow the goods, by association, with an interest the merchandise might intrinsically lack". Burns (1996, 54) quotes business writer Nathaniel Fowler, who wrote, "The old fashioned idea that goods sell upon their merits, and that merit alone is essential, has grown mouldy in its disuse... No matter how good a thing you have, its selling quality depends upon your ability to make people accept its value... It makes no difference what the article is... You must please the buyer's eye." Stores thus designed visual displays that would stimulate the desire to buy. According to Sennett (1976, 144–146), stores might juxtapose dissimilar products or place prosaic products in exotic settings. A pot, for example, might be made attractive by displaying it in a replica of a Moorish harem. He explains that the resulting aura of "strangeness", or mystification, stimulated desire to buy by investing goods with meaning beyond their utility; in this case, the pot became associated with fantasies of Moorish pleasure. Through these staged settings, consumers became accustomed to finding the unexpected, and more willing to leave the store with products they did not initially intend to buy. In the context of high-volume sales, products appeared and disappeared rapidly, which stores seized on to create the perception of scarcity. Sennett (1976, 145) describes this process by referring to commodity fetishism (discussed in Chapter 2): "The buyer was stimulated when he or she was presented with objects whose existence seemed fleeting, and whose nature was veiled by associations out of the context of normal use." Through what Haug describes as the enchantment of the senses that deflected attention from the origin or use value of products, department stores offered products as a means to create personal and social meanings.

Colour, Light, Glass

Three materials were used to "please the buyer's eye" and create a commodity aesthetic based around desire: colour, light, and glass. According to Leach (1993), department stores were the first institutions to disseminate these technologies, which changed the way that people saw and understood goods, as well as how they lived in their society. For centuries these materials were used by the military to inspire devotion, loyalty, and fear, and by religions to depict an "otherworldly paradise". Department stores used colour, light, and glass similarly, to focus attention, instil awe, and offer the promise of a worldly paradise provided by products. The manufacture of new shades and hues of colours, for example, helped advance visual advertising as well as product design and display. Wanamaker's Department Store in Philadelphia hired artists such as Maxwell Parrish to produce ads in saturated colours that created an atmosphere around a product rather than promoting its benefits. Wanamaker's partner John Ogden proclaimed in an 1897 speech that "hot pictures" were preferable to "cold type". He stated, where "printing fails, the hot picture rouses the curiosity, touches the sense of humour, appeals to the refined taste, and commands unconsciously the attention of the average beholder" (Leach 1993, 52). By the late 1880s, Abelson (1989, 44) writes, "colours became marketable commodities as the new uses and multiplicity of colours created heightened awareness of fashion and style". For example, she notes that when all six of Marshall Field's windows were decorated in red, they launched fashion's "red epidemic" in 1897 (Abelson 1989, 71). At the opening of Wanamaker's in 1896, both colours and scents were deployed to appeal to the senses, whether through using an atomizer to perfume the air in the toiletry section or through lavish displays of colourful silks.

In addition to colour, the use of glass and light also signified an important transformation. Before 1885, merchants did not "design" windows, but either crowded goods together or displayed nothing at all (Leach 1993, 55). The decorated display window became common in department stores during the 1880s, and by the turn of the century, window dressing and interior design had become common marketing tools. Window displays captured the attention of shoppers, luring them with the promise of acquisition, and drawing them into the fantasy world of consumer goods. Even then, they aimed largely to attract women. Abelson (1989, 72) writes, "Like love letters, one trade editorial suggested, windows must arouse in women the desire for more." Commodities were "staged" in store windows or in displays inside the store. Abelson (1989, 70) observes, "'Tempting' became the operative word for the successful window"; she adds, "as one journalist noted, 'windows furnish the stuff that dreams are made of'". L. Frank Baum, later known for *The Wizard of Oz* books, was an early expert in window dressing who both wrote a book, *The Art of Window Trimming*, and created a journal called *The Shop Window* devoted to the art of window display. The journal was, Leach (1993) writes, at the forefront of a new movement in merchandising designed to foster year-round consumer desire. The quality of the goods did not matter; Baum advised, "Use the best art to arouse in the observer the cupidity and longing to possess the goods," and "as long as the goods are properly displayed, the show window will sell them like hotcakes, even though the goods are old enough to have gray whiskers" (quoted in Leach 1993, 60). Through window displays, the distinction between art and commerce began to disappear.

Beginning in the 1890s, steel skeletons began to be used for the frames of stores, which enabled them to do away with inner walls and install glass fronts. By the 1900s, display windows were common in department stores, and people were encouraged to look – to the extent that merchants paid male window gazers $3 per day to impersonate men of wealth and stand transfixed in front of a display window! (Abelson 1989). The use of glass in display windows, and later in display cases within the store, also changed people's relationship to goods. For example, Leach (1993) observes that the use of glass had repercussions in terms of social class. By the late 1890s, open markets were linked to immigrants and working poor, while the department stores with their glass display windows that enclosed their merchandise signified affluence. Through display windows, the visual became amplified, while the senses of smell and touch, so essential in open markets, were diminished. Moreover, the objects behind the glass democratized desire – anyone could look, though not everyone had access to what was inside.

Baum's work helped to develop the idea that merchandise in display windows should be presented as a theatrical spectacle to exploit consumer fantasy. By creating dramatic tableaux to show off goods, merchants not only created visual focus but were able to construct associative meanings. Marshall Fields, for example, began to use papier mâché mannequins in store windows in 1913, which enabled window display decorators to create stylized social scenes. The displays both in store windows and throughout the stores often revolved around a "central idea" where design and colour were coordinated to make a unified impression. One Wanamaker decorator wrote, "People do not buy the thing; they buy the effect... Subordinate the details to one central idea... Make the whole store a brilliant showplace" (cited in Leach 1993, 83). Stores were decorated to look like French salons, the streets of Paris, Japanese gardens, Turkish bazaars, or other exotic places that were the stuff of fantasy. According to Laermans (1993, 92), "The mise en scene or presentation of goods was meant to 'seduce' the public. A successful decoration was one that not only fascinated the passers-by but also worked as a kind of fatal attraction, culminating in a desire to possess the commodities displayed."

In addition to developing a "central idea", department stores manipulated architectural space to draw in shoppers. At the end of the nineteenth century when most department stores were being built, they were designed as "commercial palaces" that commanded attention. For example, the style and use of glass in the Innovations Department Store in Brussels, designed by the renowned architect Victor Horta, was emblematic of Art Nouveau throughout its structure (Trentman 2016, 192). In other cases, design decisions were made to facilitate shopping. Doorsteps were removed because they were a potential hindrance to potential shoppers who would drift by; they were replaced by revolving doors that provided easier access. In addition, aisles within stores were widened and more entrances were added. Once inside, Whitaker (2006, 101) writes, "the spectator's senses were overwhelmed by volumes of space and heaps of merchandise, as well as the fragrance of perfumes and the frequent hum of commerce". By 1900, many stores had steam-powered elevators, typically located away from entrances so that people would have to walk past costly goods to get to them. Harrods in London in 1898 installed "a moving staircase" that expressed the modernity of the experience as well as moving 40,000 shoppers per hour (Trentman 2016, 194). Cheaper goods were located in the basement floors, as in the famous case of Filene's Basement, while salons and arcades on the upper floors catered to wealthier shoppers. Marshall Fields in Chicago had a fur department divided into cheap and expensive furs, with glass cases consisting of mixed furs running through the centre. The set-up was designed to spur impulsive buying; however, as Leach (1993, 79) notes, the display was so enticing that it was beset by shoplifters, many of whom were middle-class women who stole on impulse rather than out of necessity (see also Abelson 1989). He also adds that by the turn of the century, many court cases resulted from women who spent beyond their means, and men who refused to pay their wives' debts (Abelson 1989).

The point of these spectacles was to shift purchases from those made from necessity to those on desire and impulse. The addition of mirrors in the 1890s also served as "silent suggesters" that magnified and enhanced merchandise. According to Abelson (1989), the reflection of goods from a multitude of angles added to the illusion of the unlimited availability of things and fuelled desire. Even the use of lights within the stores served to intensify spectacle. Most stores used electric lights by the 1880s, and these added to the attraction, especially at night. Macy's illuminated Christmas window, for example, drew crowds of onlookers in New York City. Notably, in 1892, Oscar J. Gude put up the first electrical sign advertising in New York City, with an ad for the Manhattan Beach Resort on what is now the Flatiron Building, soon replaced by an ad for Heinz, which featured some of the 57 varieties in lights and an image of a pickle that flashed on and off. The Gude Company is widely cited for beginning the transformation of Longacre Square, now known as Times Square, into "The Great White Way", where by the 1920s a plethora of electric signs and billboards encapsulated the emerging culture of looking.

Department Stores and the Feminization of Shopping

Department stores changed the nature of shopping from a necessity to a pleasure. In many cases, they became leisure centres that largely catered to women. By the end of the nineteenth century, women were the primary consumers in middle-class families, and it was to them that department stores largely directed their appeals (Abelson 1989). Shopping became both a form of entertainment and, for many women, a quasi-profession. Women relied on department stores to fulfil new needs created by the wide array of commodities, while the stores created a space where consumption became a route to satisfaction. Department stores such as Macy's, Wanamaker's, or Marshall Field's provided services such as a room with writing tables, a lunch room, and a bridal salon. It was not uncommon for department stores to include post offices, hair salons, or restaurants, or to have nurseries for children and free art exhibitions (Howard 2006). Around 1900, Macy's even offered free courses and a bicycle academy for women. Siegel's Department Store had an orchestra that played music throughout the day that drew large crowds of women. The orchestra served as a device to attract shoppers, not only to view merchandise, but to become a part of the aesthetics of the stores themselves (Abelson 1989).

When Selfridges in London opened in 1909, its architecture, plate glass windows, roof gardens, lifts, and electric lighting established it as a "monument to modernity"; moreover, it was intended as a social centre where people could browse and meet. Its first advertising campaign encouraged people to spend the day; one ad, for example, stated, "Visitor's Day is Every Day at Selfridges." Not only did this contribute to the expansion of public leisure space for women, but Selfridges's advertisements stressed low prices, which helped to lure middle- and lower-class consumers into the world of consumption (Wrigley and Lowe 2002, 204).

Department stores made the phenomenon of a feminine public possible. As the new world of material goods became increasingly prevalent, shopping and consumer spending became an important element in the creation of middle-class women's identities, defining both their work and recreation. Abelson (1989) writes that middle-class women shopped constantly, both to pass time and to fulfil their domestic duties. By 1915, women constituted 85% of all shoppers (Keller 1995, 158). Many labour-intensive items that had previously been made in the home – food, clothing, home furnishings, and appliances – were available to purchase in department stores. In addition, by the early 1890s, women's attire became specialized, so that "the problem of not wearing the correct attire became one with not knowing how to shop and not understanding how clothes had been transformed into a new symbol of middle class life" (Abelson 1989, 25). Similarly, Ewen (1988) suggests that middle-class status was founded on one's ability to purchase, construct, and present a viable social self. This "self" had to be immediately recognizable through external signs such as clothing, thus fostering a "viewing culture" and increased "semiotic sensibility" (Ewen 1988, 68).

Nowhere is this connection between women and attire more obvious than in the creation of the bridal market. The rise of the wedding industry in department stores was connected to their attention to female consumers, who they believed "formed lifelong brand and store loyalties at the time of their wedding" (Howard 2006, 101). Wedding ads and events were directed to female consumers, and "Bride's Week" became a staple of department stores. In the winter of 1908, for example, Wanamaker's became devoted to the Bride's Jubilee for two weeks. Every floor was decorated in pink and white, an organist played wedding marches in the grand court, there was a cooking school for brides held in the basement where they were taught to use new equipment and gadgets, and a furnished bride's house was on display. Mannequins of brides appeared throughout the store, showing the bride at breakfast, the bride's afternoon on the porch, or the bride in the kitchen, all of which depicted scenes from newlyweds' lives to display goods. Some of the goods had a tenuous connection to marriage; for example, in the store's auditorium, a pianist demonstrated the Knabe piano as "the proper upright piano for a bride" (Leach 1993, 84). As Howard (2006) suggests, these merchandising techniques were significant because from the late nineteenth through the twentieth century they invented new traditions and transformed wedding practices, thus demonstrating how consumer culture became both constituted and expanded.

Bridal merchandising was also a way for department stores to build brand prestige, as window displays generated goodwill for the store and in-store events such as bridal fashion shows would draw large crowds. Together, these helped transform weddings into consumer rites (Howard 2006). The visual culture of early department stores demonstrates how aestheticized commodities not only appealed to consumers and created surplus value, but how they became internalized as necessities that created social identities.

Mail Order Catalogues

Mail order catalogues, in addition to department stores, helped foster the technocracy of the senses that came to define modern consumer culture. Designed to reach rural consumers, they were a uniquely American phenomenon that proliferated in the period from 1895 to 1925. Unlike department stores, there was no actual object to appeal to the senses, but only a verbal or visual representation.

Yet, mail order catalogues assembled thousands of items for the gaze of those who lived outside of city centres, bringing a world of abundance into areas of the United States more accustomed to scarcity. The mail order catalogue, as described by Keller (1995), brought the department store to the shopper, and the usually public activity of consumption was brought into the home.

Although Montgomery Ward was the first mail order catalogue in the United States, the Sears Catalogue was far more emblematic of the rise of consumer culture and the democratization of desire. At its peak, it weighed 6 pounds, was 1500 pages, and reached the homes of 20 million Americans (Keller 1995). Even its origins speak to the changes in sensibilities brought by industrialization. Richard Sears began his business while employed as a railroad agent in 1885. When a local shopkeeper refused to accept a consignment of watches, Sears bought them cheaply and then sold them at a profit. Watches had become extremely important because of the Time Zones Act of 1883, which was passed to standardize time so that trains could run on schedule and avoid accidents. Because of the need to conform to railroad standard time rather than measuring time by the sun, watches had become desirable commodities and Sears was able to take advantage.

After moving to Chicago, Sears took on a partner, Roebuck, and they began the Sears Roebuck mail order catalogue company in 1887. The catalogue was sent to rural communities, and with rural free delivery, which came into effect in 1896, goods were brought to the doors of shoppers, without the need of ever leaving their homes. The catalogue offered thousands of consumer goods: patent medicines, clothes, food, jewellery, toys, guns, books, candy, appliances, equipment, and gadgets. For example, the electric belt, which promised to heal, strengthen, and revitalize, was a Sears exclusive, alluring because of people's fascination with electricity. For those who had little access to doctors, the electric belt, like patent medicines also on sale in the catalogue, offered hope that a product could help create a better, healthier version of themselves (see also *Mr. Sears Catalogue* 1989).

Goods that promised well-being, such as the electric belt, were interspersed with ads that put new labour-saving devices on display. Many of the goods offered, such as washing machines, sewing machines, or stoves, suggested the promise of freedom from the ardours of housework that occupied the time of many rural women. However, these came at a cost. For example, rural women had often employed seamstresses to help them make the family's clothes. Sewing machines meant that this was no longer necessary, but increased their isolation from other women (*Mr. Sear's Catalogue*). Further, Keller (1995, 158) notes, "while the Sears catalogue always claimed that it addressed rural consumers on their own terms, its very structure and purpose made it an instantiation of the urbanization of that rural subject". Clothes and other stylish goods helped people in the country feel as fashionable as those who lived in cities, but as noted in *Mr. Sear's Catalogue*, this meant that rural women often wore corsets even when working in the fields.

Overall, the catalogue was known as the "dream book" that articulated desires and attached them to the outer world. It was in many ways a precursor to mass media, a compendium that presented an entire "consumption universe" of products to satisfy all wants; even those "wants" that people were not aware of until they read the catalogue (Leiss et al. 1990, 79). Sears, who wrote the copy himself, constructed narratives around products, matched by pictorial representations which constituted the image structure of desire. Up until the advent of television in the 1950s, the mail order catalogue was the most effective means of mass selling to rural America (Tedlow 1996). Along with the department store, it mediated between the industrial and consumer age, offering people a new relationship to the things that made up their lives.

Conclusion

Traditional department stores are no longer the powerful spectacles that they once were, and the Sears catalogue designed for mass audiences has been supplanted by specialized catalogues aimed at niche consumers. However, there are still some echoes of the past. The Macy's Thanksgiving Day Parade, for example, has been extant since 1924, when it first replaced the "ragamuffin" parade led by immigrant communities and instead became a celebration of consumerism that merges advertising and entertainment. The aestheticization of commodities, and of the shopping experience itself, has remained a focal point of consumer culture. With suburbanization in the post–World War II period, the shopping mall replaced the downtown department store as the centre of leisure activity, and now in the Internet age, online sites such as Amazon.com or eBay supplement both the department store and the catalogue. In 2016, Australia opened the first virtual department store, tailored to individual preferences. What remains the same is the image structure of desire, where use value has become increasingly irrelevant to consumption. The aesthetics of commodities, construed as both their sensual appearance and the appearance of their use value, have increasingly become detached from material goods themselves. People buy brands rather than products, and brands offer consumers identities through the construction of appearances. Department stores and catalogues helped to usher in this transformation.

4

Formation of the Advertising Industry: Camel Cigarettes and Marketing Controversial Products

In Chapters 2 and 3 our case studies of patent medicines and department stores explored how advertising created consumer desire in the late nineteenth to early twentieth century. Interwoven in our analyses were four themes that we further develop in this chapter: advertising's promise of transformation, its early attempts to segment markets into brand tribes, its fostering of participatory engagement, and its merging of entertainment and advertising. Here we consider how the advertising industry that emerged in the late nineteenth century worked in the formation of consumer desire for a controversial product, cigarettes. We focus on cigarettes because they both illuminate the techniques advertisers used to create positive sign values for products based on desire rather than need, and they provide an important window into how the industry evolved to evade attempts to regulate and control advertising.

To understand how cigarette advertising fits into the structure of the industry, it is important to identify both the industrial apparatus of selling a product and the dimensions of advertising in the grand scheme of contemporary consumer economies. The advertising industry consists of advertising agencies that are responsible for disseminating information about products; they are the key enablers of making a product visible. Initially, advertising agencies emerged in the mid-1800s to sell advertising space in newspapers and magazines, largely for patent medicines (see also Chapter 2) or dry goods stores. Advertising agents, called "space-jobbers", bought column-inches in newspapers and magazines for advertisers – they were in effect middlemen who mediated between the needs of the press to generate an income from their readers, the needs of the manufacturers to get their products noticed, and the needs of consumers to purchase products. At the same time, the association of advertising with the overblown claims of patent medicines created a general distrust of advertising and a sense that legitimate products need not advertise (Fox 1997). The climate changed after 1885 as factories produced a plethora of merchandise whose supply threatened to exceed demand. According to Turner (1965, 132–133), "the spectre of over-production, alias under-consumption, began to grimace at the factory window". As a result, Herskowitz (1979, 135) writes, "modern, respectable advertising took off", and "puffing" (the use of exaggerated, overblown language) was appropriated by the business world.

In the context of an increasingly rationalized commercial world, advertising agencies sought to achieve legitimacy as a profession and dissociate themselves from perceptions of advertising as a world of "carnivalesque tricksters" (Lears 1994, 90). Two figures that exemplified this transformation were George P. Rowell and Francis Wayland Ayer. Rowell, who founded the trade journal *Printer's Ink* in 1888, established procedures for setting advertising rates and, most importantly, shifted the focus of the ad agency from selling space to determining the best places to advertise to attract consumers. In addition, *Printer's Ink* offered advice on how to calculate an advertising budget and how to best package and promote products to reach diverse audiences. Francis Ayer was another innovator who established the advertising agency N.W. Ayer and Son in 1869. While initially the agency merely bought space, in 1879 Ayer developed the "open contract" between ad agencies and advertisers, where advertisers paid the agency a fixed commission based on the quantity of advertising placed. While in the past, agencies often misrepresented how much money newspapers and magazines charged for space, the open contract aligned them with advertisers in order to reap the financial benefits of an ongoing relationship. By 1884, almost three-quarters of Ayer's contracts were open, and by 1890 it was the largest agency in the United States (*Advertising Age Encyclopedia* 2003). Further, Ayer became a full-service agency as we know it today by expanding to invent the words and images that constituted the ads they placed. While in 1880 there were only two copy writers of consequence in the country, by the late 1890s there were hundreds (and by 1915, thousands). In 1888, Ayer became the first agency to employ a full-time copywriter, and in 1900 it was the first agency to hire a full-time art director to design and illustrate ads.

As it became apparent that visual images, along with words, were key in the creation of desire, images with "eye appeal" began to rival copy for prominence (Leach 1993, 43). Whether in newspapers, magazines, trading cards, catalogues, or department store windows, images that whetted appetites for goods flooded the culture at the turn of the century. Attractive packaging, along with colourful circulars and trademark labels, appeared at this time

(Leach 1993). Product packaging was a way to differentiate products, but, more importantly, it also provided an ambient meaning for a product when it was not in the consumer's immediate possession. Trademarks and brands, as we have seen with patent medicines in Chapter 2 and department stores in Chapter 3, were instrumental in the construction of desire. They became the core images of advertising and acted as the indexical links between the product and the creation of desire that advertising attempts to produce.

Through use of trademarks, logos, and the words and images that surrounded them, advertising agencies developed icons and made them rich with living energy. The agencies were thus the creative source for maintaining the presence of mass-produced products. But in order to create associations that resonated with consumers, advertising agencies also needed to have knowledge of who they were – and thus market research became another essential aspect of advertising agencies. Expertise in reading culture, as well understanding the meanings generated by and through different cultural forms, became a crucial, though contracted-out, part of contemporary manufacturing and production. With major advertisers aiming their product at widely dispersed groups of consumers, market research helped determine what kind of advertising mix would be best and most potent in capturing the attention of those most likely to buy their product. A broadly conceived differentiation of consumers into markets was endemic to early advertising.

In the contemporary milieu, media buying and placement, creative work, and research still provide the structures of advertising campaigns. Advertising campaigns are the ultimate in integrated design for an advertising agency and, in essence, become the product that is sold to companies, where the agency is knitted together into a cohesive whole that matches with the objectives of the company/manufacturer. The complexity of advertising campaigns often determines the size and type of agency that is necessary to handle a specific client. For example, as research in the 1950s identified more specialized market segments, "boutique agencies" arose which specialized in specific types of advertising or a certain aesthetic approach, as was the case with Doyle Dane Bernbach and the Volkswagen campaign that we will discuss in Chapter 6. In contrast, there are now multinational agencies with branches and subsidiaries operating on a global scale. Contained within these larger agencies are in fact completely owned "independent" boutique agencies that service the larger players of the industry. The top five international advertising agencies have names and monikers that no longer identify the personal origins of advertising agencies; instead, for instance, the mega-agency Omnicom, the largest in the world, is a conglomerate of firms with greater historical and personal detail, and its services include media planning, digital and interactive marketing, and public relations in addition to traditional advertising. Thus since 1986, Omnicom's stable has included major names such as DDB Worldwide Communications (itself a merger of Doyle Dane Bernbach and Needham) or BBDO (Batten, Barton, Durstine, and Osborn), and smaller but still large "national" agencies such as Arnell and Goodby, Silverstein and Partners.

Our case history of R.J. Reynolds' Camel cigarettes provides insight into the development of the advertising industry and how that industry has advertised the specific product of cigarettes. We focus on Camel in part because of their longevity. They originated in 1913 and were the first nationally popular cigarette brand. Throughout the twentieth century, Camel's attempt to maintain a dominant market share amid competition from other brands and growing awareness of the health dangers associated with cigarettes illuminates some of the dominant techniques that typify the industry as a whole. In our case history, we also see a number of different ad agencies for Camel Cigarettes, most prominently N.W. Ayer from 1913 to 1930 and William Esty from 1932 to 1987. In 1987 Trone Advertising, a small advertising agency from Greensboro, North Carolina, became responsible for the reinvigoration of Camel cigarettes' iconic "Joe Camel" in a campaign designed to mark the seventy-fifth anniversary of the brand in 1988 (Elliot 1991). Reynolds ran this campaign until 1997 even while undergoing a series of changes in ad agencies: they left Trone for the major New York firm McCann Erickson in 1988, then went to Young and Rubicam from 1989 to 1991, and then settled on Mezzina/Brown until the demise of the campaign. The Joe Camel campaign was one of the best-known, if controversial, advertising campaigns of the late twentieth century.

Camel and the Selling of Cigarettes

Cigarettes represent two significant dimensions of advertising. First, from their inception as a product, cigarettes have had a very long association with the advertising industry. They thus highlight the way that advertising creates sign value by creating arbitrary associations between a product and what it represents. Second, they reveal the contentious nature of advertising discourse that works to create desire for what can only be described as an unhealthy product. Cigarettes thus represent a success of the industry, and the way the industry had to retreat from its very success by the latter half of the twentieth century. Our case history of Camel cigarettes encapsulates some of this contentious history in the last few decades.

Cigarettes are products of mass consumption that emerged with industrialization in the mid to late nineteenth century. They are one of the earliest examples of branding as production became "massified" and manufacturers strove to make their products appear distinctive. Their first appearance as a product is usually attributed to an Egyptian soldier in 1832. Throughout the nineteenth century, consumption expanded in Europe, Asia and North America, with various business entrepreneurs in a range of countries, from England and Japan to Sumatra (Indonesia) and the United States stimulating their growth (Borio 2001). While the first national tobacco company, Bull Durham, emerged in the 1860s, the production process changed in 1881 when a cigarette-making machine was developed that could manufacture up to 40 times what workers could produce by hand. James Buchanan Duke, founder of American Tobacco, acquired a licence to use the machine in 1885, and by 1890, American Tobacco controlled 40% of the American cigarette market. Cigarettes were easier than cigars or chewing tobacco to package and advertise, easier to make because of the rolling machines, and easier to smoke because they were milder in the way that one inhaled the smoke into the lungs. With mechanization, 150,000 cigarettes were produced daily, which was about a fifth of American consumption at the time (Kremer 2012). While cigarettes represented only 1% of the American tobacco market in 1880 (Tate 1999), by the 1920s they passed the consumption of pipe tobacco, cigars, and chewing tobacco (Schudson 1984).

By the early twentieth century, cigarettes were advertised and promoted through two distinct strategies that have continued to define the key directions of the advertising industry into the twenty-first century. One prevalent strategy is to segment markets by creating associations that differentiate products and make them appealing. Cigarettes, in particular, have no individual identity or distinguishing characteristics apart from the image, or sign value that is created through advertising. The need for cigarette manufacturers to differentiate themselves from one another intensified after 1911 when the Sherman Anti-Trust Act broke up the Duke-controlled Tobacco Trust, which had been operating as a kind of loose monopoly and cartel (and, in fact, owned two-thirds of R.J. Reynolds). As a result, creating images associated with different brands of cigarettes became elemental to cigarette advertising throughout the rest of the twentieth century, as a small group of companies competed for market share. In this new form of competition in the industry, R.J. Reynolds Tobacco, along with the advertising agency N.W. Ayer, launched the first national cigarette brand – *Camel* – in 1913. The cigarette was an "American blend" of burley and bright leaf tobacco (with a bit of Turkish leaf for flavour and saccharin for sweetener), and thus advertised as milder than the other tobacco on the market. The package of 20 cigarettes was innovative, and imaging for Camel, created by graphic designer Fred Otto Kleesattel, was designed to establish an exotic quality and emulate then-fashionable Egyptian cigarettes. The camel on the label was based on a photograph of Old Joe, a Barnum and Bailey circus camel. The image of a camel also evoked the desert and implied that Camels were "dry" and thus easier to smoke. In terms of the advertising campaign, Ayer's strategy was to heighten anticipation for future pleasure. The Camel campaign was the first in the cigarette industry to use what is called an advertising "teaser". Well before the release of the actual cigarette, R.J. Reynolds released a series of print and display ads with taglines warning first, "The Camels are Coming!" followed by, "Tomorrow there'll be more Camels in this town than in all Asia and Africa combined." At the same time, a circus camel called "Old Joe" was driven through towns to dispense free cigarettes as a form of publicity. The campaign culminated with the line, "Camels are here!" when the cigarette was released (*Advertising Age* Encyclopedia 2003b).

In addition to creating an image that differentiates one brand of cigarette from another, cigarette advertising aims to increase market share by attracting new consumers. In this early period, cigarettes were primarily marketed to men. To capture the male market, companies linked cigarettes to the war efforts. During World War I in the United States, cigarettes became part of the daily ration packages provided to troops. General Pershing instituted this practice in 1918, and cigarettes were rationed by the market share of each brand, thus helping the already established and dominant Camel brand, which already shared over one-third of the domestic market (Borio 2001). Because of the addictive qualities of tobacco, these forms of benevolent promotion could be seen as "loss leaders" for the tobacco industry. That is, although the gift of cigarettes to soldiers was expensive, the returning soldiers became a new group of dedicated consumers, potentially addicted to cigarettes for the rest of their lives. The cigarette became associated with relief and comradeship, as well as positive conceptions of masculinity and even heroism. It lost some of its previous links with being a more feminized form of smoking in this new and very strong connection to war and soldiers.

Throughout the early decades of the twentieth century, Camel's approach made it difficult for other brands to make much impact. In addition to associating cigarettes with masculinity, Ayer also implemented strategies to present Camel cigarettes as unique and desirable. One of the most enduring slogans, "I'd walk a mile for a Camel," was coined in 1921. Ayer initially believed that the image of a smoker walking through the desert in search of a Camel would inspire brand loyalty, but then continued to use the slogan for decades.

The line became part of American argot in the 1920s and lived on as a defining slogan for Camel throughout most of the twentieth century (AdSlogans 2016).

The advertising industry was not so much involved in transforming American culture; what the industry focused on was taking ideas and sentiments that were developing in modern culture and attaching them to products. In this way, consumers would form identities based upon the values represented by a product. Specifically, the images that circulated through cigarette advertising linked it to modern life. For men, it defined a type of pursuit that matched the pace of modern life. In contrast to other forms of tobacco, it was convenient and easily stored and carried, and it had none of the elaborate preparation associated with pipe-smoking or the more obvious intrusion by smell and activity of either chewing tobacco or cigars. One campaign promoted cigarettes as more hygienic and "modern" than cigars, which were, after all, manufactured using human hands and saliva (Goodman, cited in Kremer 2012). Cigarettes became a cleaner and more urbane form of experience than other tobacco products. This shift was surprising because when cigarettes were first marketed, they were inexpensive products associated with immigrants and the working class.

Connecting the cigarette to modernity also helped cigarette companies expand the market from men to a new group of consumers – women. For middle-class women in the 1920s, smoking defined a kind of new generation of independence. Especially for females, smoking became a symbol of the "new woman" – as Schudson (1984, 196) writes, "a sign of divorce from the past and inclusion of the group of the new, young, and liberated". Ads were placed in "glossies", the new mass-market magazines aimed at women. Although women were banned from smoking in public in many cities, in 1924, Philip Morris introduced Marlboro, a women's cigarette that was "Mild as May". The copy for a 1925 Marlboro ad asked, "has smoking any more to do with morals than the color of a woman's hair?" Lucky Strike also targeted women by using testimonials from famous actresses, singers, and celebrities such as Helen Hayes and Amelia Earhart who provided aspirational points of identification. In one of the most famous examples of the association of cigarettes and female independence, Edward Bernays, working for Lucky Strike, organized New York debutantes and fashion models in the 1929 Easter Day Parade to light up "torches of freedom". Advertising and publicity functioned to legitimize and naturalize women smoking, but as Schudson (1984) notes, only by capitalizing on social changes already in play. In another example, in 1928, Lucky Strike began its "Reach for a Lucky Instead of Sweet" campaign to appeal to women's desire for a slender figure, again using ads that featured testimonials from celebrities on the benefits of substituting cigarettes for candy (when the candy industry objected, the language was changed to "overindulgence").

In 1929, Camel was the last of the major cigarette brands to actively expand into the female market. Ayer created the subtle magazine advertisement of a man offering a woman a Camel in order to challenge the conventions of propriety that only a decade earlier would have been deemed scandalous. But by 1930 Camel had lost market share to Lucky Strike, and sales were stagnating. Because of Ayer's delay in attempting to capture this new market, as well as their inability to counter Lucky Strike's powerful, if nonsensical, "It's Toasted" campaign (all cigarettes are toasted), and their failure to embrace the new medium of radio until three years after the debut of the Lucky Strikes Dance Orchestra, Reynolds dropped Ayer in favour of a new agency in 1931 (*Advertising Age* Encyclopedia 2003b).

Throughout the twentieth century, companies developed strong relationships with their advertising agencies, and accounts sometimes lasted generations. For example, Ayer held the Camel account from 1913 to 1931. However, when sales decline or stagnate, the relationship with an agency is generally one of the first to go. Part of the industry of advertising is the competition among agencies to both maintain clients and pull them away from other agencies when a moment of weakness is sensed. In the case of Camel, the first change of agency came when they left Ayer and briefly shifted to Erwin, Casey and Co. before switching to William Esty in 1932. The following year, Reynolds increased its advertising budget from $2.4 million to $10 million, and the new campaign emulated Lucky Strike by using public testimonials from celebrities, sports figures, business leaders, and society women. Testimonials and endorsements, which became popular in the 1920s, remain an important means for advertisers to foster participatory engagement when consumers make an emotional connection to an "authentic" image, often one perceived as authoritative or aspirational. As Stanley Resor, president of J. Walter Thompson, asserted, "People had always been most eager to hear about other people and to see 'virtues and vices… personified'" (quoted in Marchand 1986, 96). Moreover, Marchand adds, "the eternal 'search for authority' led people to revere whomever in a democracy could best fill the traditional role of aristocracy" (1986, 96). The use of testimonials from famous people in cigarette advertising coincided with the rise of celebrity culture in the twentieth century. Nearly 200 Hollywood stars from the 1930s and 1940s were contracted to tobacco companies for advertising (Anonymous, "Wayne for Camels"). Its spokespersons represented different types of stars, from the masculine John Wayne who appealed to men to romantic stars such as Tony

Curtis and Dick Powell who appealed to women. While the Federal Trade Commission (FTC) stipulated in 1929 that testimonials could not be used unless they were "genuine, authorized and unbiased", the tobacco industry evaded this by having film stars sign statements that they did not receive monetary compensation. Thus, despite the FTC's regulation, agencies continued to write the copy for endorsements and money was instead paid to the film studios. In an interesting blur of advertising and entertainment, testimonial ads made by stars were often timed to coincide with the release of their new films (Lum et al. 2008).

In addition to film stars, cigarette advertisements relied on testimony from sports figures to appeal to youth. Cigarettes have a long history of trying to appeal to youth. By the 1880s, cigarettes were already cleverly packaged with trading cards that featured photographs or drawings of baseball and other sports figures. Ostensibly, the cards were used to protect the cigarettes, but ultimately their attraction was to young boys drawn to the allure of the first generations of professional sports stars (paradoxically, as early as 1890, 21 states had outlawed selling cigarettes to minors). Thus in 1933, under the guidance of Esty, at a time when baseball was the most popular professional sport in the United States, Camel began using baseball stars in its advertising. At this time there were few restrictions on what claims could be made. In one case, for example, Camel used virtually the entire team of New York Giants in an ad that appeared two days after they won the World Series. Comments touted the energizing effects of Camels, with remarks from players such as Pepper Martin: "I like Camels because when I light one I can actually feel all tiredness slip away." Similarly, Rip Collins claimed: "A Camel has a way of 'turning on' my energy. And when I'm tired I notice they help me to snap back quickly." Dizzy Dean added: "A Camel sure brings back your energy after a hard game or when you're tired, and Camels never frazzle the nerves". While these claims could not be proven, there were no regulations to prevent cigarette companies from making them.

Other ads in the 1930s and 1940s focused on individual success and achievement and linked Camels with both sport and outdoor activity to tout them as relaxing. Tennis star Ellsworth Vine appeared in one 1935 ad, followed by another that featured Vine, pro golfer Helen Hicks, champion sculler Bill Biller, and water polo star Harry "Stubby" Kruger. Kruger, for example, states, "I smoke a great deal and Camels don't ever ruffle my nerves." In the same series, an oceanographer, a helicopter pilot, cowboy, a skin diver, and a sports parachutist were also depicted both doing their jobs and then relaxing with a cigarette. These ads emphasized that healthy and exciting outdoor professionals were drawn to the pleasures and calmness of Camels.

Camel's relationship with Esty continued for more than 50 years. What was valuable about Esty's approach and getting Camel to become the dominant brand by 1936 was the strong relationship and sponsorship arrangements with newer media such as radio, and later film and television. In this way, Camel was an early innovator in the blurring of advertising and entertainment. For instance, through Esty's work, Camel became linked to and sponsored young adult music programmes and thereby aimed its focus both on cultural change and on new potential cigarette consumers. Visibility of products was key to the success of brands such as Camel; but that visibility had to be attached to prevailing values and opinions. In a highly innovative approach to outdoor advertising, a 1942 billboard in Times Square featured a 15-foot-high serviceman blowing real smoke rings over the street from his Camel cigarettes (Julin 2006). Not only did it draw attention, talk, and stories, it served to link Camels to the World War II war effort and the positive sentiments associated with the armed services at that time. As was the case in World War I, cigarettes were part of every soldier's kit during the war, and sales soared when they returned home (*Advertising Age* Encyclopedia 2003b).

The connection to newer media was critical in the 1930s and 1940s for Camel as much as the entire advertising industry. Radio by the 1920s became a sponsor-controlled medium, with many programmes linked to products and their associated advertising agencies. In fact, as advertising agencies moved into producing radio programmes, they became instrumental in defining the nature and feel of what constituted entertainment in American broadcasting. In contrast to print advertising where agencies bought space in publications for their clients and therefore had very little connection to the production of the magazine or newspaper, broadcasting gradually allowed the sponsor to be at the helm of the production and therefore responsible for the creative work and how advertisements were inserted and placed within that production. Camel's whole-programme sponsorship included the popular tenor singer Morton Downey in the early 1930s on the nightly *Camel Quarter Hour*, *Blondie* (based on Chic Young's comic strip and the Columbia Pictures series) from 1939 to 1944 and the comic, singer, and best paid entertainer on radio in the 1930s, Eddie Cantor.

Countering Medicine with Medicine

Along with this strong connection to radio and entertainment, Esty continued to develop copy that competed and attempted to best Camel's competitors as well as allay any fears of the dangers of cigarette smoking. Cigarette advertisers have always been leaders in the development of ambient advertising and other sophisticated techniques of promoting their product in an environment of some resistance. Tobacco had long been thought of as unhealthy and hence was periodically banned in the nineteenth century. Throat cancer was already recognized as "smoker's cancer" in the middle of the nineteenth century, and throughout the twentieth century, studies that linked cigarette smoking to cancer continued to appear. However, by the middle decades of the twentieth century, cigarette companies were among the leading advertisers in the United States, and perhaps not coincidentally, cigarette smoking had become completely normalized. By 1949, it was estimated that 50% of men and 33% of women in the American market smoked regularly (Borio 2001). Yet, as direct medical evidence that identified the serious harm and danger of cigarette smoking mounted throughout the 1930s and 1940s, Reynolds tried to position Camels as a safe form of smoking. In part, their campaign was in response to the rapid growth of Philip Morris as a new major brand, which had enjoined the authority of physicians in their ads to allay concerns about the health issues related to smoking. R.J. Reynolds took this much further. First, they established a Medical Relations Division (MRD) in the early 1940s. Its mailing address was the side door of their advertising agency, Esty! The MRD financed research that was then referred to in the ads as "scientific". Their research identified that because Camels were slow-burning they had the health advantage of slower nicotine absorption (Gardner and Brandt 2006). None of this research made much sense, but in the tradition of patent-medicine puffery that we explored in Chapter 2, Camel worked to establish authority and legitimacy through its MRD. The research and its circulation to doctors also served as the launching point for Camel via MRD to enlist doctors' support for their brand. R.J. Reynolds began appealing to doctors by publishing ads in medical journals that touted their "scientific" research, and also by presenting doctors in ads in a flattering light. For example, in 1944, Camel began claiming that they were the favourite brand of physicians. Given that they were the most popular brand overall, and, at that time, a majority of physicians smoked, it was not a difficult claim to make. In classic advertising style, this simple link of a product to a noted and trusted authority figure – the physician – led to the powerful and provocative "More Doctors Smoke Camels" campaign in 1946 which became a mainstay of Camel's advertising for the next six years (Gardner and Brandt 2006, 1).

Camel's key strategy was to bring in the authority of science in medicine, with ads that featured doctors who advocated smoking Camel cigarettes. Doctors provided a reassuring presence, and looking back, they serve as a reminder of their cultural authority in the mid-twentieth century. A typical tagline read, "More doctors smoke Camels than any other cigarette", and the copy claimed that surveys conducted by three leading independent research organizations confirmed that doctors preferred Camel cigarettes to any other brand (see Figure 3.1). Reynolds originally announced that they surveyed all doctors, but then pulled back and listed the 113,597 doctors they contacted. In fact, the surveys were conducted by Esty, whose employees questioned doctors about their smoking preferences at conferences and in their offices just after providing them with free cartons of Camels (Gardner and Brandt 2006). Additionally, in contrast to celebrity and athletic endorsers, the doctors in the ads were never specific individuals, because appearing in advertising was not considered acceptable according to medical ethics. Thus the "doctors" were actors dressed in white coats. To further augment these claims, in radio and print ads, Reynolds and Esty advanced the idea of non-irritation as evidence of Camels' healthfulness. Ads reassured smokers with copy such as: "How Mild Can a Cigarette Be? Noted throat specialists after weekly examinations over 30 days found no throat irritation with Camels." The campaign also expanded into a "money-back guarantee" challenge where the consumer tested him or herself. These individualized tests served as further testimonials for the safety, mildness, and comparative healthiness of Camel smokers. Esty also invented the "T-Zone" to designate the area where one inhaled the

Figure 4.1   1949 Camel television ad relying on the authority of doctors

Source: "More Doctors Smoke Camels" 1949 television commercial on YouTube (https://www.youtube.com/watch?v=hxUZI0vE0FM)

cigarette, and used both attractive "ordinary" smokers and celebrities in the ads. The copy read, "'I' for taste, T for Throat, Camels will suit you to a T." Overall, the campaign's somewhat deceptive claims implied that unlike other cigarettes, Camels were healthful and would not irritate the throat.

Innovative Advertising Strategies to Create and Maintain Smokers

Looking at the advertising industry through its support of cigarettes, and in particular Camel, allows us to see some of the most innovative techniques in advertising and promotion in the latter half of the twentieth century. By the early 1950s, Camel ads shifted away from medical authentication that provided "throat reassurance", to personal verification of the pleasures of smoking, while still maintaining that Camel cigarettes were both the physicians' and America's "choice". In 1953, the first study was published that established a clear link between smoking and lung cancer. In response, the industry set up the Tobacco Industry Research Committee to prove that cigarettes were not dangerous, and launched a PR campaign that both affirmed their commitment to health and questioned the validity of the charges (*Advertising Age* Encyclopedia 2003b). At the same time, they made heavy use of the new medium of television to promote cigarettes. Cigarette companies were one of the largest sources of advertising revenue in the early days of television. Given the now complete ban of cigarette advertising on television, this appears to be just an interesting historical footnote. However, because cigarettes gradually came to be seen in a less favourable light due to their damaging health effects, advertising was one of the principal ways that tobacco companies could combat the massive negative evidence, research, and publicity. In early television, Esty ensured the prominence of Camel and bolstered their linkage to authority and sincerity. For example, NBC's flagship news programme was originally titled *The Camel News Caravan*. This association with news was further augmented through Edward R. Murrow's well-known four pack a day Camel cigarette smoking habit. Murrow was easily the most famous news host and reporter of the 1940s and 1950s. As his shows and commentary moved from radio to television on CBS, he was rarely visible on television without a Camel cigarette in hand. Esty's sophisticated approach to advertising illustrated its capacity to target the markets most likely to generate new consumers. Camel, along with most of the other major brands, focused an enormous amount of resources for advertising in college and university student newspapers in the 1950s and 1960s (Crawford 2014). Through humour, cartoons, and ads that depicted specific college experiences such as exams, Camel worked to insinuate itself into what was seen as "hep" or "cool" in the 1950s (Crawford 2014, 110). What one can see emerging via cigarette advertising is that in addition to blurring advertising, news, and entertainment, the industry was relying on greater demographic information to differentiate markets and beginning to embrace the concept of "cool" that became so important to advertising in the 1960s.

Ad copy became specifically aimed at the predispositions of specific groups within a culture. Camel's "Real Cigarette" campaign in its many variations from the mid-1950s to early 1960s highlights its efforts to equate smoking Camels with career success. Ads used endorsements from business tycoons, or, in one 1953–1954 series, Hollywood stars endorsed the brand while giving stories of how they got into the movie business, thus encouraging consumers to connect Camels with fame. Another 1956 "Real Cigarette" ad featured a testimonial from a civil engineer: "I want a real cigarette. One I can taste. That's why I am a Camel smoker and have been one since college." These ads largely targeted male college students and presented cigarettes as a pathway to a career.

During this period, Camels aimed to reach a male market as it relinquished the female market to newer brands. In order to reach mature men, Camel's ads made use of light entertainment television actors such as *Father Knows Best* star Robert Young, as well as the entire crew of *The Phil Silvers Show*, a situation comedy that overtly celebrated masculinity through its setting on an army base. The last of these, *The Phil Silvers Show* (1955–1959), and later *McHale's Navy* (1962–1966), identified a very sophisticated move in advertising. Camel became integrated into a well-developed skit-comedy routine where all of the actors performed in character, and thus the product pitch resembled the programme and its style of humour completely. The end-point of the skit was usually related to the value, the smoothness, or the intelligence of smoking Camel cigarettes as well as underlining how all of the characters were lifelong Camel smokers. Although these were clearly advertisements that were meant to blend seamlessly with the programme itself, they identified the beginning formulation of product placement – previously called "tie-ups" or "exploitations" – as a form of advertising in the entertainment industry (Newell et al. 2006). As cigarette advertising became prohibited, restricted, or banned, agencies placed products such as Camel into the entertainment itself to maintain its visibility and cultural value.

In 1980, R.J. Reynolds and Esty developed a formal relationship with a Hollywood public relations firm, Rogers and Cowan, to assist in promoting their brands through popular entertainment and to connect their product to key entertainment workers of national prominence and visibility. Camel's cigarettes were freely distributed as a form of promotion to many stars both before 1980 and after; but the critical change was the prominence of Camel in films in particular. In the famed 1982 Bond film *Never Say Never Again*, Rogers and Cowan paid just $10,000 to secure a deal that Sean Connery and others would smoke Camels and other Reynolds brands in the film (Mekemson and Glantz 2002). Likewise, in the 1988 film *Who Framed Roger Rabbit*, the animated Betty Boop character is a periodized cigarette girl who prominently displays packs of Camel cigarettes on her tray.

Sporting events were another prominent and early site for product placement, a practice initiated by James Duke in the late nineteenth century. Thus Camel became visible in various motorsports over most of the middle part of the twentieth century, from Formula One teams to sponsorship of particular events. In 1963, R.J. Reynolds sponsored eight major league baseball teams (Cummings et al. 2005). These associations were instrumental in maintaining the visibility of Camel and the other R.J. Reynolds brands when the complete ban on broadcast advertising of tobacco came in force in the United States in 1970. Along with lower-level and community-based sponsorships, advertising agencies shifted to providing ambient ads and promotions in all sorts of ways in the 1970s and 1980s. For instance, billboards along major freeways, in stadiums, and strategically placed in sight of busy intersections became a principal channel for maintaining cigarette advertising prominence.

Joe Camel, Children and the Culture of Retreat

As we have described, the tobacco industry was constantly shifting its image and type of visibility in the latter half of the twentieth century in response to the societal and governmental condemnation of its product as an overwhelming health hazard. This presented unique challenges for both the tobacco industry and the advertising agencies representing cigarette companies, which in turn produced innovative forms of advertising. From product placement to sponsorship, from target marketing to constructing a sense that cigarettes represented something independent, fun, cool, and alluring for young potential consumers of the product, cigarette advertising was a constantly moving but effective form of persuasive communication.

To complete our case history of Camel cigarettes, we address the way the controversial "Joe Camel" campaign highlights the cleverness of advertisers in a climate where cigarette advertising was in an apparent massive retreat. By the 1980s, the American government mandated that cigarette manufacturers' display ads and packaging had to list that smoking leads to lung cancer, is dangerous to pregnancies, and is a major contributing cause of heart disease and emphysema. In some countries, packaging also had to show graphic evidence of the damage that cancer produces in its users: thus, mouth cancer images in full colour were included on some packages along with related maladies on other packages. By the second decade of the twenty-first century, Australia instituted that cigarettes had to be sold in plain packages and thus eliminated any of the brand allure that promotional packaging tries to produce.

Predating these further efforts at eliminating the promotion of cigarettes was the Joe Camel campaign, which ran from 1987 to 1997. Interestingly, from an advertising industry perspective, the campaign emerged shortly after the new owner of Camel, RJR Nabisco, dismissed Esty Advertising because they had failed to expand internationally. Esty had handled much of R.J. Reynolds' business for more than 50 years, and thus this move severed one of the longest brand connections between a manufacturer and an advertising agency in the twentieth century. In 1988 Camel celebrated its seventy-fifth anniversary, and the new agency, Trone Advertising, used that event to catapult a new American mascot for the brand: thus the cartoon character Joe Camel was born. Joe was not entirely new as a Camel figure. He had a career promoting the brand in Europe for the previous decade and was linked to the dromedary image and the original circus performer who was used to promote the cigarettes 75 years earlier in its first decades as a brand. Nonetheless, this version of Joe Camel was a very recognizable and funny caricature: his snout was elongated, his attitude was hip, and he regularly appeared with sunglasses and an incredibly wide, knowing grin. A cigarette hung from his mouth, naturally. Joe Camel was used in magazines ads, billboards, and, because of his popularity for nearly a decade, on all sorts of branded clothing from hats, stickers, and cups to t-shirts and boxer shorts – many of them supplied originally as free promotional giveaways. The timing of his emergence intersected with the early Internet as well, and his image circulated widely among Internet users in the early 1990s.

What Camels achieved through Joe Camel was the creation of a cultural icon that was almost universally recognized. The Camel brand had been in decline since the 1960s, and instead of being the number one cigarette in the United States, it had less than 5% of the market at the time of the introduction of Joe Camel. Joe Camel created a media sensation for a number of reasons, but from a strategic point of view, for an industry in ill-repute it became an image that circulated widely over and above what would be normal forms of advertising. What propelled it even further was that Joe Camel was scandalous. In some ways, Joe was a mascot designed to appeal to young males: he was visible in men's magazines and sporting and cultural events attractive predominantly to males. His image was associated with ad copy that exuded cool: the predominant slogans of "smooth character" and "genuine taste, never boring" were designed to imply that both the cigarette and Joe embodied these traits. Even Joe's nose was thought to resemble male genitals. However, what made Joe Camel a veritable media sensation in the 1980s and 1990s was that his cartoonish features appealed to children. R.J. Reynolds was taken to court over whether they were deliberately advertising to children. The case was put forward for a ruling by the FTC within weeks of the launch of the campaign to decide whether the Joe Camel campaign crossed the restrictions of advertising to children because of its appealing cartoon quality (Figure 4.2). The controversy brewed for almost a decade. The *Journal of the American Medical Association* published two articles detailing how well Joe Camel was recognized by children. The second of these articles found that 91.3% of 6-year-olds not only recognized Joe but linked him to a cigarette; an almost equal number linked Mickey Mouse to the Disney logo (Fischer et al. 1991). Further damning evidence came in the publicized promotional strategies of R.J. Reynolds and how they imagined the Joe Camel campaign as the

Figure 4.2   The cartoonish Joe Camel character was widely criticized for appealing to children
Source: AP Archive, published July 21, 2015 on YouTube
(https://www.youtube.com/watch?v=b_5I5GjzF64&t=45s)

best way to enliven the brand with young adults. The wording of their strategies implied that the goal was to create new smokers. In that focus, and the general knowledge that most smokers begin the practice in their teens, it was generally perceived that the Joe Camel campaign was indeed targeting youth. In 1997, once the case was championed by the American Medical Association and well-funded, R.J. Reynolds decided to end the campaign to avoid any further controversy. In effect, after nine years Joe Camel had run as long, or longer than any campaign that Camel had produced over the last 75 years. The scandal actually defined yet another innovative way in which products can be promoted and endorsed by advertising agencies intent on making its content go what we now call "viral".

Conclusion

Through our case history of Camel cigarettes, we have detailed much of the developments of advertising as an industry. What has to be understood is that advertising is an interesting negotiated relation between companies. The manufacturers who produce the product are aided, assisted, and brokered by companies that focus their entire energy on making the product visible, valuable, and desirable in a wider populace. These brokering companies are advertising agencies for the most part, and their expertise has linked them with another range of companies that are expert at drawing audiences and readers to cultural forms, events, and practices. This third group of companies are generally thought of as the entertainment industries in their production of television, film, popular music, and a wide array of related and unrelated performance and sporting events and exhibitions. Our case history has been at study of the past and therefore has not investigated the converged entertainment and communication structure of the Internet, the Web and the related social media, games, and applications that we associate with online culture.

This chapter has described how cigarette advertisers created brand loyalty by linking their products to social and cultural values, how markets were segmented in early cigarette advertising, how cigarette advertisers used testimonials and endorsements to create engagement and participation, and how products become attached to forms of entertainment through different kinds of content, sponsorship, and space- and time-buying. This has not changed in the online era. We continue to have our entertainment and our forms of communication interspersed with online forms of advertising. What can be discerned from our case history is that the techniques that define the advertising industry all have elements that were deployed in earlier eras and marketing strategies. From the original introduction of Camel with the Teaser, we can see how movie trailers try to construct a similar enticing relationship now or how rolling animated GIFs on our various screens draw us to click on them to find out more and be drawn into a particular promotional world. Just as significantly, we can see that advertising as an industry has built and expanded through extensive market research. For Camel cigarettes, this research led to several of its campaigns. For example, its focus on men in the 1950s and 1960s was part of realizing that the market diversification in cigarette brands meant that a brand had to build a solid niche that is attached to highly valued notions in a culture. Its efforts at structuring Camel as a brand that embodied individualized and independent masculinity was a technique that appealed to the brand's tradition and responded to a very segmented cigarette market. The Joe Camel campaign underlined how constructing a cultural event – this time through an alluring cartoon image – can make any product have a greater impact. One can see these trends in advertising and marketing regularly on online platforms, where individuals and companies work very hard for their videos to go "viral" and produce meme-like variations of the original content.

Finally, it is important to see that the advertising industry is a complex amalgam of companies. Advertising now includes the marketing and promotional divisions of large corporations, the branding agents and specialists, global advertising agencies, creative advertising specialists and boutiques, audience and consumer research firms and companies that now blend with online data companies, product placement agents and specialists, and marketing companies who specialize in creating buzz and activity beyond any production of a commercial or image/text based advertisement. In some cases, with the many mergers that have occurred in the industry over the last 20 years, all of these supposed companies are often housed in a major advertising conglomerate. This structure of interrelated companies and industries defines the contemporary advertising industry.

5

Traditional and Ambient Advertising: Targeting Children through Cereal

This chapter is an exploration of both direct and "ambient" advertising techniques used to target children and, more indirectly, the parents and adults who buy for them. Our choice of case history – breakfast cereals, and specifically those breakfast products that have been primarily aimed at children – serves as an example of how even an ordinary, mundane product is advertised through the discourse of transformation; it illustrates how brand loyalty is instilled even in the youngest consumers, and it shows the growing importance of consumers actively engaging with a brand. Most importantly, this chapter illustrates how throughout the twentieth century advertisers have blurred advertising and entertainment by presenting an array of attractive images/characters/enticements to induce consumption, and how these promotional messages have been insinuated into the everyday environment through television programming and in the twenty-first century through online games and activities. We consider the way "traditional" advertisements that are clearly demarcated and non-traditional "ambient" advertising strategies work together to make a form of promotion part of everyday life.

Throughout the world, an extensive level of advertising is targeted towards children. For instance, in the United States companies spent over $17 billion on advertising to children in 2009 – more than double what was spent in 1992 ("How Marketing Targets Kids", 2016). However, one of the difficulties in advertising directly to children is that it is subjected to heavy regulation and policy debate. As we have seen in our chapters on patent medicine (Chapter 2) and cigarette advertising (Chapter 4), promotional culture is sometimes under incredible scrutiny for its integrity, its value, and its potential danger to our cultures and societies. Children are often seen to be the most vulnerable to advertising messages because they are cognitively incapable of identifying what is in their best interest. In this regard, drawing from Lee (2001), Buckingham (2011) has explained much advertising research posits children as not fully formed. Instead of complete "beings", children are "becomings" (Buckingham 2011, 49). It is perhaps a sad reality that the same critique of not understanding the true value of things could be levelled at adult culture as well; nonetheless, children have provided the focus for much of the concern, and ultimately the regulation of content.

One way that advertisers circumvent regulation is through what we call ambient advertising. This form of advertising has many variations, and when first coined as a term in the early 1990s, it involved nontraditional forms of advertising. Thus, a bus shelter, the series of ads in a subway car, or the latest variation of the ever-present video screen at checkout counters, gas station bowsers, airport lounges, and university spaces are all clear examples of the intersection of traditional and ambient advertising. Although often characterized as a separate form of advertising and promotion, sponsorships are another way for products and services to move into spaces perhaps not normally associated with the product. Thus, a major stadium may be associated with a retailer through naming rights (for example, the Los Angeles Home Depot Stadium or in Melbourne, Australia, Etihad Football stadium which promotes the airline in an ambient way around soccer and football matches). When advertising is put into the environment and is therefore not clearly targeted at children because of its "public" location, its ambient quality means that it can connect to children without explicitly targeting them. A sporting match with its massive flow of images of all sorts of products and sponsorships, from those on the jerseys of the players to the rotating images on the sideboards of the field, is not only designed for the core adult fans, they are also in an ambient/environmental way being seen by children.

The advertising industry has been very successful at positioning itself in an ambient way into youth culture. One of the more ingenious ways has been how corporations have funded and sponsored school programmes. As Toland Frith and Mueller (2010) explain, in the 1990s, the United States led the world in permitting this movement of commercial culture into the schools and classrooms as a new funding source to countervail the decline in governmental support for education. However, the movement has also advanced internationally. Corporations have sponsored programmes even in the tightly controlled French education system where "Colgate [taught] children to brush their teeth, [and] the Le Clerc supermarket chain [was used to] tell them about the European single currency" at the turn of the millennium (James 2001, quoted in Frith and Mueller 2003, 153). In the United States,

Procter & Gamble, Coca-Cola, and Levi Strauss are some of the companies connected to educational programmes as sponsors. Other companies such as General Mills, one of the major companies explored in our case history of breakfast cereals, have become part of school breakfast and lunch programmes.

Connecting to the youth market is highly lucrative for advertisers for a number of reasons. As Buckingham (2011) identifies, the money that young people have, whether in the form of pocket money or earned income, is often the most detached from household necessities. Different surveys reveal that children are playing less and shopping more, and from a very young age they are major media consumers and thus susceptible to the influences of advertisers. Moreover, advertisers know that young children can influence purchases through the "nag factor". Story and French (2004, 1) write that a child's first request for a product occurs at around 24 months of age, 75% of the time it occurs in a supermarket, and the most requested in-store product is breakfast cereal. The phenomenon of children pestering their parents towards consumption gained the name "kidfluence" in the late 1990s and early 2000s and led to at least some campaigns that saw part of their promotional efforts based on making children intermediaries in consumption. Decisions about cars, vacations, and restaurant eating have been demonstrably influenced by marketers aiming their messages at children over adults (see Schor 2004, 23–25; Sutherland and Thompson 2001). Indeed, some of the research into kidfluence suggests that in relative terms, the affinity of children to particular brands is often more powerful than that of adults (Schor 2004). Our case history of breakfast cereal is perhaps the quintessential model of how this form of advertising to children works to change consumption patterns quite dramatically in families.

Adolescence is also seen as one of the key times that lifelong patterns begin to emerge in the purchase of products. Drawing on research from the advertising firm Griffin Bacal in 2000, Schor (2004, 25) concludes that "Today's tweens are the most brand-conscious generation in history." The attachment to a brand of toothpaste, a particular breakfast cereal, or a certain type of soft drink becomes strong enough that it could be part of the consuming practices of an individual for the rest of their life. Further buttressing this status of the importance of adolescent purchasing is that it is also seen as the time where forms of peer pressure can be identified by consumer research, and also connected to by advertisers and marketers. As we will see in Chapter 11 on Dove and commodity activism, advertisers have become more and more sophisticated at creating brand tribes where people feel both authentic and part of a community defined by their connection to products, even when groups such as adolescents may appear to be quite ambivalent to consumer culture.

As children move into adolescence, many studies have identified a high level of cynicism in their reading of advertising. From one perspective, this cynicism points to their understanding of how much of advertising is interruptive in terms of its placement in cultural forms such as television or online sites. It is from this perspective that teens may perceive ads as highly annoying and to be avoided. Despite this apparent level of sophistication in adolescence, according to a wealth of literature their level of discernment of the meaning of advertisements does not match the cognitive abilities of adults (see Gunter et al. 2005, 57–61; Bartholomew and O'Donohoe 2003). Nonetheless, much innovation in advertising has been directed at this lucrative teen market as marketers and advertisers continue to develop new ways to intersect with their lifestyles. These techniques of advertising which are at least partially designed to appear as if they are not advertising at all have often been connected to the way in which advertisers appeal to the different strata of youth markets. In this way, our case history of cereal is an extended example of how, throughout the twentieth century, advertising has worked out a variety of ways to appeal to youthful consumers and become part of everyday life so that advertising becomes indistinguishable from entertainment. While our analysis of cereal advertising includes traditional and ambient advertising techniques, what follows are two principal forms of ambient advertising that, while often described as new, have existed throughout the twentieth century. These are explored with greater historical detail and context in our case history, which details how from the late nineteenth century to the present day, advertisers have combined traditional and ambient techniques to naturalize cereal as a breakfast food for children. In this way, cereal advertising illuminates the intersection of old and new practices into the twenty-first century.

Intertextual Advertising: Cross-Promotion as Ambient Advertising

Cross-promotion simply means the linking of two products for coordinated promotion. As we saw in Chapter 2 with the example of Lydia Pinkham, cross-promotion emerged alongside modern advertising. While Pinkham offered products such as perfumes or sewing kits that bore her name and/or image, in the early twentieth century endorsements by celebrities or sports figures also became a common form of cross-promotion. For example, the endorsement of a movie star such as John Wayne for Camel cigarettes (See Chapter 4) served as an example of cross-promotion because the movie star was a product as much as the brand. In more recent years, role models such as sports figures often earn lucrative salaries for their endorsement of products. This can go horribly wrong if negative news stories emerge, especially when athletes endorse products aimed at children. For example, in 2008 Olympic Gold medallist Michael Phelps appeared on Kellogg's Corn Flakes, though he was quickly fired when it was reported that he had smoked marijuana.

Beyond celebrities or sports figures, cross-promotion of food products with other forms of popular culture is probably the most visible and the most connected to children. Film promotion is regularly connected to children through both food and toys, called movie tie-ins. It should be remembered that *Star Wars* in 1977 began the now normalized trend for blockbuster films to create a series of cross-promotions with food, toys, and restaurants to expand the impact of the film's release and eventually produce what has been termed a "megafranchise" (Dalecki 2008, 148). In the 1980s, Ralston's even manufactured a cereal called Gremlins to tie in with the release of the movie. The cereal bits were in the shape of the movie's main character, Gizmo; moreover, children could purchase a plush toy, and each box included a collectible sticker.

Disney, in an even longer history of movie tie-ins, has been enormously successful at extending cross-promotion into other media and entertainment forms as well as other products, thereby extending the "franchise" quality of the original film. Theme-park rides, children's books, toys, character-linked snacks and packaged food, television programmes, musical albums, song books, musicals, and even figure-skating shows are some of the ways that a film and its characters are deployed to extend both the longevity of the value of the film and to monetize the intellectual property generated by the film. Needless to say, Disney characters such as Mickey Mouse, the Little Mermaid, or more recently, Elsa from *Frozen* have appeared on cereal boxes.

Along with regular forms of advertising, this type of film cross-promotion ensures a saturation coverage upon a film's release. McDonald's, for instance, has regularly promoted children's movies with small figurines or toys that are part of its Happy Meal. Indeed, in the American market, toys directed at under-10-year-old children have been part of the Happy Meal since its inception in 1979. By 1987, an arrangement with Disney ensured that both classic characters such as Mickey Mouse and new-release characters such as Aladdin, Simba, and the puppies in the 1990s version of *101 Dalmatians* were collectible figurines in the Happy Meal. Characters from film and television properties such as Transformers, Lego, and Teletubbies have also been part of the meal (Webley 2010). These toys, we would argue, were forms of ambient advertising in their capacity to provide an intertextual commodified link (Marshall 2002) between the fast-food chain, the entertainment product, and the child. The toy itself not only served to extend the promotion into the home; in the long history of fast food's relationship to entertainment cross-promotion, it also helped ensure a participatory engagement with the brand. Children return to these locations for the experiential connection of eating and enjoying the pleasure of first receiving the surprise "gift" of the toy in the Meal, and then the imaginative play that extends the toy into the child's life. Needless to say, this intertextual and ambient form of cross-promotion has been part of the entire fast-food industry as companies compete for movie tie-in franchises. In one of the more recent bidding wars, McDonald's successfully secured the exclusivity of the *Minions* franchise – at least in terms of fast food. One has to keep in mind that when a particular entertainment character/story gains traction, it becomes ubiquitous, and in its ambient presence in the culture it helps define the structure of feeling of that particular year/time. As we will see in our study of cereal, similar techniques of cross-promotion have been integral to its marketing and advertising.

Point of Purchase Techniques

Critical to understanding the value of ambient advertising is to appreciate its capacity to operate as if it is not directly a form of advertising. This communicative sleight of hand makes it doubly powerful as an advertising technique directed at children. Along with the forms of cross-promotion described above, perhaps the most powerful ambient advertising is called Point of Purchase (POP) or Point of Sale (POS) advertising or marketing (see Liljenwall 2004). On the most basic level, this is a form of advertising of the product itself at the point where the consumer is making decisions. Window displays of all stores represent the most obvious form of POP advertising. Actual merchandise on a mannequin attempts to sell clothes by tantalizing a buyer with future possibilities made attainable by consumption. Augmenting this display are often discount posters that increase the specialness of the moment where the product is heightened not only in its visibility, but also in the sense of the timeliness of shopper's presence at the store. In a manner that modernizes the ancient custom of barter in bazaars and markets, supermarkets work to entice shoppers to feel that they individually, by their good fortune of timing, have got a special price for a given good. What one sees in the contemporary supermarket in almost every country around the world is the sticker display of "special" everywhere. Enhancing this experience are the modern day "barkers" of supermarkets and other discount settings. For example, food samples cut up into bite-sized portions that are consumed by shoppers are designed to shift their planned purchases and lead to impulse purchases. Similarly, checkout lanes are constructed cleverly to capture further momentary desires. Indeed, the very design of supermarkets, including the checkout lanes, has been organized to attract children and thereby distract the rationality of purchasing that was at least the original objective of the shopping trip by their parents.

POP advertising has many other examples, including how even homes are advertised with grand photo displays of their interiors on every street in Australia and other countries, or the now standard pattern of providing coupons for future purchase based on your buying practices in your current shop. What is critical in locations such as supermarkets or department stores is the packaging of the product itself as a powerful form of advertising that appeals to the senses. The way in which products are designed, presented, and displayed in aisles, itemized in terms of type, and connected to related products helps define their relative success. Also, in relation to children, it is evident that products rely on packaging, with attractive characters, bright colours, and eye-level location as part of their point of purchase campaign.

Finally, as with much of advertising, ambient POP advertising and promotion has also transformed with the migration to online culture. Children's use of online sources such as YouTube and other platforms, along with their varying age-differentiated uses of social media such as Facebook and Instagram and online games, have created a whole new way to communicate products to children and a whole new generation of laws and restrictions. In our case history of cereals, we assess how online POP promotion and advertising has become indistinguishable from entertainment and, to some degree, poses a danger for contemporary families.

What follows is an extended historical analysis of how a particular product through both traditional and ambient advertising became naturalized and normalized as a product for children. Breakfast cereal advertising and promotion, from advertisements to ambient-style promotions and lures, demonstrates how advertising from the late nineteenth century to the present has connected to the elusive and sometimes protected market of children.

Case History: Cereal and Children – An Historical Case of Ambient Promotion

Although porridge represents at least a 5000-year-old precursor, breakfast cereals are an interesting modern invention. Cereal manufacturing origins in the latter half of the nineteenth century in the United States were definitively part of the "therapeutic ethos" identified by Lears (1983) (see also Chapter 2) as elemental to the emerging consumer culture of self-betterment. Indeed, the first generation of cereal makers were connected to the Seventh-Day Adventist Church and their hospitals and sanatoriums. The birthplace of Kellogg's cereal was Battle Creek, Michigan, the home of the church's sanatorium and the location where John Kellogg and his brother developed and tested the health value of their first cereal of baked grain. Kellogg saw his baked grain broken up into small hard pieces as a cure to the bad American diet and lifestyle. Post–Civil War, many people in America were perceived to be suffering from digestive ailments related to diet. From Kellogg and his mentor, it was believed that fibre was missing from people, both spiritually and in terms of food. Drawing from work done by a precursor, John Kellogg called his first cereal Granula. At first, the product was part of the therapy at the sanatorium facilities itself, where patients could go to cure themselves of ills. Soon after, the breakfast cereal became included as part of the therapies in other nineteenth-century health spas and retreats. The relative success of both the sanatorium and the cereal led to its quick commercialization. The name was changed to Granola after Kellogg was sued by the original manufacturer, a follower of the vegetarian evangelical preacher Sylvester Graham.

Very quickly, Battle Creek became the centre of breakfast cereal manufacturing. Beyond Kellogg's, by the early twentieth century more than a hundred companies were located there, producing variations of cereal and quickly improving both the edibility of the "flakes" and their durability in packaging (Lawrence 2010). Most were still vaguely connected to the Seventh-Day Adventists (William Keith Kellogg, the brother of John, broke away when he added sugar to his "flakes" and started Kellogg's) and, at minimum, were part of a very particular health food craze (a follow-on of the mid-nineteenth century Clean Living Movement) of the late nineteenth century and early twentieth century (Arndt 2013, 21). The manufacture of cereal and the expansion through advertising of its message of positive and healthy well-being allowed it to be one of the first successful mass-produced and highly packaged foods of the twentieth century.

Because of its religious roots, breakfast cereal was a product that through its promotional messages was linked to family and well-being. Etymologically, the word breakfast implied a break from a period of religious fasting from supper the night before until after Holy Communion the following morning – eating too soon or too much made you gluttonous and was one of the seven deadly sins (Arndt 2013). The benefits of a pure – in this case, vegetarian – opening to each day were reinforced in the packaging and other forms of advertising engaged by cereal manufacturers in the early part of the twentieth century. Charles Post, who was first an attendee at Kellogg's sanatorium and derived his business from the experience, was instrumental in the expansive positive discourse and selling of breakfast cereals nationally. Indeed, breakfast cereal was among the first generation of national brand campaigns. Through his first cereal, Postum/Post Grape Nuts, Post attached pamphlets entitled the "Road to Wellville" filled with the positive values that the cereal ensured. Early advertisements in newspapers similarly gave patent-medicine-inspired testimonials as to the benefits of Grape Nuts with claims that it could cure malaria and consumption, while still working as a form of brain food (Lawrence 2010).

It has to be understood that cereals were only successful as the new breakfast health food in English-speaking parts of the world. In addition to the United States, the Seventh-Day Adventists worked to expand their take-up in Australia and New Zealand as well as Great Britain. They still control Sanitarium, one of the largest cereal manufacturing companies in Australia, which is named after the hospitals and health centres that Kellogg was involved with in the late nineteenth century. Notwithstanding this limitation to the British Empire and North America, breakfast cereals in their various forms became standard by the 1920s in these English-speaking countries and literally present in the rest of Europe by the 1950s. Availability of breakfast cereal in the twenty-first century is nearly universal across the world even though it is much less popular in the non-English-speaking countries, particularly in areas where dairy products are less prominent and not commonly valued as a regular food source, such as China.

Targeting Children through Sign Value

Breakfast cereal's infiltration into the twentieth-century household was built on two important sign values that marked the transition to consumer culture: cereals were linked to the idea of healthfulness; in addition, they were presented as highly convenient – "quick" and "instant" were some of the promotional catchlines. As the origins of cereal described above illustrate, advertisers took advantage of yearnings for health and vitality by linking products to well-being (See also Lears 1983). "Natural" products such as cereal were equated with wholesomeness and goodness, in contrast to the artificial products of modern life, and the promise of a better family through appropriate consumption was part of the advertising message. A 1903 Shredded Wheat ad, for example, asked, "Mothers, do you know that children crave natural food until you pervert their taste by the use of unnatural food?"

(Lears 1983, 23). Breakfast cereal was also promoted as a healthy alternative to the heavy meat- and egg-based meals that public relations advisor Edward Bernays, working for the Beechnut Company, made into the quintessential American breakfast in the 1920s.

In addition, though advertising and packaging, cereals were presented as highly convenient and therefore part of the modern lifestyle. Susan Strasser argues that the seemingly common-sense value of convenience is one marker of the shift from pre-industrial to modern consumer culture; in pre-industrial societies where there was no division of labour and leisure, there was no need to save time or to work less (Strasser 2009, 30–31). For example, she writes that an ad for Wheatena cereal proclaimed that it could be prepared "in 2 minutes of bubbling and boiling", or another ad suggested that the virtue of Grape Nuts cereal was that it did not have to be prepared at all. Moreover, breakfast cereal's other convenient quality was its durability. As a packaged food, cereal lasted long periods of time, especially as companies began to add preservatives. But perhaps of even greater importance is that cereal required minimal supervision by parents for feeding children. This freedom from the labour of preparation and even serving dovetailed with other time- and energy-saving inventions for the modern household.

One particularly resonant ad for Post Grape Nuts from 1913 illustrates the interrelationship of the values of health and convenience. A colour picture depicts a young mother and her two preschool children on the beach having breakfast underneath an umbrella. Apart from portraying the family as from the better classes in terms of dress, the advertisement also demonstrates the new possibilities for mothers with children because of the convenience of Grape Nuts. It promises to improve the family by saving time while remaining healthful. Here was a breakfast that was easily transportable, made no mess, and, ironically, was a "natural" food made "scientifically" to provide well-being and healthfulness. The slogan was "Fresh Air and Natural Food", and the ad promised "tissue-building" and aid in "replacing soft gray material of brain and nerve centres". The closing line defined the increasing move to children as the target market for cereals: "Follow the law of Old Mother Nature – eat Grape-Nuts and cream, and *give it to the children*, at least once a day."

Children figure prominently in other early cereal advertisements. From Cream of Wheat to Kellogg's, the child is presented as an important recon-figuration and expression of the future and the present that is wedded to the desire for healthiness. With Postum leading this early charge in linking cereal with children, other cereal manufacturers such as Kellogg's worked in a similar space.

Targeting Children through Ambient Advertising: Pre-Television Cross-Promotion

By 1906, Kellogg's tried its first creative effort to expand sales through an ambient appeal to children that both encouraged active participation and presented its advertising in the guise of an entertaining book. At the campaign's launch, a children's book was offered to any consumer who would buy at least two boxes of Kellogg's Cornflakes. The promotional product was titled *Funny Jungleland Moving-Pictures Book* and branded completely as a Kellogg's product; it allowed children to manipulate pictures of comic-like animal images to create new funny hybrids. The campaign worked in what we would now term *virally*, as children and families compared their acquisitions, and children's desires spread the promotion. Indeed, the book's visibility in the family home became something highly prized. In addition, even the structure of the campaign of linking a children's product with the cereal at the point of purchase – a clear example of ambient advertising – cleverly anticipated the presence of children when mothers were grocery shopping.

In 1909, Kellogg developed another ambient advertising strategy that would later become a standard industry practice to reward children for accumulating box tops by exchanging them for a prize. By sending in box tops of Kellogg's Corn Flakes, children would receive a coupon allowing them to buy the coveted book for a premium price of 10 cents and, by 1912, 2.5 million books had been sold or given away (World History Project, n.d.) This campaign continued in some form until 1937. The campaign also generated massive amounts of marketing information as the return addresses identified the relative success of the brand in selling as well as identifying a pattern for engaging with consumers with even greater commitment and loyalty to their product.

Cereal companies either pioneered or appropriated various forms of ambient advertising and promotion throughout the first half of the twentieth century. Part of this was built on their packaging of their products themselves. The cereal package in the aisle was a form of attraction; once it was in the home, it served as a regular reminder of the product and its values as it often sat in front of the family at breakfast, working as a source of both attention and reading material throughout the morning ritual. The front, back, sides, and tops of the package became sites for promotion and, in many ways, appealed to different dimensions of a family market. Nutrition and health information worked to appeal to mothers allaying their fears of whether a product was good for their growing children; box tops, characters and promotions, although not exclusively aimed at children, were generally ways in which children would serve to "pester" the sale and future sale of the cereal brand.

After Kellogg's original *Funny Jungleland* promotional campaign, cereal manufacturers had increasing confidence in aiming their advertising and promotions directly at children. From the 1920s onwards, campaigns depended less and less on in-house advertising and more on particularly innovative advertising agencies. Premiums became a regular feature of many cereals, and more and more products related to children were produced. Kellogg's in the 1920s promoted *the Stuff-Yourself Nursery Rhyme Rag Dolls* that could only be purchased through sending box tops to their Battle Creek headquarters (Kellogg Co. 2016). Agencies such as N.W. Ayer & Son and Kenyon and Echkard, and by 1938, J. Walter Thompson, fine-tuned Kellogg's marketing approaches as their strategic targeting transformed from a focus on families to children. General Mills, one of their rivals, in 1923 worked with the agency Blackett-Sample-Hummert to both produce and sponsor *Skippy Secret Service Society*, the first radio programme and club aimed at children. The programme and club focused on the adventures of a boy, Skippy, who managed to get into a great deal of mischief. To build loyalty to the character, the agency embedded box top promotions for General Mills's sponsored brands. This programme and the follow-up, *Jack Armstrong, All American Boy*, ran on syndicated radio stations from 1933 to 1951, helped move the cross-promotional strategies aimed at children that Kellogg's had initiated to an entirely new level. Boy-targeted promotions such as the Jack Alexander Hike-O-Meter stimulated the mailing of 1.2 million Wheaties box tops to General Mills by customers who wanted the adventure toy derived from the radio show's narrative.

The structure of early to mid-twentieth century radio advertising helped define this seamless relationship between products, programmes, and cross-promotion. Unlike the era of television, advertising agencies were responsible for not only the sponsorship of programmes, but also the programmes themselves that would serve as the ultimate vehicles for attracting audiences. Radio networks provided the studios and distributed the programmes, but the show's content emerged from the advertising agencies. Performers, writers, producers, and, ultimately, programmers were thus closely linked to the advertising industry as they represented their clients.

Cereal companies in this era were generally sponsors of what could be deemed crossover markets. Adventure programmes such as the *Lone Ranger* skewed to a younger audience and were attractive for the promotion by General Mills of their newer product *Cheerioats*, which later became renamed *Cheerios*. Indeed, *Cheerioats* had an even longer link to children: it was the first cereal product advertised as an "infant's first snack food".

The pattern of American radio sponsorship was direct and unrelenting. Although promotions were scattered throughout programmes, the opening announcements quickly identified both the specific campaign and the general product. For example, *The Adventures of Superman*, sponsored by Kellogg's from 1938 and all through World War II, concluded its opening after explaining the origins of Superman with the following plug:

> Yes it's *Superman*. Before we begin today's story, here's a suggestion for you. Say gang, have you ever noticed that when fellows get together these days they often talk about aviation. That's why I want to tell you about the wonderful prizes that are in the Kellogg's Pep packages these days because it's a swell way to build up your aviation knowledge. Now this prize is a model plane made of colored cardboard and it's just as easy as pie to put together. And furthermore, on the back of the plane there are lots of pointers about that particular model. Now there are 14 different models you can get altogether. Exciting planes like the British Lanchester Bomber and the Douglas Dauntless Dive Bomber and the Russian Single Sea Fighter, the 118. And best of all, you don't have to send in a single penny to get them. Not even a box top. There's a model plane right inside every single Pep package. So gang, be sure Mother gets you a package of those delicious whole wheat flakes tomorrow. See which model plane you find inside. And remember the name Pep. P-E-P, the famous cereal is made by Kellogg's of Battle Creek. (Terrace 2004, 13)

This form of promotion became typical: the more a programme was aimed at a younger audience, the more likely products such as cereals were advertised. The radio show *The Adventures of Rin Tin Tin* which followed the boy Rusty and his trusty dog, Rin Tin Tin, was strongly linked to Nabisco's Shredded Wheat for children and their related product Milk Bones for dogs (Terrace 2004, 11). After the opening jingle of the programme which mentioned both of these General Mills products, the announcer would continue:

Announcer: The National Biscuit Company presents this week's *Adventures of Rin Tin Tin*.

Sound: Dog Barking

Announcer: You know keeping up with Rin Tin Tin is a real man-sized job. Now tell me Rusty, just how do you do it?

Rusty: Well, sir, I have a man-sized breakfast, Nabisco Shredded Wheat. And boy, is Nabisco Shredded Wheat ever fun to eat. It just looks just like a raft in your milk.

Announcer: Ah, you're so right, and believe me, those rafts of Nabisco Shredded Wheat are just loaded with energy, the energy you need to keep you on the go all day long. In fact, everybody needs the raft of energy in Nabisco Shredded Wheat.

Rusty: So be like me. Every morning sail a raft of Nabisco Shredded Wheat into your breakfast bowl.

Announcer: Kids, just ask Mom to get you the package with Niagara Falls on the end and you'll be sure you're eating the kind Rusty eats, Nabisco, the original shredded wheat. Now back to *The Adventures of Rin Tin Tin.* (Terrace 2004, 11)

In the era of American radio advertising – which was similarly structured throughout much of the rest of the world's commercially generated radio stations – there was no clear separation between promotion and programme. Given that by the 1930s the advertising industry had begun to heavily invest in motivational research, it is also likely they were at least somewhat aware of the much more direct effects of these kinds of promotions on children and the use of children in producing family-buying choices. The number of programmes in American radio directly sponsored by cereal manufacturers in the 1930s and 1940s was more than 26. By the 1930s and 1940s, most cereal manufacturers had become packaged-food industry conglomerates and were generally recognized as some of the largest advertisers in terms of budgets in the media industry. Much of those budgets were connected to the complete sponsorship of programmes. Radio programming at the time was also designed to a "general audience" which generally included children. Thus, the tone of radio was child-friendly – a kind of communicative strategy that served the family–child marketing of companies like Kellogg's and General Foods.

Building the Child Market: Sweetness and the Televisual Marketing of "Cute"

The direction of advertising that was child-oriented also helped shift the actual fabrication of the cereal as a product. Over time, through images on their boxes and advertisements, cereals promoted the practice of sweetening their basic cereal with sugar or the addition of fruits. It is important to emphasize that one of the great market leaps in cereal production emerged when one Kellogg brother overruled the other in terms of adding sugar to their original corn flakes in about 1906 to make them more palatable, and thus built the recognized and surviving Kellogg brand and company. Other cereal companies had engaged in this practice years earlier, but by the end of the 1910s, some element of sugar was pre-cooked into most cereals (Lawrence 2010, 11).

As the market for some types of cereals became primarily children, and shifted from their nineteenth century origins as a pure and healthy food source – and perhaps also spurred by the successful marketing through child-oriented radio programmes of the 1930s and 1940s – the 1950s and 1960s can be defined as the decades where pre-sweetened cereals became normalized as products and promoted exclusively for children.

The nature of this development came in several forms. The first of these can be characterized as the original marketing of "cute". *Cute*, as a type of marketing, has often been linked to the 1980s and 1990s Japanese animation and design culture, also called *kawaii* (in Japan), with hallmark brands such as Hello Kitty and Sailor Moon, along with many other similar 'cute' styles emerging from the Japanese anime and manga industries, and moving into the sale of many products and services. In many ways, the 1950s in the United States also produced a plethora of cute characters that flooded media outlets with their messages. Many of these were linked to breakfast cereals and associated snack foods and moved internationally over the decades. Some of the earliest models of cute characters included Snap, Crackle, and Pop who were the mascots of Rice Krispies (also known as Rice Bubbles in New Zealand and Australia). These characters were originally designed for cereal boxes and advertisements in the 1930s and emerged from the onomatopoeic slogan used to promote the product at its launch. The first cartoon versions of Snap, Crackle, and Pop were baker-looking elfin-like creatures who hovered over the cereal bowl and made breakfast eating fun for children (and adults for that matter!) (see Figure 5.1). Follow-up versions that Kellogg's advertising agency Leo Burnett developed appeared on the very popular children's programme *Howdy Doody* in the 1950s filled in the backstory: they came from the Planet "K" (for Kellogg's) and they were the breakfast "musketeers" who made the cereal come alive with sound. In both advertisements, the other characters were children. Cute animated characters stylistically quite close to the dominant Disney-style of the same period were a way to appeal to children and transform the rather bland product of Rice Krispies, along with sugar, cream, and fruit, into an exciting product to eat.

In a similar fashion, Leo Burnett created Tony the Tiger for Kellogg's in 1951 to promote the newly pre-sweetened corn flakes, Sugar-Frosted Flakes. And, like Snap, Crackle, and Pop, Tony became an icon of television and 1950s and 1960s culture. As opposed to being just a feature of the cereal, the animated Tony became a recognized voice, endorser, and image of the brand far beyond Snap, Crackle, and Pop. Tony's address to children was generally as an energizer for sport and exercise, and this became a prevalent theme of

Figure 5.1   Snap, Crackle, Pop in 1950s Kellogg's Rice Krispies commercial

the campaign for most of the next 60 years. His position in the rise of television worked in two ways. He was quite visible in family programmes such as Groucho Marx's *You Bet Your Life* comedy game show, and also in children's programmes such as *The Adventures of Superman*, where Kellogg's controlled the sponsorship. The combination ensured that the new cereal was visible to both mothers and children in its blatant attempt to corner the child-centred cereal market.

These two icons of Kellogg's were far from alone in the 1950s. In the development of their pre-sweetened puffed wheat cereal, Sugar Smacks, Kellogg's also advanced the seal Smaxey. Similarly, General Mills devised Sonny the Cuckoo Bird for their Cocoa Puffs brand in 1958, a cereal that moved internationally over the next 50 years and established Sonny's famous catchphrase of "I'm Cuckoo for Cocoa Puffs" (Topher 2015). Post's Sugar Crisp Cereal, originating in 1949 and regularly marketed with cartoon "sugar bears" in its earliest incarnations, also eventually developed the singular Sugar Bear whose voice and attitude were vaguely modelled on the cool and mellow sounds of Bing Crosby and Dean Martin. Through advertisements beginning in the 1960s, Sugar Bear produced little narrative vignettes overcoming villains, and a further character called Granny Goodwitch.

Attempts to blend new sugar tastes into breakfast was also part of the development of cereal in the 1950s. One of the most unique brands of pre-sweetened cereals was General Mills's Trix, first introduced in 1955, a combination of baked corn pieces, artificial colours, and equally artificial fruit-like flavours. Trix was linked to its mascot Rabbit called Tricks who was constantly trying to trick children into giving them their Trix. The slogan for every narrative from 1959 was "Silly Rabbit, Trix are for Kids", and rarely did Tricks the Rabbit actually get the opportunity to eat the cereal. Along with Lucky Charms and its leprechaun, and Kellogg's Fruit Loops, cereal manufacturers and marketers were transforming breakfast cereal into a snack food. However, breakfast cereal eating still had the quality of something essential for children – an important part of how children should start the day energized. The fruity cereals along with the chocolate-coated cereals produced a series of characters that included Toucan Sam (for Fruit Loops), a hyper-energetic monkey for Cocoa Puffs, and a crazy avuncular sea captain for Cap'n Crunch. The cute character/mascot world of the 1950s was the overwhelming way in which cereal manufacturers moved their products into the contemporary home for more than the next two decades.

Along with cute characters and sweetness, breakfast cereals became even more closely aligned with children through the development of American television programming structures. With television networks broadcasting fewer hours in the 1950s, two timeslots emerged as children's hours. *Captain Kangaroo* became a regular on CBS at 8 am for preschool children in 1954. *Howdy Doody* was designed for school-aged children and began broadcasting at 5:30 pm in 1947 on NBC. The popular *Mickey Mouse Club* began in 1956 on ABC, America's third network. All of them were loaded with commercials aimed at children, and breakfast cereals were some of the most regular sponsors. By the 1960s, American Saturday-morning television developed with eventually all three of the major networks designing their programmes exclusively for children for hours. A massive flow of cartoons populated television. The commercials from breakfast cereals with their mascots kept a seamless flow of cute cartoon stories where programme and commercial blended and blurred. Indeed, by 1964 at least one of the Saturday animated programmes, *Linus the Lion-hearted*, shown on CBS and later ABC, was created by the Ed Graham Advertising Agency for Post Cereals to sell Crispy Critters. For the next six years, many of Post Cereals's mascots were featured on the programme, including the very visible and popular Sugar Bear who promoted Sugar Crisps.

A similar cross-promotional blurring of advertising and entertainment emerged with the widely syndicated programme *Rocky and His Friends* in 1958 (retitled after its first two years as *The Rocky and Bullwinkle Show*), an animated programme distributed and owned by General Mills to advance the sales of Cheerios. The similar animation style, close affinity with "cute" characters, and, on occasion, the slippage of cereal mascots into the actual programmes themselves created a peculiar norm in children's television. It is perhaps unremarkable that when the education-oriented and non-commercial Children's Television Workshop developed their flagship programme *Sesame Street* in the late 1960s, its style resembled the flow of commercials and content on commercial-saturated television. Learning individual numbers, for instance, became an ad as each day the programme was *sponsored* by a letter and a number as animated shorts. Akin to break-fast cereal commercials, these were interspersed throughout the daily narrative of the show.

Twenty-First Century Ambient Advertising: POP through Branded Websites and Advergames

Branded websites and online children's games have now become major sites of commercialization, where participatory engagement works together with the blurring of advertising and entertainment. Cereal companies have exploited digital culture by targeting children through websites where they enter contests, view videos, vote for their favourite cereal, or play advergames, which feature products by making them part of the experience. For example, from 2004 to 2010, General Mills's site, Millsberry, targeted elementary and middle school students. The virtual world included shops, homes, an arcade, and even had a newspaper called the Millsberry Gazette that reported events in the town. Participants were required to sign up, after which they could create a character, decorate their homes, visit the shops, and play the games, which featured characters such as Lucky Leprechaun, Sonny the Cocoa Puffs Bird, or Chef Cinnamon. While Millsberry discontinued the site in 2010, new sites have emerged such as The Cereal Project at Mr.Breakfast.com, sponsored by Amazon. The Cereal Project features a mascot, Mr. Cereal, who invites children to play games such as Cereal Match game, described as "a cereal card matching games with cereal boxes instead of cards". The Cereal Project also features a video library of classic commercials, offers an online cereal museum, asks visitors to vote for their all-time favourite cereal, and even allows visitors to design and upload their own cereal box. Most importantly, The Cereal Project features a "buy" button where visitors can purchase cereal from Amazon.com.

Online gameplay usually leads to advertisements for "professional" level gameplay of the same game, new and better versions of the game, or related games. Purchase is sometimes literally a click away for children and can often lead to surprising new expenses for their parents. The "smartness" of online advertising, where a child user's searches and activity ensure that the products advertised are in proximity to their activities, seem to be just natural add-ons and flows to their online experience. As with early regulation of television advertising, online advertising actively blurs the boundaries between promotion and "content". The online search culture is designed to keep extending the experience of connections and links. By paying for better page ranking and by connecting their products to certain search words that are part of their targeted youth demographic, advertisers can be become a normalized part of the experience of watching. Each decision that a child makes in watching a particular video on YouTube Kids thus serves as direct cross-promotion for related entertainment products and commercials. Another blurred line has emerged online: unlike their use of highly regulated media such as television, children move between content and new advertisements, from show to product to purchasing, with very few visible divides.

Conclusion

The relationship between cereal, children, and advertising is an incredibly rich case history of both traditional and ambient advertising. Given the targets of this form of advertising, our case history also reveals how advertising has insinuated itself into both family life and children's play and pleasure. As the case history illustrates, this was not an inexpensive process or short-term strategy. It was built on multi-million-dollar, decade-long advertising accounts across an array of large processed-food conglomerates. These were designed to not only buy/sponsor expensive advertising space and time, but also to produce related content and programmes, innovative mascots and extensive efforts at cross-promotion, and ambient advertising to both construct a market and maintain it. Breakfast cereals may have started a health food that promised self-betterment, but as they were repositioned within the twentieth century advertising–meaning system, they quickly moved from an identity with family to a close affinity with children and mornings. The family anxiety of what children would eat first thing before heading off to school was appropriated by cereal manufacturers as an innovative space to produce "fun" snack-food-like pleasure for children, as well as convenience and happiness for the modern family. In many ways, breakfast cereal advertising identifies how advertising has worked out many techniques of connection to the contemporary consumer. With children being vulnerable to messages, as well as perhaps being the conduit to family acceptance of change and transformation, cereal advertising creatively reimagined what was acceptable.

Through their efforts, cereal advertisers gained a great deal. Their research calculated well-ahead of academic research both how important children were for success in consumer culture and how to appeal directly to children even as they were being chaperoned by adults. The success of these advertising campaigns has also led to the targeting of many of their approaches by those critical of advertising and hypercritical of the (ab)use of children for economic gain. The style of advertising employed by cereal companies led to requirements in the United States and around the world to clearly differentiate television programme content and advertising, though no such restrictions apply to online websites and games. In other cases, the industry attempted to circumvent regulations and controls through techniques such as cross-promotion, POP lures, and various other forms of ambient advertising that supplemented traditional advertisements. These ambient strategies attempt to create brand loyalty by blurring advertising and entertainment and encouraging children to actively engage with the product. These practices remain part of the larger advertising industry and continue to organize the various dimensions of cereal advertising today – especially in relation to children.

6

Volkswagen and the Creative Revolution

In this chapter, we illustrate the rise of image-based advertising based upon the creation of sign value that constructs social identities. We describe what is commonly referred to as the Creative Revolution in advertising by tracing the history of the Volkswagen, from its roots in Nazi Germany to its marketing as a symbol of the American counterculture in the 1960s. In its journey from Nazi Germany to a global commodity, the Volkswagen illustrates the way that commodities come to supply meaning and identity. The landmark Volkswagen campaign, developed by the advertising agency Doyle Dane Bernbach, is widely regarded as one of the most influential campaigns of all time and one that changed the culture of advertising (Frank 1998, 55). Rather than simply emphasizing a product's utility, social meaning, or the satisfaction it provided, it actively constructed consumer identities. It exemplifies the mutability of meaning in different cultural contexts, from the car's origins in Nazi Germany to its reinvention in the United States in the postwar period and beyond. What began in the 1930s as Hitler's "people's car", designed to make mass motorization possible by being inexpensive and widely available, became positioned as the "counterculture" car in the United States in the 1960s, and then reinvented as a brand identity in the 1990s. In the 1960s, it became an identity marker for the hip individualist who rejected the inauthentic, conformist, mass-produced consumer culture of the 1950s. In so doing, the Volkswagen campaign's self-referential, ironic, irreverent ads addressed the "alienated" consumer, while simultaneously offering consumption as an antidote to the ills of consumption.

Consumption, then, as we move into the twenty-first century, is ever more about the signs or images that a product represents that, in turn, represent the consumer. The Volkswagen Beetle campaign is a prime example of how advertising actively constructs brand tribes who form a collective identity based around a product; in so doing, it builds on the ways in which advertising promised transformation and fostered an interactive relationship with consumers earlier in the century.

Post-war Consumer Culture and Advertising

The period after World War II marked a major moment of transformation in consumer culture in the United States. George Lipsitz (2001, 46) notes that increased consumer spending, fuelled by an expansion of credit, was considered essential for economic prosperity in the post-war period. Rather than improving the infrastructure of inner cities, government spending went towards building highways, while Federal housing loan policies favoured the construction of single-family detached homes in suburbs. Both government and industry worked to stimulate purchases of cars and houses, as well as home furnishings and appliances, based on credit. While the Depression years created fears of accruing debt through instalment buying, and the scarcity of goods during wartime encouraged frugality, business and government worked to foster a new consumer mentality.

Even before the end of World War II, industries involved in defence were concerned with how to remain profitable after the war. As military production shifted to consumer production, many products initially developed for military purposes, such as aluminium, polyethylene, nylon, powdered milk, and processed foods, became transformed into consumer goods. Most importantly, industry leaders strategized that they could build the economy by creating wants and desire that promised, but never quite delivered, satisfaction. For example, at a workshop on the shift from military to consumer production, DuPont Vice President J.W. McCoy predicted that business after the war would be good because of "a huge backlog of unfulfilled wants". He added that while satisfying American consumers' desires for cars, washing machines, radios, and other products would build the economy, he also proclaimed, "A satisfied people is a stagnant people, and business will have to work to ensure that people are never satisfied" (WGBH 2012). At the same time, desires needed to be managed to eliminate financial risks. Dick Hebdige (1981, 132) explains, "Given the huge costs involved in producing a new line of goods, if crippling losses were to be avoided, the consumer had to be as carefully primed as the materials used in the manufacturing process." In other words, creating desire for a product – through image and advertising – was as important as the manufacture of the product itself.

In a context where it was important to stimulate rather than merely meet demand, advertising and marketing took on heightened importance. Advertisers worked to create rather than merely satisfy wants by using sociological and psychological research techniques to tap into people's desires and fears. Advertisers had made use of behavioural science and Freudian psychology from early in the twentieth century onward. However, in the post-war period, Ernest Dichter's motivation research, which applied Freud's psychoanalytic techniques to advertising in order to uncover consumers' unconscious motivations, gained traction, and an industry that had still been tied to providing reasons why people should buy products became an "all-out persuasion industry" (Clark 1988, 69). While a great deal of advertising remained tied to verbal arguments that proclaimed the positive benefits of a product, or warned of the negative consequences of not using it, advertisers began to more fully attend to the communicative aspects of visual images. Product design changed too, so that style became as important as function – in other words, as Hebdige(2000, 132) remarks, the image interceded between the consumer and the act of consumption. As we have seen in previous chapters, consumption is not simply about utility, but is about signs or images that evoke a range of affects and affinities. In this regard, Mike Featherstone noted how everyday life became increasingly aestheticized in the twentieth century, as advertising encouraged consumers to reject a utilitarian orientation towards commodities, and instead encouraged them to choose commodities that work together to signify a style or "lifestyle". He writes, "the aestheticization of reality foregrounds the importance of style, which is also encouraged by the modernist market dynamic with its constant search for new fashions, new styles, new sensations and experiences" (1991, 84). This emphasis on the "new", the image, and the unity of form and content distinguished much advertising in the 1960s from what had come before. Advertising shifted from appeals to masses to segmented markets. Moreover, as the post-war baby boom generation that had grown up with television and its celebration of material acquisitions began to enter young adulthood, the consumer who was critical of consumerism emerged as a market segment. Advertisers appealed to these youthful consumers by offering "hipness" as the antidote to the conformity, standardization, and materialism of the 1950s.

The "new" advertising that emerged in the 1960s thus marked an important stage in consumer culture, a stage that has further evolved in the twenty-first century as products become severed from their original use or meaning and are attached to new signs and images in an endless play of signification. Advertising both expressed a new aesthetic and addressed the "hip" consumer who took on this identity. Thomas Frank (1998, 24) stresses the importance of this shift in the 1960s: "this new species of marketing is concerned with nothing other than the construction of consumer identity, as manufacturers and advertisers attempt to call group identities into existence where there had been nothing but inchoate feelings and common responses to pollsters' questions". The consumer's embrace of this positioning marks the image-based advertising of the 1960s as a new phase of consumer culture.

Notably, in the 1960s "youth" became a consuming position defined by characteristics such as hipness, nonconformity, and individuality. Advertising addressed the "alienated spectator" (Goldman and Papson 1996, 83) who was sceptical of advertising and critical of the way it promoted the conformism and materialism that marked fifties culture. While Goldman and Papson (1996) refer to the alienated spectator as a 1980s phenomenon, we suggest that this consuming position was initiated in the 1960s by Doyle Dane Bernbach's self-reflexive anti-advertising that set up a different discursive relationship with consumers than what had existed in the past, and addressed consumers who perceived themselves as distanced from, rather than embedded in the system of, commodity signs. The Volkswagen campaign, then, was both part of and an integral constituent of the countercultural movement of the 1960s. By speaking to the "alienated consumer", the Volkswagen ads simultaneously created and reflected countercultural subject positions. Volkwagen's image of the car – and consumer – shaped a collective identity that transcended the material attributes of the product, though we share Frank's (1998) position that even these anti-consumerist brand tribes were ultimately subsumed within consumer culture.

Origins of the Volkswagen

The Volkswagen, marketed in the United States as a symbol of nonconformity, was initially developed in Germany under the auspices of Adolf Hitler, and designed to emulate the success of the legendary Ford Model T. Hitler planned to use Fordist production techniques to manufacture "the people's car" that would be affordable, reliable, and available to all for the new autobahn road network that he would build. He positioned the automobile as both an emblem of modernity and a means to bolster the German economy, and thus announced two projects in 1934: construction of the autobahn and a car for the common person. This car would, in Hitler's vision, install Germany as "an energetic, racially homogenous, highly militarized, and technologically modern 'people's community' that brought previously unaffordable consumer goods within reach of ordinary citizens" (Rieger 2013, 87). For Hitler, the "people's community" referred to Aryans who would form the cornerstone of Germany's renewal. He enlisted Ferdinand Porsche to design the car, which Porsche worked on between 1934 and 1938. In 1938, Hitler announced that the German Labour Front would build a factory to manufacture the car, and that the site would be surrounded by a model city for workers. The project was allocated to the division of the Labour Front called "Strength Through Joy" (Kraft durch Freude/KdF), whose purpose was to offer workers inexpensive outings and recreational activities designed to reenergize them and increase their productivity. The Volkswagen was initially called "The Strength through Joy Car" (KdF), and the worker's city was called the Town of the Strength through Joy.

Over the next year, with a few prototypes developed, Strength Through Joy promoted the car by inviting journalists for test drives, exhibiting the prototypes, and securing coverage in international media. In the United States, the *New York Times* was impressed by the prospect of autobahns crawling with "thousands and thousands of shiny little beetles", thus offering the earliest use of the moniker 'Beetle' (Rieger 2013, 72). There were also unconventional strategies to promote the car: the Post Office issued a special stamp, with an image of the Volkswagen on the autobahn, and there was even a family board game where players moved their cars along the autobahn. Much like Henry Ford, who had promoted the Model T as a means for workers to take their families on weekend trips to the country, promotional literature linked the car to recreation and mobility; typical images featured the car cruising on the autobahn or linked it to natural settings, with family and friends relaxing in forest clearings or enjoying the countryside next to a tent by the lake. The car was praised because it would bring "strength, happiness, and pleasure to millions of people who until now have been forced to live without them" (Rieger 2013, 76).

At the same time, the creation of sign value was undergirded by use value: literature promoted the car's workmanship, especially that the car parts were tested extensively, emphasized its streamlined design whereby worn parts could be easily replaced, and said that the car was inexpensive. Although its sign value shifted over time, reliability and low cost would continue to define the Volkswagen when the car was marketed throughout Europe and the United States after the war. To make the car even more affordable, Germans were encouraged to open a Volkswagen Savings Book Plan, similar to an instalment plan, to pay for the car ahead of time. Each time a payment was made, people were given a stamp to place in their book, with the idea that they could claim the car once the book was filled. While initially subscribers were to pay the equivalent of $2 per week, when this was too expensive, the fee was lowered to $2 per month. Despite the fact that it would take 16 years to get the car, 253,000 Germans signed up before the war broke out, and another 83,000 signed on even after the start of war (Hiott 2012, 146). However, the plan was a failure. The Volkswagenwerk factory produced no more than 630 cars before the collapse of Nazi Germany, and the few cars that were manufactured went to prominent party leaders.

The "people's car" thus had a complicated history as both an enticing object of consumer desire that symbolized the "people's community", and an object associated with Nazi Germany and the atrocities of World War II. Production of the car halted when Germany invaded Poland in 1939, and the factory shifted to manufacturing armaments and military vehicles. During the war, the factory relied on forced labour, first Eastern labourers, then prisoners of war and concentration camp prisoners. As a result, Rieger (2013, 89) writes, "Both its ideological lineage as Hitler's prestige project and the inhumane management practices at the factory during the war lent the vehicle a deeply compromised pedigree by 1945."

While Hitler's Nazi party never oversaw production of the "people's car", the Volkswagen did not disappear at the war's end (although the name of the town was changed to Wolfsburg). The Volkswagenwerk factory was located in the British zone when international forces took control of Germany. Initially, the Allies' Morgenthau plan, devised in 1944, was to remove all German potential for war by creating a deindustrialized, largely agrarian economy, so the factory was to be dismantled and the machinery shipped to England. However, no car manufacturer wanted it. An official British report famously found that "the vehicle does not meet the technical requirement of a motor-car… it is quite unattractive to the average buyer… to build the car commercially would be a completely uneconomic enterprise" (Clausager 2000). Instead, almost 2500 cars were built for the British army by the end of 1945. The "Town of Strength through Joy" was renamed Wolfsburg in 1945, and production resumed under the guidance of British officer Ivan Hirst, whose enthusiasm for the Volkswagen, despite the prevailing belief that the car was not commercially viable, is widely considered responsible for keeping the factory operating. In 1947, the Marshall Plan advocated rebuilding West Germany as a defence against the Cold War; the Volkswagen factory, already manufacturing cars, quickly became a symbol of West Germany's economic revitalization. Initially, the cars were sold domestically, though in 1949 an "improved" model was designed for export. This new Volkswagen was distinguished mainly by its design features: a glossy, synthetic resin paint that made the body more durable; and the pastel green, Bordeaux red, and medium brown colours. The factory's general director, Heinrich Nordhoff, explained that the car's colours were "characteristic of peacetime". In this way, he attempted to distinguish it from Hitler's "people's car" as well as the matte green cars produced for the English military (Rieger 2013, 115). By 1954 every other car on German roads was a Volkswagen, and it was leading Europe in exports (Hiott 2012, 325). Indeed, the car's ubiquity and the success of the Wolfsburg factory turned it into an icon of West Germany's identity: "a collective experience of success that gained almost mythic symbolic power" (Rieger 2013, 127).

The Volkswagen first became available in the United States in 1950, though initially it did not sell well. In a context where big cars signified upward mobility, Hiott (2012, 330) writes, "Drivers wanted a big white Buick or a color-coordinated pink and Ivory Olds. They wanted elongated riffs and tail-fins and a wider trunk; they wanted a smooth ride, a big upper-class tent that shielded them from sound. They wanted names like Thunderbird, Corvette, and Starlite, cars that long-legged American cowboys could stretch out in. They wanted an automobile with a team of horses up front. Henry Ford had already given the people mobility. Now they wanted their mobility in a larg-er-than-life package." Needless to say, the Volkswagen did not fit into this context.

The Volkswagen's gradual acceptance in the United States in the 1950s demonstrates how creating the appropriate sign value can make a car marketa-ble. Although people were aware of the Volkswagen's origins in Nazi Germany, it was referred to by the non-threatening name Beetle or Bug, an identity that dissociated it from its totalitarian origins. Moreover, because the car was never manufactured in Hitler's Germany, it could signify Hitler's failure and the success of West Germany's embrace of capitalism more so than German atrocities. The Volkswagen Beetle became popular in the United States in the latter part of the 1950s. As more Americans travelled to Europe and European products were becoming available in the United States, it acquired cache as a "foreign" car whose appeal was in its small size and unconventional shape.

Although by 1955 the Volkswagen Beetle's sales amounted to less than 1% of the American car market, the press praised the car for its reliability, afforda-bility ($1495), low depreciation rates, and low fuel consumption (Rieger 2013, 200). These characteristics likely aided its later depiction as a car for "anti-consumerist" consumers. It was not nationally advertised, and sales were largely by word of mouth. Rieger (2013) asserts that from the beginning, the Volkswagen's appeal transcended its use value, and many drivers estab-lished a deep emotional connection to it. It was a "cute" car, the feminine counterpart to the more powerful, masculine cars manufactured in Detroit. The Volkswagen was often purchased as a second car, driven by women who wanted access to places such as shopping malls built outside city centres, which further underlined "the unthreatening and friendly air that surrounded the car" (Rieger 2013, 202). Some people even gave the car nicknames, and Patton (2002) suggests that its headlights, grille, and bumper took on characteristics of a human face. In this regard, biologist Konrad Lorenz claims that "Even inanimate objects that mimic human features can have powerful effects... The most amazing objects can acquire remarkable, highly specific emotional values by the 'experiential attachment' of human properties" (quoted in Patton 2002, loc1917).

By the late 1950s the United States emerged as Volkswagen's most important and lucrative export market, as it "attracted a foothold among the materially secure, white middle class whose members made up the bulk of suburbanites in the fifties" (Rieger 2013, 201). In this context, the advertising agency Doyle Dane Bernbach secured the Volkswagen account when the company began to advertise in the United States in 1959.

Doyle Dane Bernbach and the Volkswagen

In 1959, as other small European cars such as Jaguar invested in advertising in the United States, Volkswagen responded by hiring an advertising agency. Although company head Henrich Nordhoff initially opposed advertising as a wasteful expenditure, when faced with competition, he hired Doyle Dane Bernbach, a medium-sized New York based agency with a reputation for innovative campaigns. Although Doyle Dane Bernbach, an agency founded by Jewish Americans, was an unlikely pairing with a car with roots in Hitler's Germany, an automobile account was a major marker of an ad agency's success, and would help Doyle Dane Bernbach demonstrate that its unconventional approach to advertising was viable. Conversely, hiring a Jewish agency helped Volkswagen disassociate itself from Nazi Germany.

Founded in 1949 by Bill Bernbach along with colleagues Ned Doyle and Maxwell Dane, Doyle Dane Bernbach was the antithesis of the hierarchical, technocratic, risk-averse Madison Avenue advertising agency predominant at the time. Doyle Dane Bernbach saw itself as a different kind of agency that broke many of the rules and conventions that they believed inhibited creativity, both in terms of their organizational structure and their approach to advertising. Like the "alienated spectator" addressed in its Volkswagen ads, Doyle Dane Bernbach was itself a non-conformist "rebel" that broke the rules of advertising. The result produced an advertising "counterculture" that became known as the Creative Revolution.

One of the main conventions that Doyle Dane Bernbach challenged was in the structure of the organization, which was a rebuke to the conformist culture of other Madison Avenue ad agencies. Most Madison Avenue agencies at the time were bureaucratic, hierarchal, and departmentalized, with a heavy reliance on scientific, fact-driven research. For example, much advertising was dominated by the hard-sell approach of adman Rosser Reeves's "unique selling proposition", determined by research to establish a product's unique benefit that would make a difference to consumers. Similarly, influential adman David Ogilvy, who had initially worked with pollster George Gallop, published a set of rules for successful print ads that also emphasized the primacy of research. In contrast, Bernbach stated his aesthetic approach to advertising in a memo sent when he worked as creative director at Grey Advertising in 1947: "I'm worried that we are going to fall into the trap of bigness, that we're going to worship techniques instead of substance; that we're going to follow history instead of making it... There are a lot of great technicians in advertising. They know all the rules.. They can give you fact after fact. They are the scientists of advertising. But there's one little rub. Advertising is fundamentally about persuasion and persuasion happens to be not a science, but an art" (cited in Dobrow 1984, 20). When his memo was disregarded, he left to form Doyle Dane Bernbach and implement his ideas.

Doyle Dane Bernbach's innovation was to move creatives – art directors and copywriters – to the forefront of the agency, gaining an equal footing with more scientific approaches based on audience research and analysis. In addition, their ads coordinated art and copy. In typical ad agencies at the time, researchers used polls, focus groups, or even motivational research to develop an angle; they would then convey this to the copywriters who would write the ad and then send it off to the art department for images. At Doyle Dane Bernbach, art directors and copywriters formed a creative team who worked together, and while they did not necessarily dismiss research findings, they were not beholden to them.

In challenging the conventions of the advertising industry by privileging creativity, Doyle Dane Bernbach offered an alternative to the consensus culture of the 1950s. In the 1950s, advertising was marked by what Jackson Lears calls "containment of carnival", but in the creative revolution of the 1960s, Frank (1998, 54) observes, "Advertising narratives suddenly idealized not the repressed account man in gray flannel, but the manic, unrestrained creative person in offbeat clothing". He asserts, "If American capitalism can be said to have spent the 1950s dealing in conformity and consumer fakery, during the decade that followed, it would offer the public authenticity, individuality, difference, and rebellion" (Frank 1998, 9). This shift in perspective became apparent in Doyle Dane Bernbach's classic ads for Volkswagen. Doyle Dane Bernbach's Volkswagen campaign thus participated in the mass culture critique and self-reflexively incorporated criticisms of advertising and consumer culture. As Patton (2002, loc 1114) notes, they "manufactured discontent" with the system of "manufacturing discontent". Their ads invited consumers who were critical of conspicuous consumption and the false promises and manipulation of advertising to adopt an oppositional posture in relation to mainstream culture, and in so doing, positioned the advertiser on the side of the consumer. As Frank (1998, 31) observes, "No longer would Americans buy to fit in or impress the Jones, but to demonstrate that they were wise to the game, to express their revulsion with the artifice and conformity of consumerism".

Doyle Dane Bernbach's initial strategy was to portray Volkswagen as an honest, trustworthy car. They recognized that the point of advertising was to interpret the product rather than represent consumer desires. The key, according to Arviddson (2006, 54), was "to find the simple story in the product and present it in an articulate, intelligent, and persuasive way". Bernbach believed that advertising had lost its credibility as a representational medium, so a good ad would not so much provide an aspirational ideal for consumers but would give identity to a product by linking it to media culture. Arviddson (2006, 54) adds, "It was important to focus on what he called the brand image, on the symbolic totality of the product's mediatic presentation." The the creation and maintenance of the brand image was a matter of artistic creativity, not scientific research.

The creative team consisted of copywriter Julian Koenig and art director Helmut Krone, with Bernbach's oversight. Lore has it that the Doyle Dane Bernbach executives, after visiting the Volkswagen factory in Wolfsburg, came up with a plan. Bernbach stated, "We had seen the quality of materials that were used. We had seen the incredible precautions taken to avoid mistakes… Yes, this was an honest car. We had found our selling proposition" (Hiott 2012, 478). Or, as Patton (2002, loc 1018) remarks, it's possible that Bernbach read a 1956 article from *Popular Mechanics* that proclaimed that the Volkswagen was "an honest piece of machinery". Rieger (2013, 216) summarizes, "DDB's ads did not singlehandedly transform the Beetle's image from Nazi car into a 'cool' and 'hip' consumer good. Rather, the agency bundled relatively loose pre-existing associations and consolidated them into a corporate iconography".

The Volkswagen Beetle, whose outward appearance did not change from year to year and which, prior to Doyle Dane Bernbach, relied on word-of-mouth advertising rather than expensive ad campaigns, was easily contrasted with American automobiles. At a time when many Americans were infatuated with tailfins and excessive horsepower, Fox writes (1997, 256) that Doyle Dane Bernbach "made virtues of the car's apparent deficiencies: basic and utilitarian, therefore cheap; low horsepower, therefore high mileage, ugly and unchanging, therefore well-crafted and less ephemeral". Doyle Dane Bernbach's main challenge was to use advertising to convey honesty to an audience that was sceptical of advertising, particularly automobile advertising. One of their most famous ads, "Think Small," illustrates their strategy.

"Think Small"

"Think Small" is perhaps the most well-known and celebrated Volkswagen ad, first produced in 1959 and run nationally in Life Magazine in 1960. The ad, like the Volkswagen Beetle itself, was a unity of form and function. Both the original Volkswagen design and Doyle Dane Bernbach's advertising were influenced by the Bauhaus design movement, which emphasized simplicity and a reduction to basics. Although Hitler shut down the movement in Germany, Porsche designed the Volkswagen based on Bauhaus design principles. According to Hoitt (2012, 109), Hitler reportedly believed that the car should "look like a beetle" because "you only have to observe nature to know how to achieve streamlining". Thus, the car's round shape, with the engine in back, was a formal element with a functional purpose to improve wind resistance. Coincidentally, Rieger (2013, 47) attributes the "creative revolution" in advertising to the graphic designer Paul Rand's influence on Bernbach when both partnered at the Weintraub Agency in 1941. Rand, whose work strove to integrate art into advertising, also adhered to principles inspired by the Bauhaus movement and Swiss modernism. Rather than making the image a literal representation of a product and overloading ads with words and pictures, as was common at the time, Rand's ads used simple, uncluttered, often geometric shapes and images. Similarly, Bernbach's aesthetic-based approach to advertising contrasted with the the jargon-filled, visually complicated, rational approach to advertising that was typical of many ads; as Samuel writes (2012, 3), "Bernbach believed there should be only one main idea to an ad, stripping down a product's many potential features and benefits to its core reason for being" (see Figure 6.1).

The "Think Small" ad's minimalist design helped to communicate its image as an "honest", unpretentious car. Instead of locating the car in an

Think small.

Figure 6.1 The "Think Small" ad was remarkable for its use of white space, in contrast to the cluttered automobile advertisements of the 1950s

attractive setting linked to the consumer, the ad was shot in black and white with no context. The picture was deliberately "naked-looking, not full or lush" (Fox 1997, 257). Instead of a visually dominant image of the car, it was set off-centre at a medium distance from the viewer, located against a white background. The majority of the ad was white space, which focused attention on the one object, the car. In a 2009 *Advertising Age* article, Al Ries (2009) compared 146 car ads from the 1950s with the "Think Small" ad and noted the differences: almost all of the car ads used people to demonstrate the pleasure car buyers might feel about their new acquisitions, used artwork instead of photography to make the cars look long and low and beautiful, and used multiple illustrations to communicate all of the car's exciting features. The difference, he summarized, was between complexity and simplicity, artificiality and realism. Its simple, informal style mimicked the design of the car, and began to create a brand narrative that helped to make it understandable and relatable.

The implicit narrative built around the Volkswagen, rather than the explicit, rational narrative that characterized conventional ads, was key to the creation of its sign value and the establishment of its brand identity. As Twitchell (2009) writes, brands are stories attached to manufactured objects with the purpose of generating an emotional response. Similarly, Hiott (2012, 423–424) quotes Allen Adamson, who observes, "It's the whole brand story that steers people's rides. That's why smart auto companies, smart auto branders, make sure that they've got a genuinely distinctive and compelling story to tell about what makes their brand of car different in a way people care about. The best of the best know how to weave the rational and emotional aspects together in a way that really sets their brands apart." Lisa Birk's (2014) following analysis of "Think Small" describes how the ad's copy used a classic four-part dramatic structure to create a compelling brand narrative.

First, she writes, it establishes credibility by aligning with the consumer. It begins where the audience is – dismissive, a little bored, but playful. But rather than extolling the product's virtues, it uses self-deprecating humour: *Our little car isn't so much of a novelty any more. A couple of dozen college kids don't try to squeeze inside it. The guy at the gas station doesn't ask where the gas goes. Nobody even stares at our shape.* According to Patton (2002, 1053), Doyle Dane Bernbach claimed to want the tone of "one person simply talking to another", which contrasted with the shrill ads typical of conventional car advertising. The wry tone spoke to the intelligent consumer who could appreciate the Volkswagen's economy and simplicity, in implicit contrast to oversized and elaborate American cars and to the exaggerated claims made in car advertisements. As advertising executive Jerry Della Femina observed, the Volkswagen campaign was "the first time the advertiser ever talked to the consumer as though he were a grown up instead of a baby" (cited in Frank 1998, 63).

Birk (2014) then notes the move to involve the reader: *In fact, some people who drive our little flivver don't even think 32 miles to the gallon is going any great guns.* She notes that the word "flivver" is both dismissive and "so retro it's hip" (flivver was also a word used to describe Ford's Model T). Moreover, the statement that the car gets 32 miles to the gallon (at a time when most cars got half of that mileage) makes the words "Think Small" more appealing. The ad then goes on to enumerate all of the ways that the car saves money: *Or using five pints of oil instead of five quarts. Or never needing anti-freeze. Or racking up 40,000 miles on a set of tyres. That's because once you get used to some of our economies, you don't even think about them any more. Except when you squeeze into a small parking spot. Or renew your small insurance. Or pay a small repair bill. Or trade in your old VW for a new one.* After the copy relates all of the car's benefits, there is the denouement: *Think it over,* which circles neatly back to the headline, "Think Small". Birk (2014) points out how in this ad the meaning of "small", in a few short lines, has shifted from a term of derision to a hallmark of smart.

Considered another way, "Think Small" addressed the alienated spectator by using a playful, ironic tone to align advertiser and consumer. It contributed to cultural critique and expressed a common sentiment not through what was explicitly stated, but through what was implied, and it assumed that the reader/spectator was savvy – and media literate – enough to understand. Indeed, the "Think Small" ad subtly refuted a bestselling self-help book of the time, *The Magic of Thinking Big*, which implied that the acquisition of material goods was the key to happiness. In a 1992 interview, Doyle Dane Bernbach Creative Director Julian Koenig made the link direct, "By buying a Volkswagen you could take an inverse delight in not having to keep up with the Joneses, in not responding to Detroit's planned obsolescence, in not being part of that repetitive, competitive culture" (Mack 1992).

The form of the copy was also a part of the ad's message designed to convey simplicity and candour. The layout was traditional: two-thirds picture, with one-third text. The text was set in three blocks with the centred headline serving to separate visual and copy. But in every other way, the ad departed from the then standard rules established by David Ogilvy of what an ad's composition and layout should be. While Ogilvy said that ad text should be in an antique typography, this was set in an informal sans-serif font called Futura. Instead of emphasizing the Volkswagen logo, it was almost hidden at the bottom right hand side of the page. The columns of text had windows rather than uniform blocking, which according to art director Helmut Krone, made the copy look "Gertrude Steiny" – in this way, reflecting a modernist aesthetic. The headline "Think Small" ended with a period instead of the more typical exclamation point – making the statement an imperative, though low-key, and creating a visual stop between headline and copy. The style was based on novelty and interruption, which Bernbach declared was "something unusual enough to stop you, make you look and listen" (Samuel 2012, 2).

The "Think Small" ad became a cultural phenomenon, particularly popular among youth who passed it around and pasted it onto dorm walls; many people bought the issue of *Life* just to have the ad (Hiott 2012). According to Patton (2002, 983), the Starch survey found that 70% of magazine readers paid attention to the copy. Throughout the 1960s, Doyle Dane Bernbach continued to produce ads that developed the Volkswagen brand narrative and addressed consumers who rejected the conspicuous consumption of the 1950s and were sceptical of advertising, whether members of the modern intelligentsia or the youthful counterculture. "Lemon" (1960), for example, featured an image of what appeared to be a perfect car, with copy that read, "This VW missed the boat. The chrome strip on the glove compartment is blemished and must be replaced." The ad both conveyed honesty by admitting failings and provided assurance of quality. It also introduced the word "lemon" as a reference for a faulty car into the cultural lexicon.

Other ads attacked the auto industry's techniques of planned obsolescence ("It doesn't go in one year and out the other"), the worship of big cars as status symbols ("Keeping Up with the Kemplers"), and the untrustworthy practices of car dealers (a 1964 ad wondered "why they run clearance sales on brand new cars", and ended by distancing Volkswagen from these practices with the disclaimer, "Maybe we just don't understand the system"). Patton (2002) notes that recurrent themes in the ads focused on invisible improvements, implicitly contrasting the Volkswagen with the superficial exterior changes offered by Detroit, and flattering consumers by implying they were intelligent enough to appreciate the differences and to recognize quality.

Many of Doyle Dane Bernbach's ads were reflexive rather than realist. They critiqued advertising and mocked its conventions, in effect appearing to empower the consumer to read ads critically. In one example from 1963, Volswagen ran an ad with no picture, no headline, three blank columns, and instructions on "How to Do a VW Ad". The instructions both critically commented on conventional car ads and reinforced the impression that Doyle Dane Bernbach's advertising addressed intelligent consumers:

1. Look at the car.
2. Look harder. You'll find enough advantages to fill a lot of ads. Like the lair cooled engine, the economy, the design that never goes out of date.
3. Don't exaggerate. For instance, some people have got 50 m.p.g. and more from a VW. But others have only managed 28. Average: 32. Don't promise more.
4. Call a spade a spade. And a suspension a suspension. Not something like "orbital cushioning."
5. Speak to the reader. Don't shout. He can hear you. Especially if you talk sense.
6. Pencil sharp? You're on your own.

As Frank (1998, 65) notes, the message from Doyle Dane Bernbach was that "all advertisers are liars… except for this one". Even though the car's external appearance varied very little over the years, they presented it as a car for people who thought for themselves and were non-conformists. He summarizes, "The Volkswagen was the anti-car, the automotive signifier of the uprising against the cultural establishment" (Frank 1998, 67).

Considered another way, the Volkswagen ads appealed to consumers who could "think small" – who saw themselves as individuals who stood apart from the materialism and conformism of mainstream culture. The ads presented an alternative view of both the world of advertising and the consumer. Hiott (2012, 373) writes, "The habitual way of living in America at the time was to think big – to believe that more and better were the answer to life's ills – and the ads turned that accepted 'fact' on its head." Doyle Dane Bernbach made viewers' scepticism about ads a part of their discursive apparatus, appealing to savvy viewers who could see through the false promises of advertising. *Adweek* critic Bob Garfield wrote, "The car that presented itself as the antidote to conspicuous consumption was itself the badge product for those who fancied themselves a cut above, or at least invulnerable to, the tacky blandishments of the hidden persuaders" (quoted in Patton 2002, 1129).

Sales in the United States suggest that the Volkswagen did indeed become the "people's car". In 1960, the year "Think Small" ran, Volkswagen sales increased 37%; by the following year, 46% of all imports to the United States were Volkswagens, and Volkswagen became the third-largest car manufacturer in the world. In 1968, the Volkswagen Beetle was the best-selling vehicle in any country anywhere. Five years later, it surpassed Henry Ford's 15-million Model T sales record and became the first car ever to reach the 20-million mark (Hiott 2012, 369).

Volkswagen and Cultural Appropriation

In the United States, by the end of the 1960s, the Volkswagen had gained a foothold among those living comfortably in suburban affluence and the members of the counterculture who had rebelled against suburbia as the epitome of conformity (Rieger 2013). While the Volkswagen signified unconventionality, this became manifest in very different ways, from the white suburbs, apolitical campus environments, auto racing circles, and California beach culture (Rieger 2013). The Volkswagen bus, which had been developed as a transporter in the early 1950s and featured a box-like body over a modified Volkswagen chassis, was particularly popular as a means for young people to travel to concerts and festivals. Many painted their cars with psychedelic swirls, and in another example of the personalization of objects, literature such as the book *How to Keep Your Volkswagen Alive* encouraged Volkswagen owners to develop a sentient relationship to their car through empathy. As the book declared, "Your car's karma depends on your desire to make it and keep it – ALIVE" (quoted in Rieger 2013, 219).

The Volkswagen was, according to Frank (1998, 68), a product marketed as "an emblem of humored alienation and largely accepted as such by the alienated". Instead of constructing idealized images of consumers, the ads highlighted the absurdities of affluence. But Frank (1998) observes that the real innovation of the Creative Revolution was to extend the life of consumerism by running forever on the discontent that it itself produced. He writes, "In the hands of newly enlightened man in gray flannel, hip would become the dynamic principle of the sixties, a cultural perpetual motion machine transforming disgust with consumerism into fuel for an ever accelerating consumer society" (Frank 1998, 68). The oppositional subject positions constructed by the Volkswagen ads ultimately became co-opted by advertising. He elaborates:

> That by the end of the decade the Volkswagen had acquired an image that was more hip than Nazi must be regarded as one of the great triumphs of American marketing. The irony that several of the creators were Jewish was trumped by the irony implicit in that Volkswagen's hipness was a product of advertising, the institution of mass society against which hip had declared itself most vehemently at odds. The Volkswagen story, in other words, is cooptation theory turned upside down, a clear and simple example of a product marketed as an emblem of good-humored alienation and accepted as such by the alienated. (Frank 1998, 68)

In the long term, the "alienated spectator" was merely a market segment, and the "hip" consumer's rejection of tradition made her or him more receptive to the endless cycles of the "new" promoted by advertising. The critique of advertising was recuperated and co-opted as another advertising technique. In regard to the long-term impact of the Creative Revolution in advertising, Frank (1998, 27) observes that "alienation became the motor for fashion". Ultimately, the Creative Revolution helped transform advertising from an industry that sold products to one that sold images and identities.

The New Volkswagen Beetle

While the Volkswagen campaign in the 1960s framed the car's symbolic meaning through qualities such as reliability, affordability, and durability (characterized as honesty and trustworthiness), these became increasingly insignificant as inexpensive, high-quality Japanese imports entered the market in the 1970s. As a result, European production of the Beetle ended in 1978, though Mexico continued to produce special edition models such as the Jubilee in 1985, which was the last model Volkswagen brought to Europe.

By 1992, even with the introduction of new models such as the Golf, the Volkswagen had lost popularity in the United States and Europe. In order to reinvigorate the brand in the United States, Volkswagen determined that they needed a "new beetle" that would embody the values Americans had liked in the old one: simple, honest, reliable, fun (Patton 2002). Their subsequent strategies indicate the extent to which sign value came to supplant use value in the 1990s, and brands, rather than products, constituted social identities. The New Beetle, introduced in 1998 by Volkswagen's new agency, Arnold Communications, attempted to attach itself to the old by reproducing its values rather than its features. Volkswagen hired a "Visual Positioning Group", SHR Perceptual Management, to research Volkswagen culture and history in order develop a visual language for the car that would help the car's designers translate sign values such as honesty or reliability into shapes. They created a design language to express these values, for example, deciding that the circle was the most "honest" shape. In this way, the new Beetle's style and design supplanted rather than reinforced its function; in brief, sign value replaced use value.

Even before the New Beetle arrived, Arnold's well-known "Drivers Wanted" Volkswagen campaign was aimed at consumers who saw themselves as individuals – as inner-directed leaders rather than followers – and those who bought cars based on style rather than safety. The ads for the New Beetle, which was introduced with a $35-million print and television campaign, aimed to attract a broad demographic by evoking the old Beetle while presenting the car as updated and new – "digitally remastered", as one ad claimed. Ron Lawner stated at the time, "There are some nods to the past.... But it's a very contemporary campaign for a very modern car" (Elliot 1998). The ads emulated the style of the old Volkswagen ads, with lots of white space, simple designs, and a tongue-in-cheek tone. For example, the award-winning television ad Flower, which was part of the Drivers Wanted series, depicted seven yellow Beetles that formed a Daisy, and then quickly sped off in different directions. The tagline read, "Less Flower. More Power." The ad did not name the car, nor did it explicitly refer to the low horsepower in the original car. As Patton (2002, 2040) notes, Arnold and Volkswagen were trying to fabricate for the new Beetle what had come easily to the old Beetle – an association with hipness, a status of "being in the know".

In addition, Volkswagen and Arnold went beyond traditional advertising and looked to "affinity marketing" as a new way to connect consumers to products. The idea, Patton (2002, 1705) explains, was to "bond customers to a company like a club, to lend some of the sense of membership, community, and belonging that Beetle owners had felt in the past – to give them a car they wanted, not just needed, and to make the purchase something more than a cold hard cash transaction". In this way, Volkswagen produced emotional engagement through participation – in effect, consumers became prosumers who actively produced the meaning of the brand. Volkswagen created an online community where car owners could participate in contests, obtain special offers, and share their enthusiasm for the car. While in the 1960s Doyle Dane Bernbach's Volkswagen ads both addressed and created a counterculture opposed to the dominant values of consumer culture, Arnold sought to shape identities principally through identification with the brand. According to CEO Ron Lawner, owning the car meant "wrapping yourself in the brand... It is an extension of your personality" (Patton 2002, 2031). In this way, the New Beetle represented nothing beyond itself as a cultural signifier for a brand tribe. Membership in the tribe was reinforced by a range of products bearing the New Beetle logo: clothing, key chains, necklaces, flashlights, watches, even a boom box with a bud vase attached. According to Patton (2002, 1990), "Best of all were sunglasses in the shape of the New Beetle logo.... It was a perfect metaphor for Volkswagen's new view of the world: looking at it through the logo."

Despite the success of the New Beetle, by 2000 sales had levelled off. In order to keep people buying new cars, the company that had once defined itself in opposition to the automobile industry's strategy of planned obsolescence began to employ "life cycle management", where they introduced new models, features, and "limited edition" colours to whet appetites. The countercultural car had become just another lifestyle marker that needed to continually reinvent itself. As we become immersed in twenty-first-century advertising, the creative revolution of the 1960s has become an historical artefact that helped shape, and was shaped by, image-based culture where sign value supersedes use value.

The Honest Car Loses Credibility

Volkswagen's residual image as an honest, trustworthy brand took a severe blow in September 2015 when the United States Environmental Protection Agency (EPA) found that they had installed "defeat devices" in an estimated 550,000 diesel engines in order to evade emissions tests. Volkswagen admitted that about 8 million cars worldwide were fitted with software that could detect when they were being tested at emissions control centres. When being tested, the cars would enter safety mode and run below normal power and performance. Once on the road again, the cars would switch back, with the result that they emitted nitrogen oxide pollutants up to 40 times what was allowed in the United States. Volkswagen CEO Martin Winterkorn admitted that the company "had broken the trust of our customers and the public" and he resigned immediately (Hotten 2015). Subsequently, the investigation then spread to Canada, Europe, and South Korea, while Volkswagen's American sales plummetted 25% by November 2015. Moreover, the Company faced EPA penalties of up to $18 billion in the United States alone. In January 2016, the United States Justice Department filed a lawsuit against Volkswagen for violating the Clean Air Act, and Volkswagen faced hundreds of class action suits. In the succeeding months, Volkswagen was unable to reach a deal with American regulators on how to fix the problem, so that in March 2016, the Federal Trade Commission (FTC) filed a lawsuit on behalf of consumers that accused Volkswagen of deceptive advertising. Specifically, Volkswagen was cited for violating the FTC's prohibition against "unfair or deceptive acts or practices in or affecting commerce". The lawsuit did not name Volkswagen's ad agencies or PR firm as defendants, but instead claimed that Volkswagen provided them with the means to deceive others. The suit sought more than $5 billion in damages, making it one of the largest false-advertising cases in American history (Bomey 2016).

From 2008 until the scandal broke in 2015, Volkswagen ran an extensive "Clean Diesel" marketing campaign that targeted environmentally conscious consumers by claiming that its diesel cars were more ecological than gasoline cars. The FTC lawsuit alleged that Volkswagen promoted its supposedly "clean" cars through a campaign that included Super Bowl ads, online social media campaigns, and print advertising (Schultz 2016). The lawsuit also cited instances of deceptive marketing such as Volkswagen's collaborations with the Nature Conservancy and its strategic use of product placement where actress Gwyneth Paltrow arrived at the premiere of Iron Man 2 in a diesel Audi (Audi is owned by Volkswagen). The lawsuit further claimed that Volkswagen's marketers studied the psychology of potential diesel customers and concluded that they "rationalize themselves out of their aspirations and justify buying lesser cars under the guise of being responsible" (Bomey 2016). Thus, specific ads asked consumers to "Do Your Part," reassured them with copy that read, "Diesel. It's no longer a dirty word," or referred to "Clean Diesel" (see Figure 6.2). In the 2015 viral hit "Three Old Wives Talk Dirty", three elderly sisters known on YouTube for their sexually charged comedy debunk old wives' tales that diesel fuel is "dirty and smells bad". Other ads were more overtly deceptive. For example, Volkswagen's, "Diesel Decaf" ad included a demonstration that Volkswagen diesel was even cleaner than other diesel fuel. White coffee filters were placed on the tailpipes of both a Volkswagen and another

Figure 6.2 Volkswagen ran print and television ads promoting clean diesel that prompted an FTC lawsuit

diesel-fuelled car. After 10 minutes they were compared, with the Volkswagen filter remaining white, while the other was stained black.

Volkswagen attempted to rebuild its image in order to keep financially solvent and stem a sharp drop in sales. In November, 2015 Volkswagen ran print ads in 30 American newspapers promising it was "working to make things right". Part of this involved corporate restructuring: six months after Winterkorn resigned, American CEO Michael Horn also resigned. Other efforts revolved around corporate image rebranding to create new sign values for the car. In December 2015, at a strategy meeting attended by 2000 group managers, Volkswagen announced that it was dropping its global advertising slogan, Das Auto (The Car). According to one manager, Brand Chief Herbert Diess, the slogan, which suggested that Volkswagen could define the modern car, was pretentious, and Volkswagen needed to show humility rather than arrogance (Cremer 2015). Its new slogan became simply "Volkswagen". Moreover, Diess suggested the old slogan failed to convey Volkswagen's aspirations in developing the electric car, an initiative begun by new chairman Matthais Muller in response to the scandal. In January 2016, at the Consumer Electronics Show, Volkswagen showcased the Budd-e, an electric-powered microbus slated for production in 2018. According to Diess, "The original Microbus was the embodiment of peace, hope, and happiness, an apartment on wheels. The future belongs to cars that make everyone happy. We want to create a new experience of mobility" (Kable 2016). In February 2016,

Volkswagen announced plans to develop the e-Golf by 2019, an electric car that would become "as iconic as the Golf". According to Diess, the car will be the "Volkswagen for the digital age". It will use cutting-edge technology at an affordable price and "will be a crucial pillar in the company's attempts to rebuild its image" (Kable 2016).

Conclusion

In the twentieth century, the Volkswagen Beetle managed to transform from the Nazi car to a hip symbol of opposition to consumer culture and the slick marketing techniques used by automobile manufacturers. It is a prime example of how advertising in the post-war era began to manage consumer desires through product images that provide identities for particular market segments; Volkswagen's appeals to the "anti-consumerist consumer" demonstrated how image-based advertising helps to define a "better" version of the self, while its affinity marketing illustrates contemporary practices that foster emotional attachment through prosumption. Throughout its history, Volkswagen has been portrayed as an "honest" and "trustworthy" brand, although its primary sign value was undermined by its duplicity in promising "clean diesel" in the early 2000s. The proposed electric car is, of course, both "clean" and a new iteration of the Volkswagen in the digital age. As was the case with the Volkswagen Beetle, the electric car defines Volkswagen as a choice for consumers who both resist and embrace consumer culture. It addresses consumers who "think small" while lured by a "new experience of mobility" characterized by technological bells and whistles that are, according to Volkswagen, designed to make them "happy". Perhaps, in a culture increasingly dominated by arbitrary signs, Volkswagen will make a clean start.

7

The Meaning of Design and the Design of Meaning: The IKEA Experience

In this chapter we consider the way objects are produced, consumed, and made meaningful through design. Design as we explore here refers to the way that products and images are imbued with meaning through the creation of sign value – that is, the way desire for products is created that extends beyond utility. Design is both a form of representation and an activity that occurs within a particular socio-economic, historical, and institutional context and, as such, is integral in the production of values and meanings that provide identities for consumers and commodities. Here, we illustrate shifting cultural meanings of product design from the nineteenth century to the present day. First, we describe how in the late nineteenth century the mass production of elaborately decorated goods democratized taste and marked social status for the emergent middle class. We then discuss the sleek and spare twentieth-century modernist design movement as a reaction against the overly embellished products rooted in the traditionalism of the past. While modernism, which was highly influential in twentieth-century design, is often associated with the principle that form follows function/utility, "postmodern" design emerged in the mid-twentieth century in response to the limitations of modernism. Postmodern design embraces a more diverse aesthetic, often celebrating ornamentation, an eclectic mixture of styles, and form for its own sake. We discuss how postmodern design principles are expressed in the contemporary cultural moment where the form of products – their look and image – has superseded function, and design has become a way to segment markets into ever more specialized niches. As Adrian Forty (1986, 12) argues, attention to needs and desires expressed in the "look and feel" of commodities allowed the design industry to flourish in the late twentieth century. In the twenty-first century, style continues to take precedence over substance, as "the preeminence of hard goods has given way to that of abstract value, immateriality, and the ephemeral" (Ewen 1988, 157). Global brands appeal to consumers through intangible values that offer a social identity, while aspects of design – whether of products, store layouts, marketing and advertising, or even a socially responsible corporate identiy – make those values seem tangible. As our case history of IKEA illustrates, brands create experiences that facilitate the formation of brand tribes whose emotional investment gives value back to the brand. Through forms of participatory engagement, meaning is created through the interaction of consumer and brand. IKEA illustrates how consumers are simultaneously producers of a brand's meaning while its practices also demonstrate the blurring of adverting and entertainment that is key to contemporary advertising. IKEA also exemplifies how design now encompasses corporate identity. Marc Gobe (2001) states that corporations are moving away from "dictated" identities that tell us the values they represent and instead are changing to become "consumer-driven, flexible, multi-sensorial expressions of not only what the company thinks it is, but also reflections of how a company wants to be perceived by people and how they want people to interact with it" (Interview, quoted in Klingman 2007, 269). IKEA, whose products epitomize the modernist unity of form and function, exemplifies the way that the postmodern design of corporate identity, commodity, and consumer experience create meaning in the twenty-first century.

Design from the Nineteenth to Twentieth Century

Historians trace modern concepts of design back to the Industrial Revolution, when the market for consumer goods began to expand and taste became "democratized". As Penny Sparke (2013, 12) writes, the modern concept of design emerged as "the visual and conceptual component of the mass-produced goods and images that facilitated mass production made goods attractive to a mass market and helped to give meaning to people's lives". For Stuart Ewen (1988), the emergence of the modern concept of design dates back to the rise of merchant capitalism with its focus on exchange and mobile representations of value. As rising incomes, leisure time, and discretionary spending created a middle class, merchants could appeal to wants and desires rather than necessities. Moreover, even messages about necessities could be designed to offer aesthetic and emotional satisfaction. Mass-manufactured goods enabled the emergent middle classes to acquire the accoutrements that signified wealth and status.

Sparke (2013) notes that for centuries, goods provided comfort and marked social status for the upper classes, but with industrialization, new levels of social mobility and increased access to goods began to blur class distinctions. Prior to mass production, stylized, decorative products created by artists or craftsmen were markers of wealth, but as new technologies enabled the production of simulated versions of artisanal goods, these became signifiers of social status for the middle classes. The marketing of Wedgwood china in late-eighteenth-century Britain, for example, appealed to a growing middle class that sought to emulate the consumption patterns of the upper classes. While Wedgwood sold handcrafted pottery to the upper classes, and thus created an association with high status, they mass-produced less expensive china as status objects for the middle classes. According to Adam Arviddson (2006), Wedgewood was aware that the socially constructed "aura", or sign value, of its china was as important as its material qualities. By the nineteenth century, a plethora of goods that had been the provenance of the upper classes began to be available to the middle classes and signalled the emergence of a mass market in style. Stuart Ewen states (1988, 32), "The new *consumer democracy*, which was propelled by the mass production and marketing of stylish goods, was founded on the idea that the symbols and prerogatives of elites could now be available on a mass scale."

In the United States, where large corporations made huge capital investments in mass-manufactured products in the early twentieth century, design was initially a way to differentiate products from their competitors, and industry paid little attention to aesthetics. According to Leiss et al. (2005, 83), "product design was informed by the spirit of durability, mechanical ingenuity and quality, and the no-nonsense spirit of the engineer". American product design was epitomized by Fordism and its corollary Taylorism in the early twentieth century, both of which became highly influential in industrial practices (Woodham 1999, 12). Taylorism, devised by Frederick Taylor in the nineteenth century, was a system for maximizing efficiency in factories; it was later used in the design of efficient, labour-saving kitchens and domestic appliances. Fordism was associated with the moving assembly line and the standardization of mass production developed by Henry Ford for the Model T. As we discussed in Chapter 6, Ford believed that a standardized, utilitarian, inexpensive car would suit all needs. He designed the Model T to be durable, reliable, easy to fix, and only one colour – black. The rationale was that there would be no reason to change its design.

But by the 1920s, as market capitalism transitioned to monopoly capitalism and new technologies and production techniques emerged, corporations stimulated consumption by creating desires for prestigious products. In this period, Baudrillard (1970) writes, advertising, packaging, display, fashion, mass media, and the proliferation of commodities led to the dominance of sign value, where values such as style, prestige, luxury, or power became an essential constituent of the commodity and consumption. In order to keep consumers buying products, advertisers encouraged manufacturers to employ designers to diversify goods and make them visually appealing. As a result, in the 1920s Ford lost ground to General Motors, which began to manufacture different car models in various price ranges, from the expensive Cadillac to the inexpensive Buick. General Motors also stimulated demand by introducing new styles and colours on a yearly basis to give the impression of change, even if the mechanical features remained the same. In this way, the automobile became an aesthetic rather than utilitarian object. Historian Ray Batchelor concludes, "In a market saturated with Model T's, General Motors sought not merely to provide transport, but to cater for, and of course trade on, the dreams of drivers" (cited in Klingman 2007, 166).

According to Leiss et al. (2005), in the 1920s, the advertising business in the United States changed consumption practices and the ways products expressed social aspirations when it discovered the significance of aesthetics and the human desire for expression. The discovery consisted of three principles: people are eager for expressive things, they are prone to organizing their objects into coherent systems, and they are fascinated by novelty (Leiss et al. 2005). In this context, style and fashion took on added importance as markers of consumer society. Goods – such as automobiles, clothing, and home furnishings – were made attractive through names, colours, shapes, and other details, while advertising, along with packaging and branding, helped to make consumers aware of products and enticed them to buy. Fashion was one way that people could be encouraged to replace goods that had not yet worn out, while the idea of the ensemble – stylistically or expressively coherent complements of goods – expanded conceptions of necessity.

Roland Marchand (1985), suggests that ensemble-based marketing was one of the key features in the development of modern consumer culture. The ensemble not only expanded the definition of necessity through the imperative that items be colour-coordinated, but it also helped to transfer elite tastes and ideas to the masses. Having a harmonious, coordinated home, or even a coordinated presentation of self, indicated "good taste" and helped consumers to navigate an otherwise bewildering array of choices. The ensemble became a way to personalize the self and express individuality through the use of mass-produced goods. As Marchand (1985, 140) writes, "Paradoxically, mass production would rescue consumers from drowning in mass society's sea of conformity. The ensemble promised to confer the authority of correct taste, yet magnify and vivify the individual personality of the consumer". As our case history of IKEA illustrates, IKEA relies on the notion of the ensemble to both design and sell its mass-produced furniture.

In the period between World War I and World War II, both urbanization and higher standards of living enabled consumption to grow dramatically in both Europe and the United States. The alliance between design and mass production served to further democratize consumption by making goods that signified taste and luxury available to the middle classes, but mass production also required a constant flow of new goods and images available for consumption. Although production lessened during World War II, by the late 1940s and 1950s it increased again in both Europe and the United States during the post-war economic boom. As we discuss in Chapter 6, in the United States, industry shifted from defence to the production of consumer goods as means for continuing economic growth. Consumers sought to improve their material conditions and social positions through purchases of goods such as homes, furnishings, cars, or clothing while the mass media – film, television, magazines, and advertising – disseminated lifestyle models for consumption. According to Sparke (2013, 102–103), "For new consumers, buying a house for the first time and equipping it with contemporary furniture, a kitchen filled with new gadgets, a large refrigerator (in a range of new colours with exotic names) and a new car in the driveway represented their primary means of proclaiming their engagement with the post-war world and of defining themselves." She adds "Increasingly, self-identification was formed through consumption and participation in the fashion cycle" (Sparke 2013, 103). In this context, Gilles Lipovetsky (1994) refers to contemporary culture as an "empire of the ephemeral", whose central feature is the extension of the principle of fashion – obsolescence on the basis of style – to material goods other than clothing and to a broad spectrum of people. He suggests that consumer culture, which depends on the expansion of needs, relies on "obsolescence, seduction, and diversification" (Lipovetsky 1994, 134–135). As we indicate in Chapter 6 with regard to the marketing of automobiles, perpetual style change – through product design, packaging, displays, and advertising, is essential to modern consumer society.

Modernism and Design

For most of the twentieth century, in both Europe and the United States, design was linked to the visual and ideological language of modernism. According to Sparke (2013), the roots of modernist thinking can be traced back to the late-nineteenth-century British Arts and Crafts movement, where "central to their ideas was a feeling of unease with what they felt to be the over-embellished, inauthentic products of the factory" (Sparke 2013, 68). Similarly, modernist design, which moved from Britain to the United States and Europe by the early twentieth century, valorized simple, minimalist forms and emphasized functionality over ornamentation, along with an adherence to rationalism and faith in technological progress. As Sparke writes, "The famous words of Chicago architect Louis Sullivan, 'form follows function, that is the law' reinforced the American search for a rational methodology for architecture and design" (Sparke 2013, 70). Rather than looking at forms in nature as a starting point for design, modernist designers looked to the machine as key aesthetic metaphor. Moreover, just as the earlier Arts and Crafts movement linked notions of good design to a good society, modernists argued that machine-produced goods that embodied their design aesthetic would contribute to the betterment of society. According to Woodham (1999, 34), "The modernists' spiritual affinity for abstract forms and new materials was also wedded to a democratic ideal whereby the majority would be able to enjoy an improved quality of life in a hygienic, healthy, and modern environment."

Modernism is also linked to the German Bauhaus School (1919–1933). When Hitler ordered the Bauhaus School dissolved in 1933 because of its Communist leanings, many teachers relocated to Europe and the United States and spread the Bauhaus ideas. The Bauhaus School's intellectual roots were with the British Arts and Crafts movement, though without its opposition to industrialization and mass production. Bauhaus designers aimed to unify art, craft, and technology in the production of quality, functional goods. For example, Marcel Breur's Wassily chair, first made in 1925 (at first named the Club Chair) was simple, lightweight, and easily mass-produced (see Figure 7.1) He made it out of newly developed stainless steel compressed tubing, initially used for bicycle handlebars, that could be bent without breaking at the seam. The chair, which has a complex appearance but a simple construction, is still made today.

Most importantly, the Bauhaus School was concerned with the social implications of design. Their work combined a vision of the social good with aesthetic principles, so that "good design" unified form and function and worked to better society. The Volkswagen, discussed in Chapter 6, was "the people's car" that illustrated Bauhaus design principles, while IKEA, which exemplifies modern Scandinavian design, was also influenced by Bauhaus design principles and similarly espouses a commitment to the egalitarian principles and social ideals of "good design".

Despite the modernist commitment to using design to build a better society, until the mid-twentieth century modernist design was largely associated with

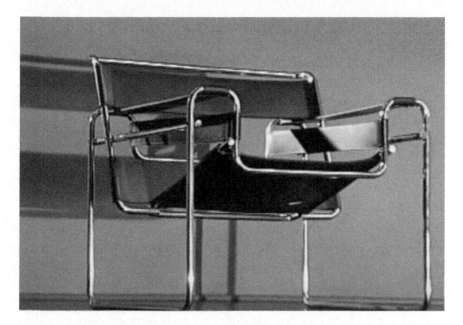

Figure 7.1   The Wassily Chair was known for its innovative use of tubular steel that made it easy to mass-produce

architecture, art, and high culture and remained separate from the world of commerce in the United States. However, as advertisers, designers, and marketers strove to create desire for goods, and markets began to expand in the 1950s and 1960s, "populuxe", or popular modernism, emerged as a dominant style in the United States. The term "populuxe", coined by design critic Thomas Hine, combines the words populism, popularity, and luxury, with an "e" added "to give it class". The term refers to the plethora of goods designed to signify the space age or "progress" (Kakutani 1986). In the affluent post-war period that Hine (1986) refers to as "one of history's great shopping sprees", even utilitarian objects were "designed" to give them the aura of opulence and to signify the modern age. According to Hine (1986), the exaggerated styling of everyday objects celebrated confidence in the future, excitement in the present, and the ability of the "average" family to share in the bounty of a prosperous time. Tail fins on cars, vacuums that looked like rockets, push button appliances, and formica counters were populuxe goods that signified "good taste" and upward mobility. In this context we can see the roots of post-modern design where form no longer followed function. Design became part of popular culture rather than the provenance of high culture. The result was a new relationship between design and culture that exists today.

Postmodernism and the Aestheticization of Everyday Life

In the postmodern cultural moment, design is part of a process that includes advertising, marketing, and mass media rather than part of art or high culture. As populuxe illustrates, in the 1950s and 1960s the division between high-modernist art and popular culture began to break down. Postmodern design, which was a reaction against the insularity of modernism, aimed to produce meaning by appropriating and rearticulating familiar, often mass-produced signs. The result was radical eclecticism, where signs that represent different styles and historical periods coexist in the marketplace. In a context marked by a plethora of goods, all of which compete for the consumer's attention, and amid the breakdown of cultural hierarchies, image (or sign value) takes on added importance as a way to differentiate products and provide meaning. Moreover, the information explosion, marked by the advent of computers, cable television, and digital technologies, facilitated the proliferation of signs, which may provide different, even contradictiory meanings.

As we saw with the rise of the therapeutic ethos, goods are markers of social status and personal happiness, but in the twenty-first century, they have moved from a promise of transformation to an expression of the shared meanings and social relations that constitute brand tribes. For example, as Stuart and Elizabeth Ewen (1992, 186) assert, "Today there is no fashion; only fashions." Within this context, designers play a central role in the construction of identities as much as products. Design has helped to create multiple, fragmented markets for goods, and has even created a market for "designer goods" that depends on the identities of designers themselves. For example, Target, a discount department store, offers inexpensive housewares by designers such as Michael Graves or Philip Stark, and clothing by Lily Pulitzer, Stella McCartney, Danili Minogue, or Jean Paul Gautier. These "branded" designers individualize and add value to otherwise indistinguishable mass-produced goods in the same way we explore via celebrities and branding in Chapter 9, while also creating the image of Target as a hip and trendy place to shop.

Design, the visual and conceptual component of goods, has become the key interface between consumers and commodities. Zygmunt Bauman articulates the relationship between design and consumption: "What is being sold is not the just the direct use value of the product itself, but its symbolic significance as a building block of a particular cohesive lifestyle – as its indispensible ingredient" (quoted in Sparke 2013, 112). A product's symbolic significance, communicated through elements of design, supersedes its practical function as emphasis has shifted from the material to the immaterial. As the immaterial aspects of goods trumps their material form, companies devote considerable resources to image production, which Mike Featherstone (2007) argues has shifted both cultural experience and modes of signification. Emphasis has turned towards the "aestheticization" of everyday life, where, rather than consumers simply adopting a lifestyle, lifestyle has become a "life project" (Featherstone 2007, 84). Body, clothes, home, leisure pastimes, and eating and drinking preferences indicate the individuality, taste, and sense of style of the owner/consumer. People both create and display their identities through assemblages of goods, clothes, practices, experiences, appearance, and bodily dispositions.

Just as on the individual level, identity is designed through assemblages of signs, brands develop distinct identities through the visual and functional elements of design. Harvey Moltoch (2005, 210) writes that branding means design made corporate, "an evolved state of taking design seriously at all stages of an enterprise". Thus, as IKEA illustrates, design involves the production of objects, but also the means of communication about objects through name, colour, logo, advertising, or literature, as well as the creation of a consistent look, feel, and integration of products into an ensemble that represents a lifestyle. In this way, the symbolic values conveyed through design tell a corporate story that makes products meaningful and enable consumers to create identities. According to Moltoch (2005, 206), "The brand also tells what kind of people the stuff is for, providing a come-on that allows the company to herd a constituency of a certain sensibility and then arrange the goods to match. Consumers will then recognize, the marketers hope, a given corporation as 'theirs' – taking the brand name to signal the appropriate pre-selection of form and function has been done."

In this way brands interpellate consumers. Louis Althusser (1970) uses the term interpellation to describe the way that ideology reproduces itself by "hailing" or addressing individuals who, by recognizing themselves in the call, take up prescribed social positions that appear to be freely chosen. In a world of multiple, constantly shifting value systems, individuals must create their own identities and find ways to signal their place in the world. Judith Williamson (1978) extends the concept of interpellation to advertising, and suggests that advertisements hail individuals in terms of their "alreadyness", or how they "wannabe". Ads address "you" as a certain kind of person who is already connected with a product or who wants to be. While the "you" is an imaginary subject, and is addressed to a plurality, individuals who are hailed take the position of the particular "you" being addressed (Williamson 1978, 50–51). Brands design their identities around emotions and values that provide consumers with an orientation and position them within particular cultures of taste and distinction. Mark Gobe (2001) even suggests that successful brands are conceived in terms of "personalities" with emotional and ethical dimensions.

In a context where sign values have superseded use values, brands have become "auras of meaning" that convey lifestyles and identities and constitute global communities of those who share interests and tastes. As Anna Klingman (2007, 56) states:

> For places and things, as for people, the most basic function of brands is to say 'Here I am', signaling a distinguished identity. Before we reveal anything in conversation, we assert ourselves through a self-constructed image: This is who I am; I'm not like that. I connect with these; I don't relate to those others.

Thus, a brand is both a personal and a social identity, an expression both of who we think we are and with whom we want or expect to be compared. Similarly, Seth Godin writes that brands today work to create "tribes"; "the goal is to discover the shared characteristics that define your tribe, speak to the changes and challenges that its members are experiencing, and create folklore and stories that will strengthen the bonds of your tribe and stoke their passion for your brand. In turn, your tribe member will help you socialize your messaging, evangelize your product, and amplify your brand" (cited in Sharkey 2012).

In this way, as brands interpellate consumers, consumers produce meaning for the brand – though contemporary brand management works to assure those meanings evolve in particular directions. Adam Arviddson (2006) suggests that in the current milieu, brands have moved beyond imposing ways of thinking about or using goods, so what is most important is what people can *become* by using them as tools to create their own meanings. He explains that when consumers interact with brands, they produce surplus value – a feeling, relation, or experience. Brands appropriate this surplus value so that consumers produce meanings that are in the service of the brand. Arviddson (2006, 69) explains, "if the brand is established as part of a particular subcultural universe, it becomes possible to act as if one was part of, or better to act *in the style* of that universe, by using goods marked with the brand in question".

Most importantly, brands involve consumers in the production of meaning through research and development. Brands such as Nike, Dove, or IKEA routinely solicit consumer feedback in the design of new products. The consumer becomes a producer of the product, though they are performing labour free of charge and receive no compensation for their input. Brands have always relied on market research through techniques such as surveys, focus groups, or neuro-marketing. But more recent practices rely on ethnographic research where people are observed and studied in the context of their everyday lives in order to assess how they use goods to produce shared meaning. IKEA regularly produces an ethnographic Life at Home report to better understand how people live and what are their emotional drivers. In 2014, for example, IKEA surveyed over 8000 people in eight different countries to learn about their routines, food habits, and wishes. They augmented their study with published research and visits to observe and photograph people's lives in and around the home. The results of the Life at Home Study are combined into a "Data Mining Board" that allows IKEA to develop new products and search for patterns that can be combined into stories that inform everything IKEA does (Yohn 2015). Their major finding in the 2014 study, for example, was that comfort and connection were the most desirable features of home. Their finding helped them design new products, such as the LATJO line of toys designed to help children and adults to play together.

Brands also use "trend-spotting" or "cool-hunting" firms, such as YouthTracker, to locate consumers who are at the vanguard of the consumer market. IKEA employs trend spotters in eight major cities: Moscow, Shanghai, London, New York, Stockholm, Paris, Berlin, and Mumbai and, based on their input, compiles reports that look as much as a decade into the future. According to Adam Arviddson (2006, 72), trendsetters are "the first to articulate and materialize what everybody subsequently recognizes as general knowledge". Once trends are identified, they are appropriated by brands. For example, based on reports from trendsetters, experts, and visits to homes, IKEA changed the design of its kitchens to account for the fact that the kitchen is the new living room, where children do their homework and guests gather as meals are prepared. Research Manager Mikael Ydholm suggests that IKEA even determines the direction of the culture by making trends mainstream: "We have such a big influence. We can actually decide, to some extent, what the future will be like" (quoted in Hansegard 2013).

In this context we examine IKEA as a global corporation that exemplifies the shift from brands as signifiers of production to brands as signifiers of values. IKEA illustrates the way that design at every level of a corporation is used to communicate a brand identity. As Kerry Carell (2005) has noted, "Perhaps more so than any other company in the world, IKEA has become a curator of people's lifestyles, if not their lives." It is a trusted safe zone that people can enter and immediately be part of a like-minded cost/design/environmentally sensitive global tribe. IKEA is a prime example of a company where product and brand identity work together to convey meaning. As a home furnishings company that specializes in modern, functional, economical, aesthetically pleasing products, it illustrates the democratization of taste and the popularization of the modernist aesthetic that characterized mid-twentieth-century design. Its branding strategies further work to enhance its emotional appeal and create the IKEA "experience" by connecting to Swedish national identity, principles of "democratic design", and commitment to social responsibility. In this way, IKEA interpellates consumers who readily identify with the IKEA image, and in so doing, help to build the brand. The following will examine four areas that work to produce the IKEA brand and shape the identities of consumers: the design of corporate identity, IKEA products, the IKEA catalogue, and the IKEA experience.

Case History: IKEA

IKEA is one of the most successful furniture companies in the world, with 389 stores worldwide and retail sales of €36.4 billion in 2016 (IKEA Facts and Figures 2016). From 1943 to the present, it has grown from a small Swedish mail order company that sold inexpensive merchandise, to a global corporation. The rise of IKEA is an almost mythical rags to riches story, though it is one of many local, family-owned businesses that emerged and then expanded as Sweden modernized in the post-war period. IKEA's founder, Ingvar Komprad, began his business by selling small discounted items such as greeting cards, pens, and pencils to his neighbours in a small farming village in Sweden. In 1943, at age 17, he formed a company, IKEA, a name that combined his initials, and the first letters of Elmtaryl, the name of his parents' farm, and Agunnaryd, the name of his village. Within two years, his business grew large enough that he began to advertise in local newspapers, and three years later IKEA began selling furniture made by local artisans. Beginning in 1951, IKEA goods were sold through a mail order catalogue. By 2015 the IKEA catalogue, one of the world's largest circulation print publications, was printed in 32 languages, with 213 million copies distributed; moreover, there were 52 million visits to the catalogue app (IKEA.com).

IKEA opened its first showroom in 1953, which allowed people to see and touch the furniture before ordering from the catalogue. This was followed in 1958 by a store in the town of Almhut. As both urban and suburban populations in Sweden grew in the post–World War II period, there was a ready market for inexpensive furniture. The IKEA store was, at the time, the largest furniture store in Sweden. Because many people had to travel a long distance, it also provided food, which has remained a key aspect of the experience.

Initially, IKEA did not design its own furniture, but the company was forced to do so when the Swedish furniture cartel, in response to IKEA's undercutting of prices, pressured suppliers to boycott it. In response, Komprad employed a draftsman, Gilles Lundgren, to design IKEA's furniture and hired Polish suppliers for the materials. Lundgren is credited with the idea for another key feature of IKEA, flat packaging, or "knock-down" furniture, after he realized that taking the legs off of a table made it easier to transport and lessened risks of damage. Flat packaging was not, however, unique to IKEA. Even in the United States in the 1800s, furniture maker Lambert Hitchcock shipped flat-pack furniture up and down the east coast. But IKEA made self-assembly a key selling point by presenting it as a way to keep costs down with the added benefit of allowing consumers to take ownership of the finished product. IKEA also began the practice of self-service in its Amhult store in 1965, and both flat packaging and self-service have remained important markers of the "Do-It-Yourself" aspect of the IKEA brand.

Design of Corporate Identity

In the 1970s, IKEA opened a store in Stockholm and expanded throughout Europe. At this time, Komprad (1976) wrote "A Testament of a Furniture Dealer" which defined IKEA culture and values, in effect establishing a corporate identity or brand "personality". This document has continued to define IKEA into the twenty-first century, although in 1985 Komprad stepped into an advisory role, and a complex corporate structure, Inter Ikea Systems B.V., began to oversee the concept and the brand. Today, the company operates as a franchise, though "the IKEA concept" is still enforced through trainings and manuals.

A key aspect of IKEA's corporate identity is its association with both Sweden and modernist principles of Scandinavian design, both of which serve to communicate its democratic values. As IKEA claims on its website, "franchisor.ike.com":

> From picturesque fishing villages to endless forests, in Sweden nature plays an important role in everyday life. At the same time, Swedish society is known for being open, innovative, caring and authentic. Yes, things are a little different in Sweden! Over the years a unique IKEA culture and set of values have developed from our roots in Sweden. The IKEA culture and values shape everything we do.

Swedish national identity, with its commitment to social and economic equality, is used as both a resource and a means of persuasion. As Sparke (2013) writes, by 1914, countries had begun to understand the way design could be used to promote national identities, both internally and externally. She states, "It was an important means through which governments and corporations could define their citizens and its consumers, and, just as importantly, through which citizens and consumers could define themselves" (Sparke 2013, 90). Germany, for example, aimed to restore unity and national identity in the wake of World War I by emphasizing industrial production and a rational model of design whose aesthetic was based on the machine. In Sweden – which had a strong craft tradition – craftsmen, artists, and manufacturers worked together to mass-produce goods. The predominance of wood, as well as a harsh climate and scarce resources, facilitated a modernist design aesthetic that was minimalist and functionalist, though based on organic materials. The bright, light, practical design of furniture and spaces evolved to make domestic environments as comfortable as possible with the materials at hand. Today, Scandinavian design still refers to "beautiful, simple, clean designs, inspired by nature and the northern climate, accessible and available to all, with an emphasis on enjoying the domestic environment" (Eyborsdottir 2011).

In the interwar period, while Swedish manufacturers remained tied to traditional applied art industries, designers adopted decorative elements from Art Nouveau. Instead of the rational approach taken by the Bauhaus, Swedish designers demonstrated a "softer, more humanist, decorative modern style" (Sparke 2013, 87). At the same time, the Bauhaus-influenced union of art and industry, and a democratic approach that aimed to make products accessible and affordable, came to represent Swedish design. According to Komprad (1976), IKEA's key concept is democratic design, which on the IKEA website is defined as "just the right mix of form, function, quality, sustainability, and low price". While a short film on the IKEA website in 2014 claimed that "democratic design is IKEA's unique take on design", the concept initially came from the the Swedish Society of Industrial Design, which advocated democratic social views and the modernist belief that design could improve society through its commitment to making functional objects of high aesthetic quality available to all. The Society's guiding principle, rooted in the nineteenth-century Arts and Crafts movement, was "beautiful things that make your life better". Similarly, the IKEA film concluded as a heavily accented Swedish designer states, "almost anybody could make a beautiful product if it could be at any cost, but the beauty is that we could make great design accessible to the many people, and that's the real beauty for me".

IKEA also positions itself through visual references to Swedish national identity. As Simon Garfield (2011) points out, in the 1950s IKEA was spelled with a French accent, and it was only when it expanded internationally that it emphasized its Swedish identity and dropped the accent in order to differentiate itself in the marketplace. Ursula Lindqvist (2009, 44) writes that IKEA is a celebration of design nationalism, "a living archive in which values and traits identified as distinctly Swedish are communicated to consumers through its Nordic-identified product lines, organized walking routes, and nationalistic narrative". Every element of IKEA's design – both the products and store layout – communicates its "Swedishness", despite its global locations and manufacture of products outside of Sweden.

While the IKEA logo was initially black and white, since 1983 it has been blue and yellow, which are the colours of the Swedish flag. Swedish identity is further reinforced by the blue and yellow colour scheme within the stores, and blue and yellow shopping bags. Stores throughout the world have restaurants that serve Swedish food, and most of its products have names that have Swedish or Scandinavian origins. There is a naming system where, for example, upholstered furniture is based on Swedish place names, beds on Norwegian place names, or dining tables on Finnish place names. DUKTIG, which means good or well behaved, refers to a line of children's toys, while KASSETT refers to media storage. Today, although most of IKEA's products are manufactured in third world countries, it is widely regarded as a national icon. The Town of Amhult, where the IKEA Corporate Cultural Centre is located, includes an IKEA Museum, an IKEA Democratic Design Centre, and even an IKEA Hotel, where drawers contain both Gideon's Bible and an IKEA catalogue.

Design of Products

Komprad's (1976) "Testament of a Furniture Dealer" begins with IKEA's business plan, which is simply a reiteration of the modernist goals initially espoused by the Swedish Society of Design: "We shall offer a wide range of well designed, functional home furnishings prices so low that as many people as possible will be able to afford them." The Testament offers several principles, the first of which declares that the company identity resides in its product range. One of the marks of IKEA has been a consistent design approach, even in global markets, so that only small adaptations are made for different countries. IKEA has about 9500 products, with 2000 new products developed per year, though some designs, like the BILLY Bookcase and POANG Armchair, have been unchanged for years. As Harvey Molotoch (2005) notes, brands require stories that lessen the need for explicit instructions every time they create an object. Thus IKEA products are divided into four sets of styles and expressions, all of which are variations on modern Swedish design: Country, Scandinavian, Modern, and Young Swede. These are then divided into four price levels: high, medium, low, and "breath-taking", and in this way form a matrix. The idea, which dates back to the early-twentieth-century notion of the ensemble, is that consumers can mix and match from the range group in a particular style and so achieve a homogenous "look". While there are choices among the four styles, and choices within each matrix, the constitution of matching ensembles is predetermined. It is also important that there are no gaps in the matrix that competitors could fill; for example, if there is not a low priced, "Country-style coffee table", the gap is filled to prevent competitors from doing so. Moreover, extremely low priced products, referred to as "breath-taking", are visually marked with yellow price tags with a red border. These reinforce the message about low prices, though there is only one "breath-taking" item allowed in each group.

As we mentioned above, a key feature of IKEA is "knock-down" furniture that people assemble themselves. While this is presented as a way to reduce costs, it is also a powerful means to interpellate consumers. The notion that making one's own objects offers self-fulfilment dates back to the nineteenth-century Arts and Crafts Movement, which promoted the idea that artisanal products would free people from the alienated labour of the factories. By World War I, the craft impulse had turned into "a revivifying hobby for the affluent" that was "dispersed in millions of do-it yourself projects and basement workshops, where men and women have sought the wholeness, the autonomy, and the joy that they cannot find in the job or domestic drudgery". The sentiment reemerged in the 1960s countercultural movement, which advocated simplicity, getting back to nature, and savvy consumerism as a form of political activism (Lears 1981, cited in Morozov 2014). IKEA's "Do-It-Yourself" ethos addresses consumers who oppose the excesses of consumer culture and contribute their own labour to "create" the IKEA furniture. In this way, they take ownership through production as well as consumption and become makers as well as buyers, even though the product of their labour is determined by IKEA. While consumers save money, they become more invested in the product and thus more loyal to IKEA, while IKEA profits from the surplus value created by their labour. In recent years, various IKEA hacker sites have emerged to guide people to produce their own designs by making new, unintended combinations of IKEA materials. IKEA did not respond well to rearticulations of their brand and threatened to close down the main hacker website in June 2014 for trademark infringement.

The IKEA Catalogue

The IKEA catalogue is its prime marketing tool. In 2009, 70% of its annual marketing budget was spent on the catalogue, while in 2012 an additional 11% of its budget was spent on interactive features (Edvardson and Enquist 2009; Elliot 2012). The print version of the catalogue is distributed in stores and by mail, though IKEA is increasingly focusing its attention on digital versions with interactive features. The catalogue is produced with a standardized layout, with similar products and overall information for every country in the world. Both the covers and the models used differ in different countries; for example, the IKEA catalogue in Saudi Arabia does not include any images of women. Up until the 1960s, the catalogue only showed the products, but as the stores began to display interiors, staged settings appeared in the catalogue too. Today, most of these setting are created by graphic artists and digitally produced. IKEA also offers an app so that the catalogue is always available on a phone or tablet. The app has features such as video clips that give deeper views of rooms and virtual walks through IKEA-designed kitchens or living rooms. The app, as well as the IKEA website, also includes a downloadable program to help consumers redesign rooms in the home. In 2016, IKEA announced a test version of a virtual reality app that would bring the user a virtual kitchen in real-life size; the app, launched on the game platform Steam, was designed to gather feedback so that consumers could "co-create" the virtual reality experience (Boerner).

Throughout the catalogue, the images are simple and unpretentious, as is the descriptive language that is both familiar and inclusive. While initially Kamprad wrote the catalogue text himself, by 2010 there were 10 staff copywriters. While the tone remains straightforward, IKEA claims that "it takes several years to learn the style, to break the code of what to sound like" (Kristofferson 2014, 26). Copy reflects the IKEA values and lifestyle, as in the following description of DINERA dinner bowls: "Understated in style, simple in shape and made of sturdy matte glazed stoneware, this is a do-everything kind of bowl. From solo snacks on the sofa to meatballs around the family dinner table, DINERA has an unpretentious and tastefully rustic look. DINERA is safe for the dishwasher and microwave, and also stacks neatly in your cabinets." But copy also hails consumers by linking IKEA products to contemporary lifestyles. For example, a photograph of an IKEA bedroom is accompanied by the text: "Happiness is… a super comfy bed, a few side tables, and a strong WIFI connection". Or a photo of the KIVIK living room features a family of three. All have mobile devices, though lest the family appear too alienated from one another, the son is looking at something on his mother's tablet. The copy reads, "Your own thing, together. If you spend more time looking at screens than one another – don't sweat it. Sometimes the most relaxing moments are the separate-together ones." IKEA validates the modern family who engage with screens rather than one another.

Even the design of typeface used in the catalogue, as well as the company logo, communicates IKEA's values and inspires strong reactions. Up until 2009, IKEA used the Futura font, which was linked to political art movements of the 1920s and fit IKEA's progressive image. But in 2009, Futura was not compatible with the web, so IKEA switched to Verdana in order to have consistent typeface online and in print. But Verdana, one of the most widely used fonts in the world, is also homogenous and nondescript. The result, Simon Garfield (2011, 74) writes, was that "instead of looking industrial and tough, the catalogue looked a little more crafted and generously rounded. It also looked a little less like a Scandinavian enterprise founded on the promise of original design, and more like a sales brochure from a company you wouldn't think twice about." The controversy led to a wiki called "Verdanagate". Despite the protests, and the fact that Futura soon became compatible with the web, IKEA materials remain printed in Verdana.

The IKEA Experience

The purpose of the IKEA catalogue is to attract consumers to the stores, which are deliberately located outside of city centres so that customers must drive there and so shopping at IKEA becomes an event. The stores themselves use sensory appeals and structured experiences in order to encourage consumption. The stores are all about "seeing, feeling, touching, and having fun" (Howard 2004). According to Pierre Martineau (1957), a store's image refers to the way in which a store is defined in the shopper's mind, partly by its functional qualities and partly by an aura of psychological attributes. As Edvardson and Enquist (2009, 6) note, "In many ways the stores resemble modern theme parks, with their childcare centers featuring large climbing structures and flamboyant playthings and their restaurants serving delicacies such as smoked salmon, Swedish meatballs, and lingonberry tarts." Store entrances have a colourful play area for children where parents can leave their children while they shop. The IKEA restaurants offer local foods as well as Swedish specialties, including organic and vegetarian options. More recently, IKEA has begun to sell its own brand of food, and restaurants offer breakfast, lunch, and dinner options. The restaurants are family friendly, with high chairs and changing areas. The result makes it a "fun" experience and encourages lengthy visits.

Throughout stores around the globe, there are the same products, though room settings in different countries are designed to adapt to local cultures. In China, for example, settings accommodate apartment balconies. But in all locations, IKEA structures the experience of navigating through the store in a manner that works to encourage purchases. According to John Stenbo (2009), who worked at IKEA for 20 years before writing *The Truth About IKEA*, "One could describe it as if IKEA grabs you by the hand and consciously guides you through the store in order to make you buy as much as possible." The stores are designed around a "one-way" winding path of arrows that direct customers through the store so that they will see and experience everything. The path curves every 50 feet or so to keep people interested. Alan Penn (2011) describes the IKEA experience as paradoxical: it is highly disorienting, yet there is only one route to follow. As Johnstone (2011) observes, "the experience replicates the confusion people feel when they are faced with home decoration and interior design – they are looking for direction, and almost without realizing it, are led down the right path".

Typical stores consist of four parts: furniture display, marketplace, cash registers, and the warehouse. The best-selling sets are located in spaces that have the most exposure to the flow of customers, while others are relegated to the aisles. Furniture is displayed in room sets that correspond to each of the four IKEA styles. People are encouraged to experience the products by touching or sitting on furniture to imagine how they would fit into their homes. The main objects in a living room set, for example, consist of sofas and storage units, though interior decorators then add elements to bring the room to life and make it appear "realistic". The displays also contain strategically placed bins that contain inexpensive items to tempt consumers, so that if a sofa is too expensive, a smaller item serves as consolation. The items are always at a convenient height to pick up and place in the yellow bags with blue handles that are placed throughout the stores. IKEA also uses a technique called "Bulla Bulla" to jumble items to give the impression of volume and thus inexpensiveness (Collins 2011).

The arrangement and design of the products illustrates the IKEA maxim that "simplicity is a virtue". As Johnstone (2011) notes, highlighting the virtue of simplicity in the design of the modern interior is part of the modernist aesthetic of sparseness, light, and minimalism, in contrast to an ornate and cluttered traditional aesthetic. But while IKEA appears to support the idea that "less is more", it simultaneously convinces us that "more is less". Johnstone (2011) states that, "By means of a sophisticated sequence of in-store placements and displays, we are led to buy not just a sofa but a lamp and some drinking glasses and some other bits and pieces as well, all the while under the illusion that the process being engaged in is not one of randomly accumulating stuff but of de-cluttering and streamlining an overcrowded life".

The experience within the stores also reflects IKEA's values. Employees are referred to as "co-workers" and are part of the IKEA "family". There are no perks such as special dining or parking places. Ingvar Komprad was known for taking public transportation and flying in coach on airplanes. There are occasional "anti-bureaucracy weeks" where executives work on the floor, operate cash registers, or even load trucks for customers. To save money, employees are used as models in the catalogues. In October 2010, IKEA's annual report justified the company's austerity by declaring; "Sustained profitability gives us resources to grow further and offer a better everyday life for more of the many people". According to Lauren Collins (2011), the report was a response to criticisms, published in John Stenbo's *The Truth About IKEA*, that the company was a billion-dollar business that presented itself as a value-driven, altruistic concern.

IKEA's stated commitment to social responsibility is a large part of its brand. Since the 1980s, IKEA has aligned itself with environmentally safe, sustainable, "green" products. In 2000, its mission statement, "The IKEA Way" (1999–2012), declared that it was a company that dedicates itself to implementing high standards when it comes to people and the environment, products and materials, climate change, social change, and the "never-ending list" of improvements that IKEA is working on. This self-definition is supported by many products made from recycled materials, the elimination or reduction of dangerous chemicals such as formaldehyde or PVC, or energy-saving light bulbs and batteries. Several of its stores provide charging stations for electric cars, and new furniture is designed with ports for charging electronic devices. While IKEA, like virtually all multinational corporations, has been criticized for practices that do not match the values it espouses – for example, IKEA products are made in factories in China – its products and corporate rhetoric reinforce its socially responsible identity as well as the identities of the consumers who shop at the store.

Conclusion

In the twenty-first century, design is a powerful tool to create brands and shape consumer identities as the look and feel of products and the values they signify take precedence over substance. IKEA illustrates the way that design at every level of a corporation works to create shared values and meanings, and in this way, provides the basis of consumer identities. IKEA's strategies and practices illuminate the importance of design as brands have shifted from production-based models to those that establish emotional experiences with consumers. IKEA's success is demonstrated by the devotion of its brand tribes who live all over the world. When IKEA began a family loyalty programme in 2012 that offered discounts and special promotions to members, more than a million people joined within a few months. When IKEA Miami opened in 2014, the event was so huge, with hundreds of people camping out to be first in line and to receive free IKEA merchandise, Dade Country officially named 27 August as IKEA Day. Similar to other global brands such as Nike, Starbucks, and particularly Apple in its ability to create brand loyalty, IKEA uses design of corporate identity, product, and experience to aestheticize everyday life. Chuck Palahniuk's dystopian novel *Fight Club* (made into a movie) even used IKEA to critique consumer culture. In one memorable quote, the unnamed protagonist muses, "The people I know who used to sit in the bathroom with pornography, now they sit in the bathroom with their IKEA furniture catalogue" (Palahniuk 1996, 43). The design of beautiful objects increases desire for things, but it is the design of identity – both of brand and consumer – that creates meaning.

8

Globalization and Advertising: The Case of Nike

There is an uncanniness when travelling in the contemporary moment. Whether you are in Dubai, Singapore, Los Angeles, or London there is a similarity in the visual landscape. An array of images from major products and services and promotion of major films dominate the traditional and electronic billboards that populate our major cities. For travellers, there is something that is bizarrely comforting and unsettling to see McDonald's within a kilometre of Paris's Eiffel Tower, or to see a Victoria's Secret shop in the overwhelming Mall of the Emirates in Dubai. Advertising provides a sign system to negotiate our international world, where transnational corporations that sell consumer goods create a partial sensorium of familiarity. Advertising becomes the means where the global shares the stage with the local.

This chapter explores the globalizing reach of advertising through the study of Nike, one of the corporate success stories of the late twentieth century. What makes Nike particularly useful in the study of advertising and globalization is that it is one of the first companies to embrace the very modern business model where its expertise and value are almost exclusively related to design, image, and message: all other elements of production of its shoes and sports apparel are contracted out far away from its home in Eugene, Oregon. This division of both labour and value not only marks much of the contemporary transnational patterns of the modern corporation, but also how essential to the expansion into international markets is the production of a product's image. At the core of Nike's image is the promise of transformation: that the shoes will provide a pathway to better the self by achieving one's best performance. Through the design and look of the product, advertised messages, endorsements by sports figures, and sponsorships that merge advertising and sports, Nike addresses consumers around the globe who value its "authenticity" and embrace the notion of transcendence through sports. Nike has been brilliant at moving its product internationally because of the way it has captured a sense of contemporary sport and athletics that has transcended national borders.

What is Globalization and What Does it Have to Do with Advertising?

Media – and advertising – are heavily imbricated in the development of the current generation of what is called globalization and yet relatively understudied by those who have been most involved in its study. It has been a hotly debated concept in international relations, in political science, and among cultural geographers and social and cultural theorists for almost three decades. These approaches have informed its intersection with media and communication studies – particularly in the first instance through international communication. The first usage in media and communication of related terms has been connected to Marshall McLuhan's reading of modern media producing what he called "the global village".

At its core, globalization refers to what has been the acceleration and intensification of the movement of culture and economy transnationally. Its antecedents can be seen in imperialism, where predominantly European cultures dominated large expanses of the planet and established what economists have labelled a centre–periphery economic trade structure that serviced the centre of the empire and allowed the "colonies" to be outposts that supported the centre through the movement of raw materials for production and consumption. To capture this imperial forbearer of globalization, it is useful to think of a few companies that operated in ways that are equivalent to modern global brands and, in some ways, far beyond this characterization. For example, British firms such as the Hudson's Bay Company or the East India Company were massive entities in the era of mercantilism, which can be concisely defined as trade that is undergirded by military support. The Hudson's Bay Company established itself through the fur trade with forts and outposts for the gathering of furs from both native and settlement cultures throughout the northern parts of North America in the seventeenth and eighteenth century. In the process, it relied on a charter that connected its activities to the British Crown and to the Crown's sovereignty over the territory that the company exploited for economic gain. Apart from establishing economic trade relations between North America and Europe, the Hudson's Bay Company's development and existence was at least an elemental part of the formation of many of the British colonies in North America and ultimately the formation of Canada itself. It is an interesting endnote to this story that the major department store now called Hudson's Bay Company is essentially the economic remnant of this grand imperial company. In a similar vein, the British East India Company was involved in the development and transformation of territories in Asia and South Asia for economic trade and territorial control by the Britain (Toland Frith and Mueller 2010). One of its essential commodities that defined its growth was the production, distribution, and trade of tea. Both of these companies were closely linked to their home governments, and their mercantilistic power was at least partially built on their ability to draw on the British military to enforce their development and expansion.

Globalization is generally seen as part of what could be described as a postcolonial world composed of hundreds of apparently sovereign nation states. In contrast to imperialism, globalization describes an economic movement of capital that links production, consumption patterns, and image culture that is primarily driven by market forces and not governments and their military. As some theorists of globalization explain, it is a new form of deterritorialization as spatially separated cultures may be linked through production and consumption practices that reconnect their experiences. On a more positive version, globalization can infer an effort to describe our world comprehensively. For example, for the last 40 years, environmental movements have encouraged us to think globally and to ponder the interconnections of our consuming practices and our lifestyles as they affect the ultimate viability of our planetary ecosystem. Similarly, the pleas and plaints derived from the work of the United Nations takes as its mission a form of global care in its efforts at global peacekeeping and its continued efforts to alleviate poverty in those parts of the world seen to be the most abject.

Rantanen (2006, 8), a self-described global mediagrapher who has tried to work out the effects of globalization through the movement of media and communication, defines Globalization effectively for our purposes here: "globalization is a process in which worldwide economic, political, cultural and social relations have become mediated across time and space". Mediation is the critical fulcrum of globalization, and advertising has served as one of the pathways for the international movement of products that have had enormous political, cultural, and economic repercussions. Advertising has been an essential component in the growth of what are now called transnational corporations who successfully sell their goods and services across the globe. The role of advertising was to expand markets beyond their original corporate home by creating desire for those products. Throughout the twentieth century, the success of the movement of particular products internationally was always twinned to advertising's capacity to help create and construct new markets.

In some of the most critical literature about globalization, the most successful transnational corporations are identified as purveyors of a more homogeneous culture. For example, American domination through products in the twentieth century was often called the "Coca Colonization" or "McDonaldization" of the planet. Both of these terms are linked to the power of advertising to shift deep cultural traits. That is, cultural traditions of eating and drinking are some of the strongest forms of identity and practice of everyday life and it is a reality that both Coke and the Big Mac are now part of the diet of hundreds of millions of people around the globe. Naomi Klein in *No Logo* further identifies how these large multinational corporations are not after diversity, but a universal monoculture in their efforts to create their products as more valuable and more alluring than any produced more locally (Klein 2000). Building on this critique, an element of the anti-globalization movement that arose in the late 1990s was clearly aimed at advertising. As product and symbol, the Nike Corporation came under scrutiny from anti-globalization activists and academics alike. What follows in our case history is a close analysis of the Nike Corporation's efforts at the production of an image that has moved so successfully internationally. Nike, in its business style, in its advertising, and in its production of a brand and logo that has now become a symbol that transcends language, is a company that has profoundly embraced the possibilities of globalization. It has extended the reach of its products around the world, both through the uniformity of its brand image and by ensuring the potency of that image to create brand tribes united by their shared values and emotional attachment to the brand.

Nike History: Building Individuality within a Corporate Symbol

To begin, it is important to interrogate what Nike makes, and, in the range of objects and images that Nike creates, what is its most important form of production. From a consumer point of view, Nike has been known for making sports shoes. Its production has gone well beyond this starting point, but its starting point is significant because it helped define the ethos of the corporation – or at least how it was expressed in advertising.

In its earliest incarnation, from 1964 to the early 1970s, the company was known as Blue Ribbon Sports and located in Eugene, Oregon. It distributed running shoes made by Onitsuka Sports, including the Tiger shoe that resembled one sold by Adidas, the leading manufacturer at the time. But two key elements developed in the early 1970s for the company. First of all, in 1971 it changed its name to Nike – the Greek goddess of victory – and after severing its contract with Onitsuka, began to expand its core business by designing, marketing, and distributing its own running shoes (Gratton et al. 2012, 58). Second, in 1972 the company developed a logo to differentiate its shoe from others. Although its design origins were humble (they paid a University of Oregon student $35 to produce the design), the Nike Swoosh emerged as it key logo.

Nike's original reputation was linked to the boom in jogging and running that blossomed in the 1970s. The name became synonymous with the emergence of the sport-specific athletic shoe over the next 20 years of its corporate life. Initially it developed credibility as a running shoe through its strong connection to university athletics, as well as its emphasis on design as critical to its product. Nike's later success was related to its ability to expand a very niche market of athletes; through strategic advertising, product placement, sponsorship, and promotion to make that prestige and product value in elite competition eventually be prized by anyone taking up running or jogging – and ultimately any other sport.

The early years of promotion for Nike were strategic links with star athletes. A distribution of the "waffle shoe" – Moon shoe – was made to track and field athletes at the American Olympic trials in 1972. These kinds of gifts were designed to create value, but also visibility for the Nike brand as elites in the specific sports and disciplines were seen by aspiring athletes and thereby created demand for their product. Augmenting these strategies, Nike embarked on star endorsements in 1973. Steve Prefontaine was the first major runner sponsored by Nike. Prefontaine was a prominent college track athlete with the University of Oregon and the connection gave greater credibility to the newly emerging brand. Also in 1973, the signing of the Romanian tennis star Ilie Nastase in the year he became the number one player in the world as well as adding the French Open to his previous US Open crown, was, without doubt, a definitive move to establish the brand in that sport, but also to allow the brand to move internationally.

The connection to college sports was also a major strategy for Nike. For instance, in the sport of collegiate basketball, Nike's domination of team sponsorship is now overwhelming. In 2012, two of the Final Four teams were Nike sponsored, 54 teams in NCAA Division 1, and 10 of the last 16 teams in the national championships were Nike sponsored (Jessop 2012). An almost identical number of teams were sponsored by Nike in 2013 and 2014. In contrast, Adidas sponsored 12 teams in the NCAA Division 1 tournament in 2013.

Sponsorship thus has been the key advertising strategy for Nike for most of its corporate life. This approach allowed Nike to claim a closer proximity to the "needs" of athletes and to convey authenticity by blurring advertising and sports. Sponsorship was designed to reconstruct the events and the athletes themselves as advertising posters for the brand *as they competed*. Thus, the Nike Swoosh logo became an ever-present symbol on the footwear and apparel of sports teams. Unlike other forms of sponsorship where companies tried to bridge their relationship to the sport, Nike's sports credentials made their sponsorship a linked and connected element of the actual athlete, team and its success. The value of this form of sponsorship has become evident when the various sporting events are televised. When Nike has sponsored an athlete or team, it is a virtual guarantee that their brand logo is visible for nearly the entire screen time which dwarfs in terms of prominence any commercial in a sports broadcast.

In contrast to its extensive and growing sponsorship, Nike refrained from television advertising until 1982. What is significant is that by 1980, and without television advertising of any sort, Nike had achieved a 50% American market share in athletic shoes. Resonating with its sponsorship arrangements, Nike produced a variety of very effective magazine and display advertisements. Its advertisements in the 1970s and early 1980s were a careful concoction of "informational" ads that emphasized technology and design, and two forms of what could be described as aspirational ads. All three types of advertisements were geared to constructing a complex contemporary tribalism: the ads worked as if they were speaking to an "in-group" of athletes who would see Nike's shoes as a pathway to achieving their best performance. The technology and design display ads focused on the distinctive value of the shoe itself and much of this approach related to cushion and support structures in the revealed shoe. As Nike developed the air pocket cushion by 1980, this kind of ad continued to feature in their arsenal for shop displays and in niche-market magazines, such as *Runners World*, that catered to the dedicated athletes in a particular sport.

The second style of print ads for the 1970s and early 1980s were divided between depicting the anonymous individual athlete and the recognizable star. Many focused on the work needed to achieve performance. For example, a billboard advertisement from 1979 shows the finish line of what appears to be a marathon. It does not emphasize the glory of the achievement, but is more related to the individual emotion of completing an objective. In the early decades, Nike constructed a long-running advertising narrative through this and many other ads of how performance is driven internally and success is also determined by an internal register of what constitutes success. This style of advertising worked to extend the ethic of the athlete to an ever-widening market of aspirational amateurs. In many ways, Nike's ads intersected with the growth of self-improvement books, television programmes, and videos that grew in the 1970s to the 1990s. Running and jogging in

Figure 8.1 Nike's 1977 "There is no Finish Line" advertisement connected individuality of spirit to its shoes

particular, but also many other sports, were characterized by companies like Nike as pathways to a better version of the self – a fitter, better-looking self. Nike's particular take on this was the journey and the realization that the journey requires both commitment and effort. Ultimately, the reward was internal – to the self and self-betterment – and not some external notion of glory.

This approach of "solo-ness" of performance can also be seen in two of the more famous ads from the 1970s that also appeared in *Runner's World* and further connected Nike to the seriousness of its shoes for the true runner (Aaker and Joachimsthaler 2000). The tag line "Man Versus Machine", originally from a 1976 advertisement, gets close to this essence in highlighting the individual activity that demonstrates an achievement of movement in the modern world of traffic jams. The second advertisement featured one of Nike's more famous slogans – "There is no Finish Line", from 1977 (Figure 8.1). This ad then spawned a series of related ads that once again built the individuality of spirit that it wanted to connect to its shoes.

Endorsements and sponsorships with leading sports figures was the other method Nike employed to produce an aspirational buying public. For a number of reasons, Nike chose somewhat outsider personalities – or ones who represented a kind of young, defiant individuality for their endorsers as they moved across sporting fields. For example, John McEnroe was signed in 1978 as he became a highly recognizable tennis star, known as much for his abilities on the tennis court as his bad-boy antics with umpires and the press (Pike 2011). The campaign, developed by Nike for McEnroe, centred around McEnroe's outsider status and the slogan pedalled was "Rebel with a Cause", which transformed McEnroe into a James Dean–like figure in

Figure 8.2 Nike's 1978 "Rebel with a Cause" advertisement related John McEnroe to James Dean in an urban setting

an urban environment (see Figure 8.2). The first advertisement in the series, however, was much simpler, with a picture of a Nike tennis shoe and the provocative double-meaning of the caption: "McEnroe swears by them."

What we can see in the early styles of advertising of Nike is its strong intersection with individualism. Using current ideas around bettering the self along with star images that underline conceptions of independence, the shoe company was surrounding itself with an interesting outsider–insider sporting individuality. The outsider signified that sporting figures were in fact inner-directed people – an understanding and an integration of the Stanford-inspired psychographic understanding of different "value and lifestyle" groups in contemporary society (Michman et al. 2003, 18–22) – and driven by ambitions that only made sense to the individual athlete. Those ambitions were also indexically connected to the highest ideals of sporting myth: the pursuit of excellence. The insider quality of Nike's early ad images signified that the pathway to those ambitions were served by Nike and its close relation to the needs of athletes. Nike was a form of insider knowledge – a visible totem of a niche tribe of aspiring athletes.

The early Nike advertising culture of the 1970s was first and foremost a form of building strong and emotional bonds of the value of their product to the various sporting leaders and athletes. Its main focus was to consolidate the meaning of Nike through very direct forms of promotion. Team sponsorship, highly prominent presence at key athletic events, close connection to athletes and coaches in university sports, and technical teams that worked within various sports and their athletes in the way pharmaceutical companies have long ingratiated themselves through free goods and information to physicians (see also Chapter 2) helped Nike build a culture of expertise and ultimately strengthened their connection to the sporting elite. As it worked to massify that original marketing work, Nike constructed a visual campaign of ads that maintained the insider/close-to-athlete/close-to-the-sport excellence ethos as a way to create a sensibility of aspiration for the wider populace to imagine that they are included in these new sporting tribes through their use of Nike products.

Nike's Business Plan: Understanding Globalization as a Management Strategy

What is evident from this analysis of the early years of Nike is that the company's emphasis was not on the factories of production. Rather, it was on design, image, and constructing a relationship to an elite in a sport in the hope that these strategies would allow the company to grow with larger groups of physically active people choosing Nike to express their desire for betterment. Goldman and Papson (1998, 4) identify Nike as a "hollowed corporation":

> In the global dispersal of business functions the actual manufacture of goods no longer forms the central axis of such corporations; instead the production process is broken up, farmed out, and spatially dispersed. Conversely, the hollowed corporation is heavily dependent on the circulation of images or sign values to generate profits.

In early advertising culture, as department stores developed (see also Chapter 3), images of the factories that produced the products that consumers purchased were very important. People seemed to want to know that something substantial was behind their products, and the actual factory image made these products more authentic. A similar ethos was behind the establishment of banks where they relied on an iconography of weight and history. For example, many banks in North America and Australia used Corinthian columns to construct a façade of longevity and security. Nike, however, heralded a business model that became ever-present in the 1990s: outsourcing and contracting the manufacturing work and, in some cases, the servicing work to parts of the world where the work could be done more cheaply, and focusing their business entirely on design. The actual corporation was a shell that designed for first-world markets and provided the templates to outsourced factories to make their products according to exacting specifications in poorer countries. Nike developed the ultimate divide of physical and intellectual labour: its home headquarters, along with its associates in advertising firms, constructed and engineered various prototypes of products, as well as the way those products were going to be presented via advertising and sponsorship to the public.

By 2013, 42% of Nike's shoe production was with Vietnamese contractors, while Chinese contractors produced 30% and Indonesia 26% (Nike 2013 Annual Report, 51). As with their original Blue Ribbon Company, Nike actually makes no shoes. Similar independent apparel factories in 28 countries were contracted to make Nike sports garments and other products.

Here, in its summary of its business in its 2013 Annual Report, Nike is very similar to its nascent business model when it was incorporated 45 years earlier. The structure of the globalized, "hollowed" corporation is made explicit:

> Our principal business activity is the design, development and worldwide marketing and selling of athletic footwear, apparel, equipment, accessories and services. NIKE is the largest seller of athletic footwear and athletic apparel in the world. We sell our products to retail accounts, through NIKE-owned retail stores and internet websites (which we refer to as our "Direct to Consumer" operations) and through a mix of independent distributors and licensees, in virtually all countries around the world. Virtually all of our products are manufactured by independent contractors. Virtually all footwear and apparel products are produced outside the United States, while equipment products are produced both in the United States and abroad. (Nike Annual Report 2014, 47)

As chronicled by Naomi Klein and many others, Nike's business success was a source of major critique. In the late 1990s, as part of the emerging anti-globalization movement, Nike was targeted as a company that heavily exploited its production workers in this model. Goldman and Papson (1998, 11) note that in 1996 an $80 pair of shoes "contained $2.60 in labour costs". Other researchers have claimed that the labour costs were even lower. Whatever the actual truth about production, it is evident that Nike has profited by its globalized business model.

Here is its rough structure. Despite these outsourced labour costs, Nike still employs 48,000 people, with 8000 at its Beaverton headquarters in Oregon. These are divided into different groups: research and design, management, sponsorship programmes, and selling the shoes internationally. The company now owns one of its old competitors, Converse Shoes, as well as a sporting and lifestyle apparel company, Hurley, that is most strongly identified with skateboarding, snowboarding, and surfing cultures. Along with these new products, Nike's growth in employees has been principally through its expansion into retail outlets. While Nike ran signature stores in key locations like New York under the banner of Niketown in the 1980s and 1990s, it now runs factory outlet stores totalling 201 stores in the United States and 437 stores internationally. Over and above this work, Nike also distributes its shoes to key retail chains such as Athlete's Foot domestically and internationally, as well as sports specialty shops, and department stores globally. Augmenting this form of sales, Nike's online business also creates and extends its international profile.

To cater to its global profile, Nike has 16 international distribution centres. It divides its operations into North America, Western Europe, Central and Eastern Europe, Greater China, Japan, and what it calls "emerging markets". In all, Nike's reach is massively global. In 2013, 55% of its revenues were from non-American sources, and some of its largest increases in revenues were occurring in China. To get a sense of the dimensions of this internationalized corporation, its 2013 revenue was $25.3 billion, with between 40% and 45% of that registering as company profits or income (Nike 2014, 62, 67–76).

Yet, as all of its annual reports underline, its most valuable assets are its various trademarks. Some of its original patents related to the air cushioning are no longer protected after 25 years, and Nike has now worked to design new patentable variations. Because it sells so many products – thousands of shoe designs for many sports, thousands of clothing designs for different sporting activities, and hundreds of related sporting products – it is dependent on the power of its logo to convey their value. Given that these products are in fact manufactured very cheaply, the logo and trademark Swoosh, as it is known, are the means and method of conveying the quality of the brand. More than the technology of design, the Nike Swoosh defines the very identity of Nike internationally. In the hollowed-out globalized corporation, the brand, as we shall see in Chapter 10, is not only the identity of the company, it is what the company protects, upholds, manages, and ultimately disseminates.

In this model, advertising and promotion are central activities that help give weighted value to their products so that consumers see them as more desirable. Yet, the reality of running-shoe manufacturing, as we have seen, is that the product can be produced very cheaply. Knock-offs and clones of any particular running shoe are also an always an ever-present risk to a hollow corporation like Nike. As such, careful maintenance of their brand's image is pivotal to continued success. They have to make consumers believe that the image conveyed by their logo provides a guarantee not only of value but superior performance. Thus, the Nike athlete, at whatever level, is somehow imbued with the connotation that they are a serious athlete and the choice of buying a Nike product is a convenant (in their own mind at least) to that seriousness of intent. Advertising and promotion are the lynchpins in holding this corporate pyramid of value together. As Nike's advertising expanded heavily into television from the mid-1980s, one can see a corporation that protected this unique value of its product as it successfully expanded markets sport by sport and ultimately nation by nation.

As an advertising- and sponsor-focused corporation, Nike has developed its image with great care. Given its focus on the athlete, and that this relation to the athlete is constructed as *unmediated* and *close*, partly because of the emphasis on endorsement and sponsorship relations to athletic stars, Nike's advertising has had to tread a very fine line. As it emerged as a major recreational goods international corporation in the 1980s, it had to manage a new era of cynicism related to how audiences perceived advertising, an ever-growing cynicism that, as we see in our study of Volkswagen (Chapter 6), advertising began negotiating with as early as the 1960s as a promotional strategy. As a hollowed corporation, its integrity of being was dependent on its advertised messages. Nike's style of advertising has often been an acknowledgement of this cultural cynicism and has paralleled the negotiated aesthetic styles that dominated advertising in the 1980s and 1990s. Like its fellow corporations, it reached for forms of authenticity in a variety of ways. One was to appropriate and colonize musical and cultural styles that were believed to be authentic. Another was to occasionally translate the cynicism of its audience into forms of humour. Although many slogans developed over the course of its corporate life, through its advertising agency Wieden+Kennedy, it developed an enduring and powerful expression that populated many of its display advertisements and a majority of its television commercials. The phrase "Just do It" emerged in a 1988 campaign for Nike; embedded in those three words was a sense of the internal and individual drive to achievement that transcended the experience of the most elite athlete to the weekend amateur warrior. "Just Do It" appealed to the unmediated. As a slogan, its success in advertising made it iconic in the late twentieth century and so closely associated with Nike and its desire for athletic legitimacy that it eventually was proclaimed by *Advertising Age* as one of the two most influential expressions/taglines and number four advertising campaign of the twentieth century (*AdAge* 1999). Its introduction was twinned with the visuals of 80-year-old Walt Stack running shirtless across the traffic-laden Golden Gate Bridge and describing his daily 17-mile jog. "Just Do It" then became the fabric, that along with the Swoosh, knitted into the meaning of Nike and formed a kind of unity across sports, gender, race, ethnicity, and nations (it was not generally even translated into other languages in international campaigns) as the words served as a powerful form of anchorage/closure for each mini-narrative that Nike created.

The Meaning of Jordan: Basketball and Beyond

As we have already detailed, Nike's promotional strategy has been wedded to sponsorship and endorsement of the most elite athletes. These athletes provide Nike a pathway for the expression of their brand so that its wider consumer market is first consolidated and then expanded. Advertising, it must be understood, does not work in the production of true images of these figures, but rather the images depicted are transformative of the athlete into forms of representation for a consumer market. To get at this mutation of the athlete into an advertised image that has clear purposes, it is useful to call this version or persona of an athlete an *image-athlete*. Because of sport's strong pre-existing narratives of drive, objectives, goals, and perseverance, Nike is able to harvest the sediments of what sports mean and work to inject them into the very constitution of their product. Naomi Klein has described that advertising reaches for "a feeling of authenticity" (Klein 2000, 36), and, as Smart (2005) identifies, sports and their players provide the sensation of something authentic through their very basic essence. The athlete then personifies this authenticity and draws us into an orbit of desire that connects this authenticity to the product and by implication to the consumer.

Although Nike had many endorsement contracts that predated 1985, the signing of the basketball star Michael Jordan actually worked to provide the running template for how sport stars are used by Nike. Indeed, there have been many popular and academic articles about Michael Jordan's relationship with Nike and there is no need here to present that work again. What our case history of Nike is focused upon is how advertising intersects with globalization, and we will limit our look at Jordan to how the relationship has informed this globalized strategy.

Michael Jordan was brought into a sponsorship and endorsement relationship with Nike in his rookie year in 1985. In what was at the time an unprecedented contract of $3 million for five years, Jordan's signing was itself a media event that attracted attention. For Nike, it began to define the way in which it imagined how it would maintain its profile in the market and in consumers' minds. Jordan's own persona – as much as it was shaped by his achievements as an NBA star with the Chicago Bulls – was moderated by how Nike presented him and how it associated him with premium products. Over a series of images, commercials, and posters, Jordan's athleticism was made synonymous with flying. This was represented in the model of shoe named Air Jordan, which drew on his seemingly supernatural ability to hang in the air before he completed his dunk shot. In terms of advertisements, one of the first commercials depicted Jordan on an outside deserted concrete basketball court in an inner-urban neighbourhood. Following his run-up, his launch into the air and eventual slam advances entirely in slow-motion where Jordan appears to be in the air for more than 15 seconds. Parallelling this movement and launch, we hear the accelerating high-pitched sounds of a jet about to take flight. The advertisement concludes with Johnson's query as a voice-over: "Who said man was not meant to fly?" The commercial is then captioned and anchored with what it is selling: "Air Jordan, Basketball by Nike".

The creative development of this advertisement is attributed to Nike's advertising agency, Wieden+Kennedy, who have been instrumental in establishing the entire visual conceptualization of the Nike brand, and Air Jordan in particular. The original banning of the Air Jordan for its colour combination by the NBA facilitated in constructing the "outside-the-ordinary" quality of what Nike brings to sport. The following ad series after "flight" by Weiden+Kennedy continued to expand this meaning of extraordinary where it used similar images of Jordan in flight and the tagline "Air Jordan: It's all in the Imagination" to emphasize how the impossible is possible. As further generations of Air Jordan appeared, the relationship to the supernatural continued with tagged commercials implying "Flight School" among other ideas that emphasized how both the shoe and the man permitted something clearly extraordinary. The beauty of the campaigns is that they worked to make the technology – the air cushion in all Nike shoes – highly visible, and apparently highly involved in exceptional leaps of flight and imagination in sports. Interestingly, in 1998 an almost summary poster of Jordan entitled "Wing Span" was produced by Nike to keep the connection to air and flight both visible and valuable for the Jordan brand.

Over time, the commercials, ads, and posters of Jordan produced by Nike were instrumental in making the athlete transcend the sport. His ads in 1988 and 1989, directed by the then highly visible film director Spike Lee, featured a series of humorous vignettes which connected Jordan and Nike to aspects of contemporary culture that moved further than basketball. The use of various types of musical soundtracks – from beatbox to hiphop – also allowed the commercials to connect via different pathways to audiences. These pathways permitted an international movement as much as they worked internally within the contemporary culture and contemporary cultural politics of the United States. Thus, Jordan worked to create an incredible desire for Air Jordans among urban youth in the late 1980s and 1990s, where, at least in the United States, the shoes themselves were so coveted they led to muggings and spectacular forms of thievery. Even these news events that were connected to Nike's products served to internationalize the desire for Nike's premier brand of basketball shoe.

Operating at the centre of all of this increased activity, and both national and international value, was Michael Jordan himself. As we have indicated, what Weiden+Kennedy produced for this international movement of product was not Michael Jordan, but the "image-athlete" of Jordan – a highly aestheticized and mythological persona that in its embodiment of athleticism was able to literally take both Nike and basketball into flight to produce international value. Although there has been some debate about the level in which basketball has been internationalized in the last three decades, there is no question its reach was massively extended in the 1980s and 1990s. By the year 2000 for instance, 70 countries carried NBA games through their television networks. And Jordan, through this "image-athlete" construction, was the ambassador of the sport as his image moved into the very fibre of popular culture during that period in virtually every country on the planet. Nike capitalized on international events such as the Olympics to further globalize the reach of products such as Air Jordan. The 1992 American Olympic basketball team – often dubbed the "Dream Team" – was filled with Nike-endorsed basketball stars, including Charles Barkley and Jordan among a host of others, and their star value certainly helped expand the brand of Nike. By the London Olympics in 2012, Nike was the official sponsor of the Olympic basketball teams from 17 countries. This is a further example of the international presence of Nike in the sport of basketball, at least partially a result of the endorsing work of the image-athlete persona of Jordan.

In addition to these obvious efforts at global expansion through the star-athlete sponsor and brand, Nike's advertisements also worked to draw attention to Nike in two other related ways: quality and an appeal to cultural/political issues. On one level, the Weiden+Kennedy strategy with Nike has been embedded with quality throughout its 30-year history of making Nike commercials. As we have mentioned, the Spike Lee ads of the late 1980s and then their reincarnation when Jordan retired for the second time in 1999 are exemplary of this strategy of quality. But some of the other commercials were more significant. What is known as the 1997 "Failure" Michael Jordan advertisement is part of this very sophisticated strategy. In dark, subdued colour tones and downbeat music, we see Michael Jordan dressed stylishly in dress clothes in an obvious pre-game arrival to a stadium. Here, he is readily and positively acknowledged as a superstar, as he contemplates his life. The voice-over of Jordan describes how he has missed 9000 shots, lost almost 300 games, and 26 times he had been called upon to take the game-winning shot and missed. It concludes with the following lines: "I have failed over, over and over again in my life … and that is why I succeed". The ad looks beautiful and carries a mixed message about sport performance: like a Hollywood studio, Nike is constructing a film to capture awards in its capacity to convey these complex meanings, all in 30 seconds.

Other Nike commercials have actually garnered international awards. One of these was the kinetic commercial usually labelled "Freestyle", where pure movement of basketball players is constructed in a remarkable montage using the squeak of their movements on the floor and the bounce of the basketball to serve as its innovative soundtrack. In 2002, Nike won a commercial Emmy for its "Move" commercial where in match-cut structures, the commercial conveys the possibility in human movement of sheer beauty. Sports like hockey, basketball, soccer, and tennis are intercut with running, free-basing, diving, long-jump, speed skating, and snowboarding in a remarkable montage drawn together by the synergy of the images and the simple piano and sound-of-human-effort soundtrack. Stars are present, but not foregrounded in the flow of images. However, Nike's footwear and apparel are evident as they are seamlessly integrated into the various athletes' movements.

On a more basic level, Nike ads have been sophisticated in their use of video and digital technologies. Paralleling the Jordan commercials, Nike also led in the late 1980s and 1990s with a series of ads known as "Bo Knows." The ads, meant to highlight Bo Jackson's ability to play multiple sports, are set in a locker room where images of the athlete wearing different sports attire are superimposed, with the effect that all the versions seem to appear together and converse with one another.

Nike has also attempted to intersect with political and cultural issues, and has used sport as a way to convey their support for human effort. It is a sophisticated approach that never loses its endorsement of individuality and individualism, and how Nike fits into these dreams of success. Thus, it is very clear that Nike has used athletes as outsiders and as forces of change and has taken those images of the outsider's success as emblematic of their own out-sider and individual attitude to performance and excellence. In tennis, for instance, Andre Agassi eventually inherited the "rebel" moniker for Nike from McEnroe and built the international men's Nike shoe and apparel market effectively for 15 years. Tiger Woods was also deployed in how his skill tran-scended what would be apparent racial divides in the structure of the sport of golf. Beyond Jordan, Nike endorsed some of the most individual athletes in basketball, including Dennis Rodman. Circulating around its endorsement structure in its advertising strategy has been a sentiment of "giving back". Via its athletes and its various social sponsorship programmes such as Biketown and the #BeTrue campaign to end anti-LGBT bias in sport, it has constructed an international tapestry of goodwill. Indeed, sponsorship itself of Olympic teams and other highly visible national athletes in various settings has allowed Nike to intersect with a very sophisticated role-model position in contem-porary culture. As a corporation, its commercials convey these connections to race, class, and gender politics through emotionally charged images and grabs of related popular music in a manner that conveys positive sentiment but no clearly defined egalitarian politics beyond how sport and merit allow some sort of transcendence of inequalities. Nike's overall efforts are towards providing what Goldman and Papson (1998) explain as an *image philosophy* that replaces other forms of morality, and through its appeal to authenticity and challenging false images through humour and sincerity and attacks on other forms of image/consumer culture, an equally powerful *philosophy of the image*. Thus, Nike reaches for a transcendent philosophical approach through its advertising that opens up the promotional vistas transculturally and transnationally through the vehicle of sport itself.

Conclusion

The uses made of Michael Jordan as an image-athlete have led to many other directions in the development of the globalized corporation that Nike has become. It is important to understand that the globalized corporation has the obvious objective of growth: the internationalization of Nike's selling of products is its central pathway to maintain its remarkable run of often double-digit growth in year-on-year revenues for most of its corporate life. Central to its strategies have been incredible sponsorships of athletes who can transcend national markets. Jordan, partially through Nike, became what Halberstam (2001) labelled the "new athletic-cultural-commercial empire" (Halberstam 2001 in Smart 2005, 98). Certainly, Nike has not stopped with this effort, and, in effect, intensified it over the last 30 years. From the mid-1990s, Tiger Woods became another image-athlete that, with the exception of his fall from grace in 2009 and 2010 because of a sordid sex scandal and related marriage breakdown, was instrumental in both carrying golf globally as well as the presence of Nike in the sport. The combination of individualized sponsorship with global reach was equally at play in the long-term sponsorship of Roger Federer in tennis, where his sponsorship with Nike by the second decade of the twenty-first century had surpassed $91 million. In one of the more recent large-scale deals, the 2013 number one golf player, Rory McIlroy, was signed to a 10-year $250 million complete sponsorship with Nike (Fordyce 2013).

Nike has also targeted specific large and seen-to-be untapped markets. Through the pursuit of sport stars in China, for example, Nike has worked hard at establishing its connection to regional desires and aspirations in order to maintain its own growth and expansion. Yao Ming, the first Chinese national to play in the NBA, was pivotal for the expansion of basketball into Asia and, at least originally, for Nike to colonize that space of expansion as well. Yao Ming's sponsorship was abandoned by Nike after his rookie year in 2003, but it managed to sign the second NBA-bound Chinese athlete, Yi Jianlian, to a multi-year sponsorship. Paralleling these forays was the long-term relationship Nike developed with Li Na, by far the most successful female Chinese tennis player in the sport's history. Nike's strategy also included sponsoring tours by leading professional basketball athletes. For instance, LeBron James and Kobe Bryant have both done national tours of China on behalf of Nike. Matching these strategies are the sponsorship of sporting teams and future individual athletes in China that have the potential to become international image-athletes.

Nike's presence internationally is demonstrated by its now complete efforts in colonizing soccer and even more recently a growing presence in cricket. At the 2014 FIFA World Cup in Brazil, Nike not only held sponsorship arrangements with superstars such as the Brazilian player Neymar (at $1 million a year for 11 years), but its support of teams established their strong connection to national programmes and its ubiquity at virtually all matches in some form or another (Marcial 2014). Much like basketball, Nike is involved with professional club team sponsorships that establish the tribal connection that they desire to foster with the related sport consuming public. With cricket, Nike has moved further into markets such as India and Pakistan where the sport at times rivals national religions. It has been the Indian national team "kit" sponsor since 2005, beginning its sophisticated but grounded development of connection to authenticity through one of the most powerful pathways to the millions of Indians who play cricket.

The breadth of Nike can now be overwhelming. It is difficult to imagine how one corporation sustains so many of its sporting "balls" in the air. As we have detailed, Nike has managed to infiltrate through endorsements, clever sponsorships at grassroots level, and advertising, virtually every sport from ping pong to extreme sports. It has moved its signature Swoosh from its orginal home on athletic shoes up the body to much more visible sporting wear, and it uses these tops and bottoms as a further form of advertising, whether through their prominent sponsored superstars or through the mundane presence of the Swoosh in children playing any of these sports. It surrounds each sporting event with ambient advertising not only through its athletes, but also through its outdoor advertising and even its highly prominent signature stores and its ubiquity as a legitimate brand in thousands upon thousands of retail outlets.

As we have explored in this case history, Nike has used a variety of advertising and promotional techniques to achieve its incredible reach as a globalized corporation. Through its philosophy of individualism wedded to self-improvement and self-achievement, Nike has modelled a corporation where its ideas have worked their way into what is valuable in hundreds of national and regional cultures. This process of appending Nike's ethos to other national cultures essentially defines how advertising and globalization work. Via sport and through the value of sport in each national culture, Nike has infiltrated meaning systems with its image. It has made its symbols connected to other powerful symbols of national or local pride, and these symbols quietly become linked. Similarly, it has worked at defining the individual athlete as a consumer who has parallel desires to the elite athletes in a sport. Its simple designs thus become valuable for the individual as a form of expression of desire, potential, and possibility.

Circulating through these various sentiments are the Nike advertisements that serve to maintain the meaning of Nike for all these "users" of the brand. In its current incarnation, Nike has successfully migrated to representing these images of well-being and aspiration through online culture. Its new products such as the Nike FuelBand work to maintain a new generation of tribal connection to self-improvement individualistic values. Through "viral videos" such as the original 2005 Ronaldinho YouTube video of the soccer star foot-juggling a soccer ball for over two minutes after he puts on his new Nike boots, Nike makes its connections to new forms of authenticity and ways to circumvent the way ads are still viewed with cynicism.

Or one can be amazed at the stable of athletes that are associated and affectively connected to the Nike brand through a series of powerful advertisements of these stars wearing fashionable sportswear: in one advertisement we are introduced to the smiling tennis icon Maria Sharapova, the female basketball star Skylar Diggins, the rising tennis star Grigor Dimitrov, and the American female soccer star Sydney Leroux. In another even more overwhelming commercial, the array of stars captures the transnational flow of Nike's identity. Through intertitles and associated moving images of related streetscapes, we are told that we are in various cities of the world – Miami, Los Angeles, New York, Cleveland, Milan, Sao Paulo, Chicago, London, Munich, Houston – connecting to the lives of these star athletes. To the tune of *Stop the Rock,* by Apollo 440, we see the athletes smiling – and wearing Nike gear such as the Tech Pack collection – and casually moving through their individual star photoshoots. The commercial concludes with a "listing" of the stars with their names punctuating the music, as a roll-call in a movie trailer. As viewers, we are invited to identify the stars at the beginning, while the end confirms our knowledge of particular stars: Jon Jones, Rory McIlroy, Paul Rodriguez, Perri Shakes-Drayton, Theo Walcott, Jack Wilshere, Adrian Peterson, Kevin Prince-Boateng, Rafael Nadal, Alex Ovechkin, Maria Sharapova, Kyrie Irving, Matt Kemp, Neymar Jr, Serena Williams, Allyson Felix, Li Na. The video is almost two minutes long and does not really fit into the structures of television network advertising. It is something different, as it displays the global reach of Nike. With 819,000 views after a year of play on YouTube, the commercial video on its own moves in a parallel and affectively associated way with the star athletes it depicts.

In combination with these highly visible athletes, Nike's advertisements come alive and move into our consciousness wherever we may be. Nike has established the capacity of a contemporary corporation to be built on image; its conceit was it was able to do this through a sense that it was more authentic than image – the ultimate achievement in the complex world of advertising, value, and consumer culture.

9

Advertising and Politics: Selling Presidents as Soap

Back in 1952, American presidential candidate Adlai Stevenson remarked disparagingly about the expanding world of political advertising into television commercials: "I think the American people will be shocked by such contempt for their intelligence. This isn't Ivory Soap versus Palmolive" (Beschloss 2016). By 1980, the future successful presidential candidate Ronald Reagan fully accepted his status as a product and commodity that resembled soap and needed to be sold that way. Upon meeting his campaign advertising team called the Tuesday Team, Reagan remarked: "If you're going to sell soap, you ought to see the bar" (Beschloss 2016).

The idea that selling presidents as soaps has become mythologized as a watershed moment in the history of American politics both domestically and internationally has come to represent how powerful advertising has been in shaping politics. Adlai Stevenson can be identified as the last American presidential candidate who refused to appear in television commercials in his 1952 campaign as he competed against Eisenhower's impactful commercials (Museum of Moving Images 2012), a series of advertisements which even included endearing Disney-made animation. Indeed, Stevenson's political aide, George Bell, was oddly prescient when he added to the analogy between selling soaps and presidents that "presidential campaigns will eventually have professional actors as candidates" (Museum of Moving Images 2012). The actor Ronald Reagan, a matinee idol of films of the 1940s, was the first entertainer elected American President in 1980. Perhaps it is needless to add that Stevenson lost the election of 1952, and although there are many reasons for that loss, at least one of them relates to his resistance to media advertising.

This chapter investigates the relationship between advertising and politics. Its case history is an analysis of the political advertising campaigns of Barack Obama and how his particular use of what can be described as viral and online forms of promoting messages came to represent a new watershed moment in the organization of politics that parallels the television advertising watershed moment of 1952. What is key here is how Obama brought a sophisticated tribalism to the political sphere through digital technologies designed to cultivate a sense of belonging and connection. In so doing, he relied on his supporters to actively participate in building his brand – that is, to demonstrate their commitment by promulgating and amplifying his message through social media. In order to understand and contextualize Obama's political advertising campaigns of 2008 and its legacy for 2012 and beyond, it is useful to trace how politics and advertising developed such a close and vital relationship by examining promotional strategies in political advertising.

Promotional Strategies in Political Advertising

Both the online transformation of political advertising of 2008 and that of the use of television in the 1950s are never so immediate and spontaneous as the mythologies would lend one to think. In other words, it is important to realize that techniques for promoting politics emerge from elaborate histories. For instance, although 1952 represents the moment in American politics where television advertising "spots" transformed the way a population perceived their candidates, television advertising was predated by radio advertising, which certainly served as its model. In the American context, 1952 was the last campaign where both of the major political parties spent more on radio advertising ($ 3,111,050) than television advertising ($2,951,328) (Jamieson 1996, 44). It should also be remembered that print and display advertising have always been a major component of political advertising. Whether in Canada, Australia, Asia, or Europe, one of the signals of a major election campaign is the blanketing of public and private spaces with posters of parties and candidates. Even in the flawed elections of what are perceived to be dictatorships, the flood of images of leaders' faces along with slogans have been used throughout much of the twentieth century.

Thus, techniques of promotion that predate either radio and television need some exploration to identify how these elements are also integral to the relationship and practice of politics and advertising as they have embraced newer media forms. Before advancing further, we will discuss three political promotional forms – slogans, products, and political events – that predate and inform the contemporary structure of political advertising.

Slogans

In contemporary Internet terms, there is an understanding of particular content going "viral". Equally, other online content is described as a "meme", which essentially means that either a particular segment of content has proliferated and been shared through various networks or a particular piece of content has served as a creative source for variations of its content by users (Shifman 2014). Both of these terms refer to activities that can easily predate online and social media platforms. For instance, it is very clear that slogans developed for different politically related campaigns are examples of virality and, in some cases, memes. The exclamation in American culture of "Remember the Alamo" is an example of an enduring viral expression or slogan that has transcended its original historical moment and conveys the sense of commitment to a mission no matter what the consequences. Similarly, the origins of "Eat the rich," a humorous, leftist expression, predate the eras of promotions as it was drawn from the French philosopher Jean-Jacques Rousseau's aphoristic phrasing, and perhaps a loose connection to the emerging politics of the French Revolution of the late eighteenth century.

Political advertising tries to reproduce these moments of potential virality by making slogans attached to campaigns This activity is similar to any advertising campaign where a jingle, or an expression, enters into everyday discourse and essentially becomes both ubiquitous and popular. In political advertising, the objective is that the slogan becomes attached favourably to a candidate or a political issue. Some of the most memorable slogans have actually been developed for political campaigns by advertisers. For instance, in 1972, the Sydney, Australia advertising agency of Hansen-Rubensohn–McCann–Erickson generated the slogan "It's time" through a variety of platforms – a jingle, posters, and a commercial that showed many popular Australian performers singing the song – that ultimately captured the imagination of the electorate with its focus on youth and change to propel a Labor Government and Prime Minister Gough Whitlam into power. In contrast, the New York advertising firm of Doyle Dane Bernbach was associated with the 1964 campaign of Lyndon Baines Johnson, and the slogan that grew with the campaign's winning spirit was "All the way with LBJ". However, as much as the rhyme of the catchphrase has endured, it also migrated into a "meme" with different meanings: as the quagmire of Vietnam engulfed

Johnson's presidency, the phrase was changed to "No Way with LBJ". In the Australian anti-war movement, "All the way with LBJ" became a wry and powerful critique of the Australian government in the 1960s for its unswerving solidarity with American foreign policy.

Buttons and Lawn Signs: Politics, Promotional Products, and Ambient Advertising

It may seem innocuous, but one of the most enduring forms of promotion and advertising in politics is the type that declares allegiance and endorsement. It is a technique in modern culture that is very much linked to making visible one's network and network of influence and announcing those connections more broadly. Via Facebook and other forms of social media, an individual can very easily through visual shorthands of "likes" and "dislikes" establish a full tableau of what they endorse and that with which they have committed themselves. Historically, in political advertising, this form of endorsement has been developed through two simple artefacts of campaigns: the campaign button and the lawn sign. One of the problems and issues in political advertising is ensuring the visibility of candidates. In local elections, establishing that visibility is sometimes as simple as name recognition. Thus candidates in democratic elections have attempted to make their name known during the campaign by having individuals appear to have committed to the candidate by wearing a campaign button, or in many elections, having a lawn sign on their property. The campaign button in American politics was first employed as a button lapel with Lincoln's image in 1860 and proliferated for the next 130 years, and it served as a way to make the face of a presidential candidate visible.

The endorsement element in both buttons and lawn signs is extremely valuable in contemporary politics as it uses endorsers as an extension of candidates themselves. In a national election, despite the best efforts by candidates, it is an impossibility for a candidate to visit or connect with each constituent. The endorsement becomes a parasocial connection that makes the candidate come alive in the local community. Lawn signs similarly identify that a particular person has literally staked allegiance to a candidate in the most visible of ways by attaching it to their property. In any election, as some of Shannon Callahan's (2012) research has explored, if a certain community is blanketed with campaign signs for a particular candidate it can serve to imply that that candidate is "speaking" for that particular community. What is achieved is a highly visible scene of connection for the candidate. In terms of advertising, items such as posters, lawn signs, and buttons are forms of ambient and environmental advertising as they reconstruct the landscape with persistent and prevalent messages, and most prominently, the candidate's name. Much like how billboards work or how brand logos on promotional products such as hats work, these political promotions establish the ubiquity of the political message. By their sheer volume, buttons, posters, and lawn signs also provide an indexical sign of the popularity of the candidate – a powerful form of influence in any electorate.

The Political Event

One of the simplest and most straightforward ways of attracting attention in politics is constructing some type of event – a staged spectacle that serves to invite the citizenry to observe and experience. Thus, the soap-box pontificator in Trafalgar Square in London is a rudimentary example of constructing a political event to attract attention to a cause. In the contemporary moment, constructing an event is often the way that a cash-poor but idea-rich movement works to build its constituency. In recent times, this may have been the Earth-first protestors chaining themselves to trees to stop their logging; or Greenpeace's Rainbow Warrior lurking in the South Pacific to prevent the French government testing nuclear bombs in the 1980s; or the Sea Shepherd's small ship confronting Japanese whaling vessels. All of these examples are actions in and of themselves; but fundamentally, their drama – the David countering the Goliath – drew media attention to these causes and created a flow of financial and voluntary support. Political events then are the core of promotional campaigns. The more dramatic they are, the more effective they are at drawing citizens to causes, whether those causes are the election of an individual or the support of a political position.

Political speeches and rallies thus represent the classic way to draw a crowd by giving an event to promote. In American politics, other techniques have been used to draw attention to a presidential candidate. The whistle-stop tour allowed candidates to work through a number of cities and municipalities on a rail line, where the actual event was heralded by the train whistle and an eventual speech on a platform car specifically made for such events. Political debates among candidates have become another common technique to draw crowds to events in many democracies. Over the last half-century, political debates have been televised. Political conventions, where leaders were chosen or nominated by their party members, have also become a standard way in which to corral media attention.

Any of these techniques provide a different form of promotion that does not require paid advertising but works to produce what has been described as media events that draw the news media to cover the proceedings. The contemporary campaign ensures that some event is organized each day of the campaign – as simple as the candidate being at a factory opening or attending a country fair – so that the news media is drawn to focus on the campaign's issue. News organizations have become complicit in this game of political events by ensuring that each news service has a journalist on the "campaign bus" – a bus that is literally provided by each of the political parties working to elect their nominee.

The Role of Advertising in Political Campaigning: A Comparative International Perspective

The techniques described above – slogans, products, and events – are basic forms of political promotion and marketing. In contemporary politics they are closely aligned to professionally run campaigns that are orchestrated by advertising agencies and professional campaign teams. However, it must be understood that political advertising is very differentiated internationally; what may be commonplace in the United States is unheard of in how things are done in say, Switzerland. For instance, television advertising has been powerfully present in American politics since 1952. However, it is not permitted in either South Africa or Switzerland for reasons of costs and the potential elimination of groups/movements and parties who could not afford to participate if the benchmark was the production of a political commercial. Indeed, in Switzerland it has been at least partially a way to sustain advertising dollars for newspapers (Holtz-Bacha and Kaid 2006, 5).

Another common differentiation internationally is whether time is given for free on broadcast outlets – and thus the parties merely have to make their commercials – as a way to ensure equity in promotion. A further distinction is whether commercials are only shown on private broadcasters or whether the public and national broadcasters are also compelled to show commercials (Holtz Bacha and Kaid 2006, 9–10). In Canada, commercials populate all media forms with an effort at relative balance with free airtime guaranteed on stations. In contrast, in Australia, public broadcasters show no advertisements and the political advertisements populate the commercial stations (Stewart 2006, 273). The United Kingdom, Portugal, and Spain allow no purchase of airtime on either public or private networks (Scammell and Langer 2006, 65–82; Connolly-Ahern and Herrero 2006, 97–108).

In almost every case internationally, with the exception of the United States, there are clear restrictions on political advertising and most specifically on television ads. These restrictions are either in terms of time and/or in terms of how much money can be spent. What this underlines is how politics is peculiarly situated in contemporary consumer culture and how advertising is perceived as potentially skewing rational political debate. The scepticism with which advertising has been treated in international politics reveals how politics is in fact not seen as something that is sellable like soap or cereal: it carries much more gravitas and is shrouded in the idea of fairness. One can see how this idea of the seriousness of politics has led to very particular types of political programmes. In many countries such as Mexico, political announcements or spots are apportioned rigidly according to the current political status of a party. In other countries, laws were in place that ensured political ads were much longer than normal commercials. Germany, for instance, for many years permitted political free-time ads to be either 5 or 10 minutes in duration; it took decades for the 30-second political spot to emerge in that country.

The American system is ultimately the most open-ended, which may not be the most fair. In other words, the American system allows a potential infinite number of purchases of advertising time. It has further allowed different associated groups and Political Action Committees to purchase time related to issues that further augments the amount of political advertising that occurs in the United States. Moreover, unlike most other countries that operate under parliamentary systems of government, there is also no restriction on when a campaign begins. Over time, the American presidential campaign has become an increasingly protracted affair and is easily, for any serious candidate, a 2-year ordeal. In contrast, countries such as the United Kingdom or Australia mandate that their election campaigns are no longer than five or six weeks. This difference in political campaigns severely transforms the amount and range of political advertising that is employed.

Positioning and Posturing: A Brief History of Political Campaign Spots

Despite all these international restrictions, television in most countries has represented the most powerful form of political advertising for the past 60 years. In the United States, advertising campaigns have in some ways been used to summarize the power and success of politicians. For instance, perhaps the most famous political spot of all time is the "Daisy" spot by Tony Schwartz of the New York advertising agency Doyle Dane Bernbach for Johnson in his campaign for the presidency in 1964. The ad itself was issue-based, but managed to strike, what Schwartz would later title his book on advertising, "a responsive chord" (1974) with the electorate. The ad begins with a young child counting while picking daisy petals from a flower; it then shifts to a very militaristic countdown and concludes with the universally recognized atomic bomb mushroom cloud image as Johnson's voice-over explains the risks and stakes in the world. Without one word about his opponent, the ad was able to evoke that Goldwater and his hawkishness on the use of nuclear weapons was actually threatening and dangerous; also implied was that Johnson was the safer option of someone to lead the country.

This style of ad is often called "negative or attack advertising" (Haynes and Rhine 1998) in politics and represents one of the most dominant forms of advertising in American politics. Moreover, attack advertising transcends the political spectrum. In 1984, Reagan produced the famous commercial "A Bear in the Woods" as he tried to present his opponent, Walter Mondale, as someone who could not stand up to the threat of the Soviet Union and communism. Although it is notoriously inaccurate to say a particular ad led to a given election outcome, the "Bear" ad and the earlier "Daisy" ad transcended their places as paid advertisements as they were also heavily repeated in commentary in a variety of media forms, and on television news programmes themselves. In other words, part of the success of the commercials was their capacity to become part of popular political culture. The ads in effect probably worked more at galvanizing opinion than changing votes.

Along with negative advertising, the other dominant form of television political advertising, particularly in American presidential politics, has been image-forming ads. These ads often provided a narrative of how the individual is connected to American values. For instance, Clinton's "humble" beginnings were regularly shown in his 1992 successful campaign ad "The Man from Hope", as a contrast to George Bush's relative wealth. The ad featured Clinton as a young man meeting President Kennedy, working his way through law school and making a difference back in his home state of Arkansas (see Figure 9.1). Conversely, George H.W. Bush's ads tried to build on the patriotism that only a year before had catapulted him to the highest approval rating in presidential polling after the 1991 Iraq war. Most of these ads are drawn from the longer political campaign films that have often been used to launch the final post-convention stage of the campaign. Although it is difficult to characterize such a large group of ads over half a century, it is a general truism that the image ads work at attaching the candidate to positive and uplifting emotions of achievement, determination, and caring as they connect the candidate to the people in the most affirming way.

Figure 9.1   A young Bill Clinton shakes the hand of President Kennedy

Over this long history, American political advertising in these dominant forms, and in their attempts to crystallize issues and provide a shorthand for opinion formation, has become a normalized part of contemporary politics. As voters, we now expect to be persuaded by the techniques of campaigns, and, given the hundreds of millions of dollars they cost, we expect these campaigns to be as sophisticated as the most intricate of advertising campaigns: after all, presidential campaigns can be generally thought of as the most expensive single-advertising campaigns – well beyond the money spent on any other product or service in the normal flow of advertising. Even as early as 1980, $18 million per campaign by Reagan and Carter were spent just on television advertising (Devlin 1981, 3).

Case History: Obama in 2008 – A Transformation of Connection

Much of the literature that has analysed Barack Obama's original presidential campaign strategy have considered it unique and remarkable. One writer described it as a "fractal campaign" in its capacity to engage with the citizenry and the electorate quite differently than past efforts (Campbell 2010, 121). Others have described it as exemplary in terms of how to connect to an online generation. Some of this heralding of what Obama achieved in terms of the campaign itself is accurate. This case history will investigate how these new dimensions of campaigning changed the organization of contemporary political advertising. What needs to be emphasized is not so much that the techniques developed by Obama were entirely new; instead, this case history reveals how these new directions are more accurately a transformation or even a translation of connection where past techniques of building allegiances and investments in an electorate are now reorganized into what the campaign may have described as connections to the "Net Generation".

Although the rhetorical strategies of advertising are not a perfect match for those of politics, there are some areas that allow advertising to be the best way to express political desire. As evidenced in our study on the puffery and false promotion of patent medicines in Chapter 2, advertising has always been shrouded with the idea that false claims and overstatements are part of how the messages get consumers to finally purchase products. In traditional marketplace thinking, if the advertiser's claims are too overblown, those false claims are corrected when consumers do not return to buy the product again. If we extend that analogy to politics, political advertising is often filled with promise as to what the politician will do and what they will not do; for example, a mantra of Republican politics is often "no new taxes" and smaller government bureaucracy. Once elected, whether the politician fulfils their promise is always debatable and it is the option of the electorate to not re-elect a politician because of unfulfilled promises (and certainly any opposing politician will publicize these failings regularly and often in their political advertising). The sad reality of the electorate "buying" the message, and thus the political product by electing a politician, is that particular politician is in office for two years in Congress, four years in the presidency and six years in the Senate. In other words, it is very difficult to go back on a political purchase. Moreover, at least in American politics, incumbency is one of the only guarantors of election. In a survey of the 2012 election, 90% of House members and 91% of Senators were re-elected (Giroux 2012) and re-election rates have remained close to these percentages for most of the last century (Phillips 2012).

The 2008 Obama campaign was filled with extraordinary levels of promise – levels that had not really been seen in presidential politics since 1972 when anti-Vietnam war sentiment coalesced around the failing candidate George McGovern. How Obama's promise moved through the electorate was differently constituted because of how the campaign privileged online connections in their building of volunteers. Nonetheless, what Obama was able to produce was a sense of an historical and cultural moment that had clear momentum, a kind of momentum that felt unstoppable in its power and force. In the following analysis of 2008, we will isolate the key differences from tradional advertising that the Obama campaign produced.

Difference One: The New Electronic Grassroots – The Original Canvassing of Support

In 2004, the former governor of Vermont, Howard Dean, created a remarkable stir in the early primary season of the presidential campaign by shifting the way a candidate built resources. Through a predominantly online campaign, Dean led the field in late 2003 and early 2004 in campaign donations by building an elaborate network of small donations of often $5 and $10 that were solicited and collected online. These small donations demonstrated a commitment to his organization as he campaigned most visibly against the Iraq war. Dean developed the move from online connection to real-world gatherings through Meetup.org, an online program that helped organize meetings. The combination allowed Dean to raise $50 million in donations to his candidacy. Though its short-run ended in March 2004, he became, at the time, the most successful presidential candidate fundraiser. What became obvious at his campaign stops was that his supporter base skewed young. Dean had captured a new generation through techniques Obama's 2008 campaign built upon.

Dean's unsuccessful 2004 campaign served as the model for the development of Obama's run that began well before 2006. While presidential candidates in the past had had elaborate websites for at least a decade before Obama, Obama's organization made these sites come alive for direct involvement by supporters in a manner that was truly unprecedented. The timing of the 2008 campaign interestingly paralleled the growth of social media, and Johnson and Perlmutter (2011) have called it "the Facebook Election" for its capacity to produce a fundamentally interactive online campaign. While Obama's opponents also had Facebook pages, blogs, and websites, Obama's organization added techniques of involvement that were relatively underutilized prior to this campaign. In essence, Obama's online platforms developed ways in which voters could demonstrate their commitment through clicks and other virtual forms of participation. What Obama's organizers achieved is what Wagner and Gainous (2009) had tentatively labelled in their analysis of the 2006 Congressional campaign "electronic grassroots". Something intrinsic to the Internet was producing a different relationship and proximity to a campaign by supporters. The online connections, if managed well, were producing a younger cadre of supporters, and also provided a channel for finding committed voters who could extend the campaign outwards.

According to Rainie and Smith (Carpenter 2010, 216), by 2004, 46% of Americans accessed the Internet for their political information. The percentages of younger Americans using the Internet for political information was much higher and continued to grow. Obama tapped into this changed flow of information by not separating the digital campaign from the main directions of the campaign; instead, he allowed the digital developments to inform other developments of the campaign. This simple strategy also intersected with the new flows of information of a younger electorate. Obama's digital team, which included Joe Rospars (2014) from Digital Blue, worked hard at forms of campaign integration.

Campaign strategies, however, do not exist in isolation from some of the key messages of the campaign. What Obama's campaign emphasized was the newness of its approach. Obama's candidacy resonated strongly with newness and innovation. After all, Obama's charge to the presidency, while not the first by an African American, was definitely the one that had the greatest chance of success at achieving the different stages from major party nomination to final election. Because his major challenger in the Democratic Party, Hillary Clinton, could also be defined as the first female president if elected, one of the intriguing elements of the campaign was how Obama's recruiting structures – what could be called his digital savviness to produce a very powerful group of volunteers – actually helped underline the newness of his candidature. Clinton, in contrast, relied on her connections to party machines and forms of fundraising that had carried her husband into power 16 years earlier. In other words, despite initial appearances, Clinton actually looked like the establishment candidate. Obama's online style, his resonance with a new and powerful rhetoric that came to the surface as a force when he delivered a speech to the 2004 Democratic convention, his insight to speak of unity as opposed to difference, and his capacity to allow his followers to feel at a fundamental level part of the development of a movement, and not just in support of a candidate, all provided ways in which online forms of promotion came to be defined as youthful, different, distinctive, and innovative.

Because of the Obama campaign's efforts at shifting campaigning itself, there was an emphasis to make sure there were connections to all states, not just the ones that were perceived as winnable. This strategy in and of itself represented a fundamental shift in resources and resource allocation. For the latter, these new resource allocations were not necessarily the most expensive but instead were volunteers of highly committed people. Then, to manage the diversity of messages emerging from these volunteers, the campaign had to expend resources to ensure their individual and small collective stories fed into the messages of hope that operated as umbrella-like slogans around the campaign. For example, the institutional websites MyBO and MyBarackObama were not simply sites for the expression of the central organizers of the campaign. Throughout the sites, pathways were set up that ensured videos from the smallest of organizing teams were visible and privileged. The local organizers were thus encouraged to video their work and share it, thereby becoming part of the content and meaning of the campaign itself (Campbell 2010, 126).

Difference 2: Personalization – Social Mediatisation of Political Campaigning and a New Level of Parasocial Interaction

Even the Obama website's name – MyBO – was an interesting play on the social media precursor of Facebook and Myspace. Indeed, MyBO was designed to allow for the personalization of its use, where a dashboard could be constructed by users: the upper banner consisted of Obama and Biden's campaign images, but the rest of its construction could be tailored to the user's home state, their own name, a listing of comments and a connection to comments from friends or one's personal network of friends. The entire structure of MyBO resembled Facebook, but with all the content – whether generated by the campaign or generated by the individual –related to the presidential campaign. MyBO transformed campaigning from the blog and official website structure of online campaigning of the past into something that both personalized the campaign and more accurately social mediatized the campaign. It comes as no surprise that the digital advisor for Obama was Chris Hughes, one of the four founders of Facebook. Hughes joined Obama's Chicago-based digital campaign as early as February 2007 and began setting up this strategy (Stelter 2008). What Hughes brought to the campaign was a core social media logic: like the original Facebook which was born from an invested community of students at a particular university, Hughes worked on building the connections to the Obama campaign through a connected community. Individuals interested in Obama established their own social networks that used the MyObama platform to facilitate that interest and maintain their connection as well as expand it. It is important to realize that although social networks like Facebook were popular in 2008, they only had between 50 and

100 million users worldwide (Associated Press 2013), not the estimated 1.23 billion monthly users when the company celebrated its tenth anniversary in February 2014 (Ross 2014).

The repercussions of this type of campaigning were overwhelming. The site itself was a social media platform that during the primary campaign already had 900,000 users with their own individualized sites (Stelter 2008). Its structure worked like Facebook – or at least what Hughes described at the time as The Facebook, the primitive early version of Facebook before it dropped the "The". What this meant is that its power depended on the invitations to others. Friends thus invited other friends to join and through that linking and invocation the numbers expanded. Having 900,000 people connected and cross-connected, informed by the campaign directly through daily feeds, but also informing the campaign as to what they were doing related to the campaign, delivered a based unrivalled by the Republican party. Augmenting its power, the site was able to crosslink accounts on MyBO with users' Facebook accounts and thus the campaign built on the power of Facebook's friendship connections quite directly.

In the sincerest form of flattery, Obama's opponent in the full election, the Republican John McCain, worked very hard by September to build the kinds of interactivity and friendship structures that MyBO had in place for more than a year, on his similarly named site, McCainSpace (Stelter 2008). Unfortunately for McCain, this move to digitally replicate Obama was perhaps too late to be effective. Obama's early work meant that he ultimately was able to turn the virtual connections into real election-day volunteer staff that could literally get the committed voters to the polls right across the country. By the end of the campaign in November, MyBO had 2 million accounts. More significantly, the process was instrumental in generating 35,000 groups of volunteers and countless events. Adding to these internally directed elements that spawned self-directed related campaign work by volunteers, Obama had built 10 further Facebook accounts that scaffolded across to his MyBO with each account identifying some micropublic or connected movement to the political campaign.

It should be added that Obama also was involved in Twitter and has to be seen as an early adopter of Twitter for political campaign purposes. His "@barackObama" was fundamentally a campaign site with its creation on 5 March 2007. While it is unlikely that Obama generated any of his early Twitter feeds, his tweeting nonetheless further established his connection to the online cognoscenti and demonstrated his understanding of how information moves through youth culture more generally. Twitter further personalized the campaign and buttressed the online social media artifice that this leader was both visible and available.

In combination, Obama's social media activities via MyBO, Facebook directly, assorted other smaller social media sites, and Twitter served as a dual form of personalization. First, it worked to allow his followers to present and reveal themselves interpersonally, and thus, personalized the activities of the campaign. Second, it performed a powerfully new form of parasocial interaction unrivalled in the pre–social media era and perhaps unmatched even by the most savvy celebrity. Obama regularly presented himself through texts, Tweets, and updates on MyBO and Facebook, and the hourly feed of what he was up to allowed his followers to feel affectively connected to him regularly and often. This affective connection of knowing where Obama was and what he was thinking produced a new personalized connection between supporter and political candidate. This emotional connection worked powerfully at maintaining involvement throughout the campaign.

Difference 3: The Generation of Usable Information and its Campaign Implementation

As the campaign advanced and intensified, the number of staff that were part of the digital campaign expanded quite dramatically. In the first year, 25 staff were involved in the set-up and channelling of the website and associated social media platforms. By the end of the campaign, that number had grown to about 100 (Aaker 2010, 20). Much of that work was developing ways to track information. As we discuss with regard to YouTube in Chapter 12, commercial social network sites are concerned with monetizing the activities of their account holders by generating information for clients and advertisers. However, in political campaigns, the goal is to locate predispositions in voting behaviour and work very hard at targeting people likely to change their vote. The programme the Obama campaign developed was called Neighbor-to-Neighbor, which was launched two months before election-day. The programme generated information and then recalibrated it for online access, so that volunteers on MyBO could see a list of undecided voters who lived in their neighbourhoods. Volunteers then contacted five undecided voters each. Ultimately, the programme allowed for an effective get-out-the-vote as volunteers were fed information on getting likely Obama voters to the polling stations. Leading up to the election day, the digital team also worked to connect their information about users of MyBO and events that would help coordinate getting voters to the polling stations. Much of the zip code information that was derived from original registration on MyBO actually allowed for focused efforts in what were perceived to be the 25 "battleground" states where the likely winner of the state's electoral votes was in doubt right up to election day. This kind of mobilization ultimately was critical in the campaign itself as the wealth of digital information, from location of volunteers to prox-imity to favourable undecided voters, was detailed and developed.

The data on volunteers and the ease with which they could be contacted was also valuable in fundraising. What made Obama's campaign different than past campaigns was not only the sheer number of donors – estimates put the number just under 320,000 (see The Center for Responsive Politics 2009) – but that the constant connection to these donors and their involve-ment in the campaign led to record numbers who donated more than once. About 40% of the contributions to the campaign were small individual donations (The Center for Responsive Politics 2009). Ultimately, Obama's campaign was the first presidential campaign that declined government funds and raised $745.7 million dollars throughout the campaign. The digital and social media connection was the pivotal factor in the campaign's structure of continuous, relatively small donations to the campaign over two years.

Difference 4: The Development of a Layered and Nuanced Visual Media Campaign

As our analysis has revealed, much of the material for the Obama campaign was generated by volunteers. In contrast to past campaigns, because this mate-rial was generated from online platforms and because the "account" identities of volunteers gave basic demographic and geographical information that could be used to identify areas to concentrate energies, Obama's overall cam-paign was able to highly target its paid-for messages. On one level, the Obama campaign maintained a 50-state strategy – in other words, it was highly visi-ble and active in all 50 states and, in this way, had taken on the approach that Howard Dean had championed in the party. This high visibility, however, in the primary campaign was predominantly through online structures, and at least partially user-generated content. For example, Black Eyed Peas frontman will.i.am created a high production value video to demonstrate his support for Obama. In its content, the video expressed the idea that Obama was more than a candidate and represented a movement. The video, using Obama's 2008 Concession Speech in the New Hampshire presidential primary, was built on the slogan "Yes We Can" and presented a series of vignettes of celeb-rities speaking and singing along with Obama's words, with a simple acoustic guitar providing a unifying coherence to the images and sounds. The black-and-white moving images split the screen between the stars and Obama's address in an elegant visual montage. The video was originally uploaded on YouTube in February of 2008, but it moved virally well beyond this through links and sharing. Within a week, it had been viewed an estimated 21 million times, which by its sheer reach had an impact on the campaign in the early primaries. But Obama's election team had no involvement with the video (Figure 9.2). In a similar vein, another viral video moved through YouTube and was shared massively during 2007, and once again, it had no connection to Obama's official campaign. The "Obama Girl" video, as it was known, consisted of a song entitled "Crush on Obama", where the actress Amber Lee Ettinger lip-synched the song. The video, which garnered over 2.5 million views in its first week, was designed to have "fun" with the campaign. It was in fact a promotional video created by Barely Political, a company hoping to build a business around similar humorous videos. Nonetheless, it served to create a further emotive connection to Obama – and again without any actual campaign funds used in making and distributing the video. The Obama Girl video became a meme over the next two years as a series of crushes on other performers and politicians played off the original Obama-themed song; even

Figure 9.2   will.i.am and Barack Obama in 2008 "Yes We Can" music video

the original actor performed in an equally popular sequel entitled "Super Obama Girl" in early 2008.

Of perhaps greater significance was the very specific campaign of MoveOn.org, one of the most significant national online activist organizations. With 3 million members, MoveOn.org has the ability to generate significant direction around political issues and has made concerted efforts to help construct the political agenda in American politics (Ragas and Kiousis 2011). Significantly, MoveOn.Org endorsed Obama's candidature, the first time it had endorsed a presidential candidate in its 10-year history. MoveOn added to this by generating significant user-generated content by sponsoring a contest entitled "Obama in 30 seconds", a follow-up to its smaller and very negative contest, "Bush in 30 seconds", designed to get users to generate ads before the 2004 election. The contest, which began in late March and concluded near the end of the primaries, invited people to make an ad in support of Obama in order to propel his candidature to the Democratic nomination. The contest's one clear stipulation was that it could not be a negative ad and therefore could not use content that lambasted other candidates. The winner was guaranteed national airplay of the commercial. The contest was remarkable on two fronts. First, it generated over 1100 entrants, and even the least-viewed ads attracted some attention, while the winning ad had more than a half-million views on YouTube. The contest itself elicited 5.5 million votes, which meant that millions of people viewed many of the ads. And second, it established, as Ragas and Kiousis's (2011) research reveals, a way in which the agenda of the presidential campaign was set. The issues of importance to the "Obama in 30 seconds" contributors correlated strongly with those of MoveOn.org and resonated with the directions of the Obama official campaign advertising as well (Ragas and Kiousis 2011). Ultimately, the contest created a wealth of high quality advertisements that populated the online presidential campaign for several months. With its affirming focus, it dovetailed thematically into the hope and "Yes We Can" slogans of the official Obama campaign. The winning ad demonstrated this with its title, "Obamacan", and its simple testimonial of a lifelong Republican and former army staff sergeant endorsing Obama for president.

In striking contrast to this strategy of user-generated content, Obama's official campaign actually generated more commercials and political spots than any campaign in the history of American politics – probably the world. This may seem contradictory to its grassroots movement and user-generated strategies that have become the mythology around Obama's 2008 campaign; but this scaffolding of political advertisements defines Obama's later stages of his campaign. In October of 2008, because he had generated so many millions in donations from the digitally inspired grassroots movement, Obama was able to literally flood the airwaves with paid political messages. It was estimated in those final weeks that Obama was buying four times as much commercial time on television nationally than his opponent McCain. In fact, Obama was averaging more than 30 million dollars a week on television advertisements in the final month of the campaign (Rutenberg 2008). In the final accounts, Obama had spent $352.3 million on media buys, almost $11 million on media production for his advertisements, $21 million on web advertising, and another $20 million on print advertising. In total, media-related spending totalled $422.2 million, or 56.6% of all the money raised and spent in the campaign (The Center for Responsive Politics 2009).

The nuance of Obama's campaign was its capacity to connect to a large number of people as committed supporters (a number that far surpassed most of the campaigns of the last 50 years) and then use very directed advertising campaigns to draw the targeted uncommitted voter into the movement. How this was done was a further bifurcation of the political campaign. In contrast to McCain's visible and sometimes perceived level of negative advertising about Obama's ability to govern, Obama's campaign used its online viral savvy to generate counter-messages related to any negative campaign that McCain generated. Often, the most negative ad campaigns generated in a presidential election are sponsored by Political Action Committees and thereby somewhat distanced from the official campaign. For Obama, his counter-ads and commentary were produced by his online supporters as they counter-attacked the false statements around his foreign birthplace and his religion along with a host of other efforts to damage his reputation. From September 2008, one of the key negative ad campaigns that McCain's team circulated was trying to belittle Obama's candidacy and persona as merely a celebrity – a candidate who lacked the substance to govern. However, the direction of this campaign strategy partially fed into the overriding idea that Obama was exciting and represented clear change. It is one of the legacies of the 2008 campaign that although factually both candidates ran negative advertising campaigns with over a third of their commercials, McCain was perceived as the candidate that was seen as negative as opposed to affirming.

The massive number of ads that blanketed American media in September and October 2008 worked to maintain the spirit of change and hope that Obama's candidature had embodied so effectively. To solidify this sense and direction, Obama bought 30 minutes on three of the major national networks at 8 pm on 29 October 2008, six days before the election, a $6 million media-buy strategy that had not been seen since 1992 when the independent and independently wealthy Ross Perot bought a series of 30-minute spots (Schifferes 2008). The 30-minute ad presented a series of vignettes with Obama as the voice-over narrator who provided solutions to American stories through the key issues of the campaign: tax breaks, energy, education, health care, economic downturn, Iraq, and family. In the grand tradition of the campaign film, Obama's infomercial was richly layered with inspiring violin, acoustic guitar, and rousing piano as background music to produce an emotional connection to the candidate for the audience. The quality of production of the "film" rivalled the most carefully constructed Hollywood film. The advertisement concluded with a live speech from a political event in Florida, a technique to emphasize Obama's inspiring speaking abilities that were foundational to the meaning of the Obama candidacy. The liveness of the closing sequence was also used to identify the power of the message to sway and convince as the rousing applause, along with the closing orchestral music, provided a sense of uplift that matched his defining campaign slogan: "Change we can believe in".

In addition, in the month before the election, the Obama campaign circulated issue-themed ads that built on the positive emotions that the majority of the campaign had established. As the Global Financial Crisis took centre stage in October 2008, the Obama campaign ensured that it ran its 31 ads on job creation and 35 on taxes, 205,000 times and 126,000 times in the month, respectively (Schifferes 2008). In contrast to the national strategy of the 30-minute ad, these themed and issue-based ads were targeted in local markets where the race was seen to be close. For example, Philadelphia was blanketed with $11.9 million in local ads designed to counter the McCain campaign's almost equal spending in the same market of $10.3 million as they battled for the state of Pennsylvania (Schifferes 2008). The combination of the targeted ads and the national ads provided a way to use issues and political agenda-setting to convince the undecided how to vote. By territorializing a strong correlation with an important issue among the voters in a given state, the Obama campaign was working very hard to give reasons for voting for their candidate in the final days of the campaign.

Conclusion: Speed, Tone, and the Legacy of Obama 2008

There is no question that Obama's 2008 campaign was a watershed. To summarize what his campaign had achieved, it is important to isolate the tactical translations of political promotion and advertising and separate them from the political style that Obama injected into American politics. In other words, through a number of techniques, Obama 2008 transformed the speed of American political promotion and campaigning as well as transforming, translating, and structuring a new tone of American politics and campaigns. Each of these translations – speed and tone – will be addressed here in terms of the 2008 campaign. We also consider how these affected Obama's 2012 campaign, and also how these will no doubt shape future contenders for the presidency.

The key ingredient that Obama has added to the process of the presidential campaign is speed. The speed at which his campaign constructed an online network of committed voters and volunteers was a phenomenon of tapping into the emerging social media use and converting and tailoring that culture to the needs of the campaign. Moreover, there was considerable speed in also creating real events from these online connections. And finally, there was considerable speed in the generation of content – from volunteer-generated videos and blog posts, to constructing advertising spots that were designed very carefully to nestle into the key decision points of undecided-but-leaning voters. At the core of this development of speed was the rapid development of information and its subsequent deployment for the needs of the campaign. The digital dimensions of the campaign were instrumental in developing very usable and, because of its connection to geo-located volunteers, very targeted forms of information that became the "intelligence" and knowledge of the campaign. This intelligence led to the expensive stage of the campaign – the final two months – when traditional advertising, along with some targeted ads online and via game sites, was used through sheer volume and focus to gain the advantage in battleground states that Obama needed to win in order to be elected president. Integrated into this structure of speed was the testing of ads and their effect, and the effective online phone system of contacting targeted voters. Both of these extra dimensions of speed permitted the Obama campaign to change and adjust much more rapidly than past campaigns.

The speed legacy that Obama passed on to his 2012 presidential campaign was a realization that data management was critical to success. Thus, Obama expanded his digital team to 175 in 2012. The repercussions of this added focus were astounding in terms of their new levels of targeting. Based on extensive information about their most likely voters, Obama's team ended up buying advertising time quite differently to capture these voters. That is, instead of focusing on ads during local news, they bought extensively on daytime television and some cable channels. Their campaign went against the idea of buying time on programmes of relevancy to the campaign and worked on what their potential target voters were actually watching – engendering a more sophisticated demographic profiling of voters than ever before

(Delany 2013). Similarly, their data managers moved to what Delany (2013, 17) described as "granular" in their focus by individualizing voters in terms of likelihood to vote for Obama and their likelihood to actually get to the polls, and a numerical score was assigned to each. This kind of very particular and individualized information led to on-the-ground work to get the vote out on the day that was massively more effective than previous elections. Ultimately, Obama's 2012 campaign spent $1.1 billion; however, in contrast to 2008, he was outspent by the Republican candidate, Mitt Romney, who spent just over $1.2 billion (Center for Responsive Politics 2013). Although Obama had produced a better version of an online and mobile campaign in 2012, he still spent massively in traditional forms of advertising and commercial time.

Related to this production of speed was the other true legacy of the Obama 2008 campaign. In a variety of ways, it transformed the tone of presidential elections. On one level, the campaign was heralded as the most sophisticated form of advertising and marketing. Presidential candidates had finally been transformed resolutely into the language of the sale. Throughout 2007, and particularly in 2008, it was common to hear the term "Brand Obama". What Obama had achieved was a branding identity through a variety of advertising and promotional strategies that made a lesser-known and relatively inexperienced Illinois senator into the most recognizable personality on the planet. The techniques of this form of branding have been detailed in this chapter. It is worth underlining that the advertising industry itself recognized the profundity of the presidential campaign. *Advertising Age*, for instance, voted Obama "Marketer of the Year", ahead of companies that have the likes of Apple or Coca-Cola and their highly successful brands (Creamer 2008). In addition, in June 2009, the Obama 2008 campaign was lauded with two Cannes Lions International Advertising Awards. The campaign won the Titanium Grand Prix which is awarded to the best campaign that uses three or more media at a "high standard and state-of-the art". In addition, it won a further prize for its focused campaign ad starring Sarah Silverman called "The Great Schlep" to increase Obama's Jewish support in the election (Sweeney 2009).

The brilliance of this branding identity was how Obama also constructed a sense of difference and change in and through these new advertising and marketing strategies. This tonal element, which can best be described as a dramatically engaged blend of politics with the tonality of evangelical salvation, is ultimately what set Obama apart from his opposition in both the preliminary rounds of primaries and into the final election. His oratorical style, which was certainly foundational to his rise to political prominence, was able to maintain a sincerity of conviction that hearkened back to Martin Luther King with a sense of inclusiveness that through the rhetorical flourish and cadence of religious-inspired performance was able to maintain its authenticity.

What is remarkable is that in a two-year campaign, this tone was able to be maintained through different promotional forms. So, not only were the commercials in long form, or in their 30- and 60-second spot versions, able to maintain the consistency of this message of transformation, but Obama was also able to hold this message with his literally millions of supporters who also produced resonating forms of media content through the website, through social media and through forms of blogs, texts, and videos. The relative coherence of the message – the tone of sincerity and the link to the slogan/message of the campaign – was, without doubt, the most powerful form of political persuasion that Obama achieved. Through the power of advertising and promotion powered by social media strategies and that was connected to building a devoted group of followers – a congregation of supporters – Obama transformed American politics.

The longer-term effect of Obama in 2008 can be seen in the 2016 American presidential campaign. The originally surprising successes of both Donald Trump and Bernie Sanders in the primaries' campaigns are directly related to lessons learned from 2008 and the way that presidential candiates can be positioned strategically. There is no question that central to Trump's campaign was a sophistication with the way in which the new structures of an online attention economy operate and focus interest. Trump's version of "tone" was a form of aggressive posturing that served to situate him as a form of clear opposition to other candidates and thereby present his own candidature with the highest prominence and media value. It was a complex weaving of social media tweeting and public address that focused the traditional news media to use Trump himself and his aggressive negative sound- and image-bites to attract attention to their media programmes and associated websites. A remarkable rising prominence of Trump left the other candidates battling over sometimes less than 50% of primary voters.

Similarly, Sanders's campaign deceptively moved into online spaces and patterns of engagement and voluntarism that resembled Obama's 2008 campaign but tonally reconfigured as challenging politics as usual and oppositional. The stark contrast of Sanders's age with the youthful and online dynamism at the epicentre of his campaign led to what were perceived as "surprising" public events due to the sheer number of supporters present. What Sanders regularly was able to advance with the speed of online connections and networks was the way political campaigning and promotion had taken the idea of flash mobs and orchestrated a sense of political momentum.

From the vantage point of observation of the 2016 campaign and beyond the specificity of the actual value of any particular political position, the Obama 2008 transformation of political advertising and promotion is further validated as a political watershed.

10

The Institutionalization of Branding and the Branding of the Self

As we have observed through the case histories in this book, branding is at the centre of advertising. Liz Moor's (2007) historical research has further unveiled that branding has been one of the principal ways in which goods were moved from production to consumption. Thus, branding became an essential feature of the developing mass-market and mass-consumer culture that emerged in the late nineteenth century and continues in the twenty-first century (Moor 2007). Historically, branding has been linked to identifying ownership (as in cattle and sheep, and, perhaps more provocatively, in the human slave trade), and legitimizing and authenticating authorship and value (as in imprints on gold and silver jewellery and artefacts). For the last century, however, branding can be characterized as a principal way in which we make sense of our product-saturated world and an equally valuable way that corporations make sense of their own product in a complex economy. As Moor (2007) explains, brands serve to "inscribe meanings, rather than simply describe or indicate origin" (Moor 2007, 17) that usually complement and intersect with the development of advertising. Consumers identify with brands and develop emotional attachments that link their own identities to how they conceptualize a particular brand. This power of brands sometimes makes particular brand names become part of language, and advertising, as a practice, is often dedicated to assisting in the production of this strong association. Thus, a product name such as Kimberley-Clark's Kleenex becomes synonymous with facial tissues and is now included in both Merriam-Webster and Oxford dictionaries as such.

Critiques of the expansion of what is often described as "brand culture" have become legion in the last 20 years, led by the most visible of these,

173

Naomi Klein's *No Logo* (Klein 2000). Part of this general critique is that brands dominate our visual and cultural landscape so completely that it is becoming difficult to imagine areas of our lives that are not filtered through branding. Of even greater impact is how brands have become a recognized form of value that becomes an asset in contemporary business culture. Major research and consulting firms operate in today's culture to constantly determine the value of brands over and above the material value of a particular company. Arvidsson (2005) has argued that this added value comes from what he describes as the immaterial labour of consumption: our actions as consumers, our form of attracted attention, and our loyalty and work on making the brand meaningful actually produce a form of capital. Thus in 2013, Interbrand estimated that the top 100 best global brands are collectively worth $1.5 trillion and are led by what they describe as the number one and two brands, Apple and Google, respectively (Interbrand 2014). Brand value is now an essential part of the financial and accounting system of value as brands: they are instrumental in assessing how much a company is worth when it is sold or when it is exchanged via stocks.

There are many ways we can interpret and analyse brands. One very profitable way is to understand brands as constructions of identities. Corporations produce a number of identities via their various products. For example, the corporation Kimberly-Clark has to produce an identity that is related to its business acumen, which is much different than its brand-product identity of the softness and strength of its Kleenex tissues. Both the corporate brand and the product brand are identities. These identities can be likened to personalities, and in effect, much of a corporation's business is managing these identity personalities so that they remain appealing to the consumer. In short, the brand is the personality of the advertising identity.

This chapter will advance on how branding has moved beyond the product or even the corporation and has flowed back into the formation of the identity of the person. Self-branding will be explored from different avenues, all of which coalesce around our key theme of how advertising lures consumers with the promise of fulfilment and articulates possible futures attainable through consumption. First, we will explore how highly branded individuals operate in the contemporary economy and generate their own forms of exchangeable value. We will begin with a historical account of the development of celebrity from the nineteenth century to the present. This account of branded personalities is an analysis of our star system and celebrity culture and how value is generated when the "self" is advertised and sold in some form of product. We can see how particular celebrities construct stylistically diverse identities and resell them, a complex technique of engaging consumers so that their individual decisions of personal comportment are somehow linked to idealized celebrity images. These celebrity images orient consumers to imagine an improved version of the self that is attainable through the product.

From that vantage point, we will investigate the related world of endorsements where the valuable and marketable self, derived generally from the entertainment industries, is somehow integrated and connected to other brands via advertisements. In that study, we will focus on famous individuals who are closely associated with products for some form of mutual benefit: specifically, the perfume industry will be explored for its construction of branded prestige and allure. Our concluding analysis will look at how self-branding has become a normal practice well beyond the famous and for an increasingly large part of our population. Via online culture and social media, and via the changes in work and how we find work, collectively we are increasingly normalizing the branding of our own identities. Our personalities become at least partially defined by a kind of commodity and exchange identity. This widening construction of self-branding is then investigated in terms of how it feeds back into a changed advertising and promotion industry that monetizes our attempts at branding ourselves.

Self-Branding and Celebrity Culture

It is important to realize that self-branding is not necessarily new. People have promoted and advertised themselves for a variety of purposes since time immemorial. After all, prostitution, which is often thought of as the oldest profession, has for millennia advertised the self through provocative dress and streetwalking. What is new is the acceptance of this very commercial metaphor around property, ownership, and identity as a normal activity. The way we have arrived at this normalization of a form of advertising the self is derived from what we have privileged and celebrated in our culture. Related to individual identity, we have developed a highly visible system that focuses an elaborate attention economy on the most famous. Indeed, the most famous become famous through the operations of what can be called a celebrity system or apparatus.

Although it is obvious that our celebrity system is deeply connected to advertising and promotion, it has rarely been studied as a precursor of self-branding. In this analysis, we will focus on what are the elements of this system of celebration of individuality that have informed the emergence and extensions of a branding culture to the self. Stars are historically linked to the entertainment industry as it has developed over the last two and half centuries, first with theatre and literature and then expanding outwards into the mediated industries of film, radio, and television in the twentieth century. Principally, stars have been used to pre-sell any cultural production through their perceived influence and prior visibility. Theatrical stars from the eighteenth century, like the British actor David Garrick, built a profile through acting and managing theatres, which allowed their fame to support the next production and beyond. Through promotional techniques such as portraiture via equally famous artists such as Joshua Reynolds, stars such as Garrick expanded their visibility to achieve what we would now call celebrity status (Thomson 2005). In Britain, actress Sarah Siddons reached the heights of "achieved celebrity" (Rojek 2001, 112) during her career which spanned from the late eighteenth century to well into the nineteenth century (West 2005). Critical to that development were the emerging media forms which advanced and publicized stories of the famed and thus gave a prominent status to actors in a transformed public sphere. In the American context, P.T. Barnum has to be seen as the most influential publicist in nineteenth-century entertainment culture. Through advanced publicity that constructed his audience's desire-to-know, town by town and city by city, Barnum was able to make his marquee players, such as Colonel Tom Thumb and Jenny Lind of his travelling show, household names (Marshall 2014/1997, 208).

Two elements can be highlighted from the historical emergence of stardom and celebrity prior to the twentieth century. First of all, actors, performers, and even writers to a lesser degree, became heightened signs and symbols of individuality. As much as their own incomes were dependent on theatrical companies, impresarios, literary publicists, and/or agents, their roles in society had a developing sense of independence. By the end of the nineteenth century, their media portrayal via newspapers and magazines conveyed their mythological difference from the mass and industrialized society that was in formation throughout the same period. Second, stars from this period also cultivated an equally powerful sense of desiring allure, as if their lives had greater value and significance because of their fame and notoriety.

By the second decade of the twentieth century, new media technologies such as film had already developed a very sophisticated star system for the promotion of their productions. Supported by magazines and the relatively new capacity for the reproduction of images, stars became a powerful vehicle for advertising films through the circulation of publicity stills for publication (Wolfe 1991). The larger-than-life quality of cinema exhibition of star images along with the deployment of the close-up in film performance further accentuated film actors as significant representatives of the contemporary moment. Profiles of stars populated weekend newspaper feature coverage as well as the burgeoning picture magazines in the 1920s, 1930s, and 1940s. This power of stars, which is probably best understood as their economic power beyond their films that translated into the wider culture, defined their celebrity status: celebrity can be understood then as the conversion of an individual's public presence beyond their primary work into an elaborate presentation of their personality, their presence, and what would be construed as their private world. Currid-Halkett (2010) has more recently described this as the celebrity's "residual value": what she means by this term is that some public individuals are able to make their presence convertible and exchangeable into other domains beyond their primary activity (Currid-Halkett 2010). Thus, a film star who possessed what could be perceived as a celebrity residual would be of interest to magazines in and of themselves and be the subject of stories and profiles of their everyday lives. This interest produces, in effect, new cultural productions – in this case magazine stories and covers which by their link to the star, now a celebrity themselves – generate audiences and income for this different cultural form.

In many ways, the emergence of celebrity-stars throughout the twentieth century defined a new form of promotion that was beyond the promotion of the original entertainment entity. Celebrity-stars of films thus were very much the images that helped films achieve their audiences and box offices. Over the first 50 years of the twentieth century, the film industry operated as a loose oligarchy known as the Hollywood Studio System and very much part of Classical Hollywood. Within that very powerful structure, they helped manufacture stars, held those stars as contract players for their individual studios, and controlled and structured their publicity in support of the films with which they were involved. These stars were well-paid for in general; however, it should be remembered that the studio system was constantly producing new potential stars – for example, through bit parts or chorus lines in musicals – that could be built into a new generation of stars. The production process of the studio system was as equally adept at building a promotional structure of stars to continue to attract and maintain audiences as it was in securing clear patterns of exhibition and distribution.

Over time, the studio system's success at producing stars actually developed the elements that led to the partial breakdown of the studio system. Stars, as we have detailed above, began acquiring "residual value" that was beyond their productions or films: they became celebrities whose lives themselves were a form of cultural production that was fabricated, bought and sold, and narrativized through various media forms. These extracurricular exchanges and values were instrumental in star-celebrities becoming autonomous and independent, and a whole new industrial economy of film production developed in the latter half of the twentieth century to accommodate this shift in power and influence. The most powerful star-celebrities in the middle of the century, such as Gregory Peck, Jimmy Stewart, Burt Lancaster, or Bette Davis, were no longer conjoined to a particular studio, but rather chose their film projects individually and regularly moved from one studio to another based on the project. Agents, who represented these stars, operated as the intermediaries in negotiations and became more central to the brokering of rosters of talents. Thus, an agent would perhaps represent the actors as well as the directors and writers in putting together new production teams that were then contracted for the individual film. The development of television as an alternative source of production was also a factor in this dispersal of studio power and the ascendancy of the individual star in Hollywood's power structure.

Throughout the twentieth century, film, television, and even popular music have built quite incredible systems of individualized structures of fame that have dwarfed most of the other systems of visibility in the twentieth and twenty-first centuries. Moreover, each of these areas has constructed stars who have achieved some form of celebrity status that allows them and others to mine their residual value in other ways. Thus, what clearly develops along with cultural productions is a very elaborate ancillary industry where the public personas of the most famous celebrities are circulated in support of other products, commodities, and cultural forms. There are many dimensions to the ancillary industry. One dimension is directly related to the power of these celebrity-stars' profiles and information to be valuable in and of itself for the expansion and circulation of media forms. In different generations of this celebrity culture, there emerged magazines and programmes that in a direct sense fed off their aura: in early Hollywood, there was *Moving Picture World* and later *Photoplay* as key magazines. In pre-teen and teen cultures of the 1960s and 1970s there were specialized magazines such as *Tiger Beat* and *Seventeen* that predominantly focused on celebrity, and their covers were attuned to their audience's current affective attachments in their depiction of stars. From the 1930s and 1940s, picture magazines such as *Life* and *Look* provided the lenses and images for audiences to observe the activities of various famous people from a variety of vocations and avocations. In a similar vein, *People* magazine, a spin-off from *Time* magazine's section feature, captured in a generally positive light celebrity culture from the 1970s onwards. An explosion of magazines from the 1980s and 1990s which included *Hello!, New Weekly, Heat*, and a host of others concentrated on scandal – manufactured or real – of celebrities to sell their magazines that grew from the tabloid press of the 1970s such as *The National Enquirer* and *Midnight Globe*. This kind of discourse of newsworthy scandal occupies a privileged position in current online culture via Perez Hilton, TMZ, Celebrity Stalker, and other popular sites for exploring the latest images derived from paparazzi and videographers who have surveilled the movements of our celebrity figures in all their minutiae (McNamara 2015).

Television itself has also colonized celebrities for their own success in attracting audiences. In most talk shows, the premise of irreverent humour is twinned with the presence of these high profile celebrities to produce an attractive enough formula to lure regular audiences to programmes such as *The Daily Show* or *The Tonight Show*, which have countless permutations in similarly formatted television programmes throughout the world. One of the key differences between these television programmes and predominant magazine and online culture is that on these shows, celebrities are both present and willing participants. That is, the famous are on television specifically to promote their latest production, performance, or event, and in this way, television has come to represent one of the principal channels for celebrities to advertise themselves in a manner where they sense they have greater control of how they will be perceived.

Brands with Brands: Endorsement Culture in the Perfume Industry

All of the above elements underline how the original star system and the associated and expanding celebrity culture have been instrumental in advancing the idea of self-branding. Celebrities work very hard on producing a public version of themselves, a portrait and story that is marketable and valuable in popular culture. It is individualized as it goes well beyond a film, book, or song and transforms into a discourse about the desirability of the self. Marketing the self as a brand certainly works for actors in procuring more roles, but it also works to attract the interest of other brands that need to build or maintain their own public visibility. Celebrities linking their personal brand with a product has become one of the most interesting developments in branding culture over the last century.

Endorsements occur across a wide range of product lines. As we saw in Chapter 8, sports stars are often aligned with apparel and equipment related to their activity, and in most professional sports, the elite athletes earn far greater money through endorsements and sponsorship than their salaries or prize winnings. The tennis professional Roger Federer is an obvious example of this. Forbes identified Federer as the second-highest-paid athlete, with $71.5 million in 2013, and 90% of those earnings, or $65 million, was derived from sponsorship deals. Over $40 million of that sponsorship was tied up with 10 companies, with 5-year deals developing with sports brands such as Wilson and Nike. What is more interesting is that Federer also has long-term deals with brands outside of the sporting arena, including Mercedes-Benz, Rolex, and a recent addition of the champagne company Moët & Chandon, all very elite, luxury, and exclusive products (Forbes 2013). Although many other products are drawn to celebrities for endorsements, when one looks more closely at products that rely on famous individuals to sell their identity and value, two industries are overwhelmingly connected to celebrity branding – the perfume industry and the luxury watch industry. Here we investigate endorsement culture in the perfume industry in order to see more clearly the operation of this elite level of self-branding.

From the most cursory view of the perfume industry, it is apparent that any fragrance is associated with a personality. Tour any department store, pharmacy, or duty-free shop and one is overwhelmed with the sheer number of famous faces that appear on posters and products. On the left where classic brands are located, one sees Julia Roberts and Charlize Theron adjacent to Nicole Kidman. In the sections associated with youth, one is more likely to see music stars such as Rihanna, Beyoncé, Lady Gaga, One Direction, and Justin Bieber. The men's section provides little difference – although it is interesting to note that Bieber and One Direction are designed for females and not males – with Eric Bana, Ryan Reynolds, and Jared Leto endorsing perfumes related to high-status fashion brands such as Hugo Boss. With the older brands, famous names as scents linger: Gloria Vanderbilt, Charlie, and Elizabeth Arden still hauntingly prevail; their visages are hidden, but the visibility of their names continues. In 2012 alone, 85 celebrity perfume brands were launched, in contrast to only 10 in 2002 (Larrabee 2013). As much as media personalities fill the visual landscape of cosmetic and fragrance sales, at the highest end of this market, virtually every leading fashion designer is equally present. Thus, you will see names such as Gaultier, Boss, Yves-Saint Laurent, Versace, Stella McCartney, Kate Spade, Donna Karan (DKNY), Marni, Jimmy Choo, Hermès, Marc Jacobs, Oscar de la Renta and Dolce & Gabbana (Wischhover 2013). This three-way connection among fashion, design, and perfume is not only connected to the fragrances produced. Branding is very much about product design, packaging, and its display in the marketplace, and thus the actual bottles and containers that are developed for all of these perfumes are highly designed to intersect with the mood, design flare, and sentiment of these fashion houses. Indeed, famed mid-century artists such as Magritte and Dali designed perfume bottles (Moor 2007) – two artists that could be seen as experts in themselves in self-branding and extending their brands.

Our case history will maintain our focus on film stars, though as noted above, sports, music, and fashion also rely heavily on celebrity endorsements and the branding of film stars represents only one dimension of the branding practices of the perfume industry. We differentiate the branding of film stars from other areas because of the way stars are linked to the production of glamour, an unattainable, manufactured ideal defined by Gundle (2008, 45) as "an enticing image, a staged and construction image of reality that invites consumption". What follows is a table that links film stars to perfume brand and personality, and it is by necessity suggestive rather than exhaustive (see Table 10.1).

Historically, Hollywood has been known as a "glamour factory", where magazines, photographs, and advertising work together to create an aura of stardom that is predicated on the gaze of a desiring audience (Hautala 2011, 10). As Marshall (2014/1997) writes, film stars have established something of an aura of distance in their allure, and the perfume industry has mined that kind of cultural power very directly. Indeed, the images of film stars produced by the perfume industry are in many ways more utopian and idealized, more beautiful, seductive, and alluring, than any type of promotion and advertising produced for a major Hollywood film. Stars are spokesmodels or representatives of existing brands and are there to create the allure of these products. The allure is very much connected to the way Hollywood has constructed

Table 10.1 Celebrities and Their Perfume Labels

Celebrity	Perfume
Elizabeth Taylor	Elizabeth Arden – *White Diamonds*
Brad Pitt	Chanel – *Chanel No. 5*
Keira Knightley	Chanel – *Coco Mademoiselle*
Isabella Rossellini	Lancôme – *Trésor*
Penelope Cruz	Lancôme – *Trésor*
Scarlett Johansson	Dolce & Gabbana – *The One*
Emma Watson	Lancôme – *Trésor, Midnight Rose*
Charlize Theron	Dior – *J'adore*
Nicole Kidman	Chanel – *Chanel No. 5*
Robert Pattinson	Dior – *Dior Homme*
Natalie Portman	Dior – *Miss Dior Cherie*
Hilary Swank	Guerlain – *Insolence*
Ben Affleck	L'Oréal – *Lynx*
Jude Law	Dior – *Dior Homme*
Ryan Reynolds	Hugo Boss, *Boss*
Coco Rocha	YSL – *Elle Intense*
Liv Tyler	Givenchy – *Very Irresistible Electric Rose*

glamour – associated with qualities such as beauty, sexuality, theatricality, wealth, dynamism, notoriety, movement, and leisure (Gundle 2008, 45) – as being one of the key "products" it has sold throughout the last century. The close association between cosmetics and Hollywood glamour has also been connected to the transformation of the female body into an object of desire, as Dyhouse (2010) has developed in her work. What Hollywood stars produce via their sexualized allure then is a kind of distant public intimacy or "extimacy" that Thrift (2010) sees as both the essence of what glamour means and what consumer culture promises through its array of goods and what they can bestow on the individual.

Actors as spokespersons for perfumes bring more to the selling of the perfume than an attractive face or body manufactured as an object of desire. Their branding makes use of the meanings established in their roles as Hollywood celebrities in interviews, red-carpet appearances, and other sightings along with the actual roles they have played onscreen. Co-branding themselves with perfumes appeals to stars because these products are monikers of quality. The self-branding process for film stars via perfumes is very much about presenting a controlled and highly constructed image, but it is an image created through association rather than identification. In self-branding terms, the perfume is a vehicle to present the star by association as not just alluring, but of the highest quality of allure and value. Some of the most enduring perfume brands are thus the most likely "hosts" for a high-profile Hollywood star. For example, Chanel No. 5 has established a series of leading spokesmodels derived predominantly from film stars. From the 1930s, Chanel No. 5 has had an international profile as a fragrance, but in many ways its global movement has been the result of how well it has attached to recognizable stars. Because Chanel and its founder/designer Coco were dressing Hollywood's most famous women in the 1920s and 1930s, Coco herself was branded as the model of sophistication for the perfume in advertisements. In 1954, without any endorsement or sponsorship, Marilyn Monroe conveyed in an interview that "five drops of Chanel No. 5" was all she wore to bed, and an accompanying dramatic photo made this connection more concrete. Chanel's strength as an emotive brand was attached primarily to how French fashion defined sophisticated glamour throughout most of the twentieth century. Although several stars, including Suzy Parker, Jean Shrimpton, and Lauren Hutton, had been photographed for Chanel magazine advertisements, the spokesmodel/personality branding relationship was only made real with its employment of the famed French film actress Catherine Deneuve in 1971 in a famous ad that featured only the face of the actress, the bottle of perfume below and to her right, and the name Chanel No. 5 along the bottom of the ad.

Judith Williamson (1978) explains how the ad creates sign value through the juxtaposition of the perfume with the already meaningful image of the star established in films and magazines, so that Catherine Deneuve becomes associated with Chanel in the world of consumer goods. Although there is no necessary link between the two, we assume a connection and transfer Deneuve's "meaning" to the perfume. Williamson (1978, 25) writes, "The ad is using another already existing or mythological sign system, and appropriating a relationship that exists in that system between signifier (Deneuve) and signified (glamour, beauty) to speak of its product in terms of that same relationship; so that the perfume can be substituted for Catherine's Deneuve's face and can also be made to signify glamour and beauty."

From that point on, Chanel worked very hard at constructing its high-end fashion house relationship to its perfume, first by producing very expensive and provocative commercial series released each year prior to the Christmas gift-buying season, and second, by attaching the glamour of a series of elite and classically beautiful film stars as their brand ambassadors: the French Film star Carole Bouquet assumed the role after Deneuve's defining 20-year run. Nicole Kidman has represented Chanel since 2004 and Audrey Tatou of Amelie fame since 2009. Chanel's recent move to have their first male spokesmodel similarly appeals to the most exclusive, as well as makes an effort to be at the perceived cutting edge of fashion. In 2013 Brad Pitt, who along with Angelina Jolie represents current Hollywood A-list royalty and reputation, appeared in a series of commercials with Pitt ruminating on the meaning of love. Brad Pitt's value of course is his continuing appeal and allure to women and Chanel. Twinned with this development is the reincarnation of Marilyn Monroe as spokesmodel for Chanel as her image is redelivered in its intimate connection to Chanel No. 5.

This structure of exclusivity and glamour is at the core of the identity of perfumes that are attached much more clearly to the designer end of the fashion industry, as the example of Chanel above demonstrates. Dolce & Gabbana, for instance, have branded themselves through their fragrance "The One" with the American film star Scarlett Johansson. The fashion house Dior has a similar relationship, but with much more visibility, through Charlize Theron. Outfitted in a remarkable gold gown, Theron's classically glamorous image transforms billboards internationally as cities are awash with her luminescent association with Dior's J'adore perfume (see Figure 10.1).

Dior utilizes the looks of Robert Pattinson and Jude Law to brand their male fragrances. The male fashion house Hugo Boss has a similar array of handsome male spokesmodels which includes Eric Bana, Ryan Reynolds, and Jared Leto.

Figure 10.1   Actress Charlize Theron in Dior's J'adore perfume advertisement

Maintaining exclusivity and cultural cachet has drawn the perfume industry to what is seen as the aura of film stars. At the origin of this branding connection was the film icon Elizabeth Taylor, who established a branded perfume with Elizabeth Arden called "White Diamonds" in 1988 and it continues to sell well beyond her death. Celebrities in general can see branding with a fragrance as a way to control their image completely. Taylor's later career – in other words, by the time her perfume was launched – had already become a visible and highly mediated caricature of herself through her image in the tabloid press and beyond. In contrast to the many images of her yo-yoing weight gain, her younger male friends, and her defiant support of the increasingly bizarre Michael Jackson, Taylor's White Diamonds image maintained a constancy of her inner value and her apparent enduring glamour. Today's celebrities and stars are hyper-exposed through media and online culture; but often that exposure is out of their control and the images conveyed are less than flattering. Along with the sheer lucrative value of endorsement deals, branding as a spokesmodel for a major perfume and fashion house is one of the best ways to generate a utopian version of your public self, airbrushed, Photoshopped, and choreographed to provide the visual essence and epitome of attraction (Marshall 2016, 506–507).

As much as the perfume industry gains value from its relationship to these stars, it is also the case that the stars are working on their own constellation of reputation and meaning. The techniques used by the fragrance industry that we have explored also point to techniques of managing one's own brand identity. Popular stars, even though the process of manufacturing a fragrance is highly industrial and even far removed from the distribution companies that negotiate with these stars, imagine that their fragrance is a form of personal public identity – a key way to construct the most positive and controlled image. This image is strongly connected to the performance persona, directly and as a form of integrated promotion. For film stars, the process is one of maintaining the value of distance, the value of aura itself. Their branding is there to produce the sign value of glamour, and to indicate that their public persona is able to express alluring desires without allowing themselves to be pulled from sensuality to the messiness of sexuality. Film stars as brand spokesmodels present idealized versions of themselves and thereby are hired personas who work to maintain their wider appeal to the film and entertainment industry. Like corporate brands themselves, celebrities, at least in this world of endorsements, are highly designed and engineered.

The Expansion of Self-branding: Making the Self Visible

The example of endorsements and self-branding that pervades the perfume industry is replicated in much of the rest of contemporary culture. What we are seeing particularly in online culture is an expansion of selling and advertising the self. Many of us are engaged at different levels of intensity in ways and means of making ourselves more visible. Why we do this is an interesting story about how branding has expanded and become a means to make oneself at least appear to have value in our changed economy and culture. In part, self-branding is an inevitable consequence of the therapeutic ethos discussed in Chapter 2. The therapeutic ethos provides the ground for the belief that gratification and self-fulfilment can be achieved through consumption; in Lears's words, consumption fulfils the soul (Lears 1994). In this context, the quest for self-realization has become the highest aim of human existence, and self-creation and the search for fulfilment an ongoing project. Thus, while not necessarily associated with glamour per se, self-branding is also concerned with the production of an idealized image designed to be "alluring".

The self-help movement represents one of the key origins of what we now understand as self-branding. Over the course of the twentieth century, different authors in different contexts developed programmes and books on self-improvement. Some of these have been about improving the body and health, and one of the earliest progenitors of this approach was Charles Atlas and his powerful advertisements in comic books and youth magazines aimed at adolescent boys from the 1940s onwards.

Rich in text, Atlas's ads explained how he used to have sand kicked in his face as a "97-pound weakling" and how through his fitness and strengthening programme, he was able to achieve a physique that could not be intimidated – a strong man figure that could be replicated by anyone. Out of Atlas's own transformation – which included a change in name from Angelo Siciliano to something both American and classically mythical – he was able to build a business related to fitness and health training with great success that even has outlived him. Atlas, along with key figures in American culture such as Dale Carnegie who expounded very successfully on the virtues of "winning friends and influencing people" (Carnegie 1984), was what would be described as a 'self-made man'. According to Micki McGee (2005), this self-help movement by the end of the twentieth century had expanded dramatically into a publishing and promotions industry that generated almost $2.5 billion a year by the early twenty-first century.

As economic uncertainties have become exacerbated in the climate of the twenty-first century, the constant quest to create a "new and improved" self has become a modern anxiety and a perceived necessity. According to McGee (2005, 13):

> changing economic circumstances – declining real wages and increased uncertainty about employment stability and opportunities – created a context in which constant self-improvement is suggested as the only reliable insurance against economic insecurity. Self-invention, once the imagined path to boundless opportunity, has become a burden under which a multitude of Americans hoping to fast track their careers, or simply secure their basic necessities, have laboured.

The idea of self-invention is certainly at the core of the therapeutic ethos, but it also dovetails into the changed working structures that have developed over the last two decades. For instance, unions, which are collective representations of workers, have been in decline for more than 30 years. The focus on individuals to construct their own work pathways has expanded and perhaps even accelerated since the Global Financial Crisis of 2008. One way to describe this change is that a greater portion of the workforce has to engage in work that resembles that of the entertainment industry. Entertainment workers, from actors to writers and technicians, move from project to project, and they must build a recognizable profile to ensure that another project will be offered to them in the future. This manner of work can be called portfolio culture (Marshall 2014). It lacks security and depends very much on building an image that is visible and accessible.

As portfolio culture has expanded as a necessity, so too has the means to present oneself publicly. The expansion of the Internet has paralleled this increasing focus on the presentation of the self. In the early days of the Web, personal websites became beacons of identity. With the advent of the interactive Web 2.0, web logs and blogs superseded them. Blogs were generally highly personalized sites for writing and expressing oneself. Indeed, the development of social media from the first years of the twenty-first century built on this personalization of presentation by making the production of a personal variation of a homepage effortless. What social media added to the mix were three elemental functions that serviced the development of a culture of expanded visibility. First of all, it allowed for the interlinking of status updates: thus the uploading of personal images, links, or remarks that were available to others. Second, and related to interlinking, it established systems of following which were simultaneously visible in terms of categories such as friends, followers, and following. Third, and again this is related to both functions above, it quantified, and to a degree qualified, those connections. These three related elemental functions may seem on the surface very simple and innocuous; but when one looks more closely at social media forms such as Facebook or the microblogging format of Twitter, one can see that the amount of personal information generated by these structures is truly phenomenal. Facebook, for instance, in its original modelling on socially connecting students from particular colleges and universities, provided a system that not only provided personal details but a very structured way of updating those personal details as they relate to everyday life. By tagging, as people are linked and summoned when they are part of a photo in Facebook, or using @ and hashtagging (#) on Twitter, the continuous pull of these social networks to contribute regularly is powerful and works as a form of allure to participate as well. The quantification of friends and followers constructs users of these sites into being highly conscious of their presence among others. Thus Facebook friendships number on average 300, a pattern of use that is established in early adolescence. When one realizes that the number of Facebook users worldwide is very nearly 1.3 billion, one can see the reach and extent of this kind of presentation of the self. This push to continuous visibility is instrumental in the related push to brand ourselves and to use social media to continually define our public self. As much as we know our own numbers in terms of who follows and friends us, we are also aware of how this form of connection begins to determine our relative influence and value.

Facebook and related services such as Instagram or Snapchat are often forms that we associate with our leisure time and personal entertainment. However, in the contemporary moment, social media is designed very much to cross the boundaries between work and leisure regularly and often. Much more work-oriented sites such as LinkedIn or academia.edu for academic professionals, Doximity for American doctors, or the more recently launched and tenuous Esqspot for the legal profession make it clearer that visibility on these social network locations is designed to maintain one's work status, advertise and promote, and/or build the possibility of bridges to other potential employment. LinkedIn, for instance, with its focus on work and the value of professional work connections, has 277 million users, of which 84 million are in the United States alone. Whether individuals subscribe to these work-focused networks, it is a modern truism that many people, businesses, and institutions use both Twitter and Facebook to maintain professional visibility as they allow their online selves, institutionally defined or personally defined, to be promoted simultaneously through exposing both their work and pleasure pursuits.

Self-branding, where we are aware of both our presence and the value of that presence, is endemic to contemporary culture. Corporations have emerged that work specifically on charting the visibility, reputation, and influence individuals have on others. Companies such as Klout, which work in a networked way with existing social networks, monitor and then display what they call the Klout score, which is a measure of online social influence. The very existence of monitors of social influence has increased the focus and intensity of self-branding. The higher the Klout score out of a maximum of 100, the greater the level of influence. Thus, heavily visible celebrities on social media sites have high scores, such as Justin Bieber's score of 95 (11 March 2014), while leading scientist Stephen Hawking has a Klout score of 60 (11 March 2014). The developing of metrics around influence and reputation has expanded over the last five years to a much broader range as these metrics combine individuals' online and social media activity with their capacity to 'infect' or affect other individuals into related actions.

Re-reading this capacity of an individual to infect or affect others, as these social influence monitors attempt to do, leads one to realize that the individual in these transactions is being recalibrated into the language of advertising and marketing. Their activity, their movement of content from themselves to another, in this changed world celebrates and heralds the techniques of promoting through the self. Characterizing a range of activities – from online content generation and sharing to building an online portfolio and persona for further exchange – as self-branding helps us understand how a general promotional culture, with advertising as a prevalent mode of communication, becomes part of our everyday way of expressing ourselves. Self-branding on one level is a pragmatic answer to a changed economic environment where there is a general feeling that each of us has to promote ourselves individually in greater domains of our lives. On another level, self-branding is ultimately one of the key techniques to include greater and greater numbers of people in presenting information and data about themselves for use by the advertising industry itself. Our individual and networked uses of social media such as Facebook generate the kind of information that allows these same firms to connect and link what could be called smart and person-sensitive advertising to our own sites. Increasingly, as Turow (2011) foretells, our online "work" and activity is a source for determining our "value" to companies as a form of influence on others as well as the way in which we can be reconstituted with incredible precision to determine our likely future buying practices.

Conclusion

Branding is the personalization of the message of a corporation and its expression of its core identity. This definition highlights the fluidity with which the idea of brand has moved through our culture. As a practice, it represents the essence of an advertising strategy in order to build loyalty, recognition, and corporate value. In the late twentieth century, the increased focus on branding also identifies a shift in emphasis in advertising in the contemporary corporation. In addition, as our case history of perfumes and celebrity endorsement has underlined, branding has extended from the celebrity to the individual. At the high end of this self-branding, celebrities produce carefully constructed public identities that are used to endorse other products, but these identities also become usable and valuable brands and products in and of themselves. At the more everyday level, self-branding is a practice that defines the current condition and anxiety that pushes individuals to build their visibility and reputation. In some cases, this self-branding produces an individual brand value that rivals those of very high-end celebrities: when a particular YouTube video goes viral and attracts millions of views, there is the possibility that the individual may have a brand value that is convertible in some way in our elaborate attention economy. Generally, however, our self-branding operates as a contemporary and dominant mode of being, particularly as we allow our online and social media personas to be "fed" and maintained with images, texts, and connections that define our identity and how that identity is related to others. Ultimately, this self-branding has been instrumental in developing the material for the generation of a new and more direct form of targeted advertising and marketing as our information feeds back into consumer culture.

11

Advertising and Social Action:
Dove and Real Beauty

In this chapter, we continue to explore how advertising provides a transformative discourse of the self while simultaneously linking people who share common interests and consumption values. In the current milieu, brands, rather than products, provide the means for consumers to express their individual identities, as well as their collective tribal identities. Sarah Banet-Weiser (2012, 4) writes, "More than just the object itself, a brand is the perception – the series of images, themes, morals, values, feelings, and sense of authenticity, conjured by the product itself. The brand is the essence of what will be experienced; the brand is a promise as much as a practicality." Brands thus reflect our most basic social and cultural relations; they provide the "ambience", or context, for everyday living, individual living, and affective relationships (Arviddson 2006, 13). In our case study of the Dove Real Beauty campaign, we note how paradoxically, in contemporary culture, brands have become the means to construct an "authentic" self that is positioned in opposition to mainstream culture. Much like the Volkswagen campaign discussed in Chapter 6, Dove hails consumers who oppose mainstream culture, though in this case opposition is to unrealizable beauty standards rather than conformity and materialism. Unlike Volkswagen, Dove aligns itself with a particular socio-political agenda and engages viewers by fostering their participation in the brand – whether to answer online surveys, join their online self-esteem workshops, host a workshop in one's community, or spread their viral videos. As we mentioned in Chapter 1, we refer to this active engagement that helps build the brand prosumption. The consumer is no longer a passive recipient of an advertising message but is actively involved in creating the brand, whether through their emotional connection that gives the brand meaning, or through their immaterial labor in providing web content or circulating videos. In the case of Dove, engaging with the brand becomes a political action. Dove blurs the lines that differentiate advertising and political action, so that in brand culture, there is no contradiction between a consumer acting in their self interest, and a citizen acting for the common good.

Advertising and the Quest for Authenticity

In an era where everyday life is virtualized and experiences are prepackaged, "authenticity" has become an advertising buzzword. But the marketing of authenticity is hardly new. As Lears (1983, 6) notes, the desire for authenticity coincided with the rise of consumer culture, where the proliferation of mass-manufactured goods and social amenities engendered a sense of unreality as people felt cut off from "the hard, resistant reality of things". He writes that by the early twentieth century, "Americans began to imagine a self that was neither simple nor genuine, but fragmented and socially constructed" (Lears 1983, 8). Thus began the constant quest for a coherent identity and "authentic" selfhood that exists outside of a pre-constituted sociality; as Goldman and Papson (1996, 142) write, "Today authenticity represents the search for individuated space outside of the commodity form and outside the 'spectacle'."

The notion of modern life as spectacle harkens back to Guy DeBord's (1995) *Society of the Spectacle*, where he critiqued the dominance of predetermined meanings. For Debord (1995, 13), "The spectacle is both the outcome and the goal of the dominant mode of production. It's not something added to the real world... it is at the very heart of society's real unreality. In all of its specific manifestations – news or propaganda, advertising or the actual consumption of entertainment – the spectacle epitomizes the prevailing model of social life." In DeBord's (1995) writings, spectacle refers to a mode of social life based on the promise of fulfilment through entertainment and consumption. In the society of the spectacle, authentic life has been replaced by prepackaged experiences so that "everything human beings once experienced directly had been turned into a show put on by someone else... immediacy was gone. Now there was only 'mediacy' – life as mediated by through other instruments, life as a media creation" (Lasn 1999, 26). DeBord's critique emphasizes how the commodity form mediates experience and shapes common-sense conceptions of the world. Although DeBord wrote in the late 1960s, his analysis has become an increasingly apt description of contemporary brand culture as dominant mode of social life. As Arviddson (2006, 12) writes, "It is no longer meaningful, as it may have been in the thirties, to distinguish mediated experiences from more direct and authentic ones."

Arviddson (2006) writes that brand management – through advertising, product placements, corporate sponsorships, logos, and the like – developed in the 1990s as a response to Generation X. This demographic had grown up with the complete media saturation of everyday life, and also had experienced the disintegration of traditional institutions and securities that had grounded previous generations. He states that in this void, brands "are primarily to be understood as resources for the construction of a self and its social moorings" and "people use brands to build solidarity, meaning, experiences – all things that are no longer provided by the social context to the same extent, or in an equally straightforward manner as before" (Arviddson 2006, 82–83). Brands fill a void by providing meaning; in so doing, they produce an "ethical surplus": a social bond or common identity that "enables a person to become a subject" (Arviddson 2006, 83).

According to Thomas Pardee (2010), writing in *Advertising Age*, transparency, authenticity, and relevance are now key marketing terms to reach the members of Generation Y – those born between 1980 and 2000. Even more so than Generation X, these media-savvy consumers see through the "old school linear marketing ploys" and dislike interruptive advertising. As a result, brands reach these consumers by creating "authentic" messages that foster affective relationships and provide experiential opportunities for interaction, particularly through social media and online platforms. According to Carol Phillips, founder of market research group Brand Amplitude, "If I can add value they'll tell my story for me… it puts pressure on marketers to return to their roots – it's about engaging consumers with your message" (cited in Pardee 2010). In this way, brands both mediate and constitute social reality by providing a pre-structured space within which consumers simultaneously create their own identities and build the brand.

Jamming the Brand

For many leftist thinkers and social activists, brand culture is the epitome of spectacle because it replaces authentic experiences with commercially oriented ones and presumes to arbitrate cultural meanings. As Goldman and Papson (1996, 142) state, "Advertising is less about lies than about inflection – the bending and redirecting – of social and cultural meanings to serve commodity brand names". In the 1960s, Guy DeBord and the French Situationist movement proposed detournement, the rerouting of spectacular images to reverse or subvert their meaning, to combat the dominance of spectacle. Movements documented in books such as Kalle Lasn's *Culture Jamming* continued the

Situationists' efforts to "devalue the currency of the spectacle" (Lasn 1999, 108) by advocating techniques to disrupt spectacular relationships. Culture jammers work to "detourn" the dominant messages of consumer capitalism by offering counter-images that jolt consumers and prompt them to re-examine brand messages. *Adbusters Magazine*, a culture-jamming publication, offers parodies of advertisements. For example, their version of Calvin Klein's Obsession perfume depicts an image of a bulimic model hunched over a toilet bowl (see Figure 11.1). A transformed Absolut Vodka ad portrays the aftermath of an auto accident, with the tagline "Absolut End". The aim, according to Serazio (2013, 65), is "to contest, appropriate, and subvert the message of branding by peeling away the brand veneer so as to expose the unseemly backstage machination behind the glamour and artifice of the advertisement and to destabilize branding's claim on becoming some kind of 'authentic' cultural resource". In other examples of culture jamming, groups such as The Billboard Liberation Front deface billboards by changing their messages, the Yes Men impersonate corporate spokespersons, Negativland make sound collages that rework commercial jingles, or the Reverend Billy heads the Church of Stop Shopping and, along with his congregation, proselytizes on city streets. Jamie Warner (2007) argues that *The Daily Show* was another example of culture jamming that confronted the structure of spectacular society by undermining it from within.

Yet, these strategies of resistance are themselves subject to appropriation. As Serazio (2013, 65) notes, "if, however, advertising – and for that matter, capitalism, a spectre of broader ideological menace to advertisers – has proven anything over the course of its history, it is that today's rebellion is tomorrow's mall fashion: what starts out as controversial ends up as a Hot topic". In this way, Christine Harold critiques Adbusters' use of parody and irony as strategies of protest. She explains that advertisers themselves use parody and irony to convey authenticity by subverting traditional advertising tropes, so that both share the same logic and rhetoric. Parody, according to Harold (2009, 350), "derides the content of what it sees as oppressive rhetoric, but fails to attend to its patterns". As a result, Liz Moor states that culture jamming "has often been said to dismantle the master's house with the master's tools – and then provide the master with blueprints for a better house and better tools" (cited in Serazio 2013, 66). Harold (2009, 353) favours rhetorical pranksters who, like comedians, are "playful explorers of the commercial media landscape"; rather than didactic culture jammers who try to reveal Truth, they "diagnose a specific situation, and try something to see what responses they provoke". But even the rhetorical play that Harold (2009) lauds is appropriated – the Yes Men make movies for HBO, Reverend Billy and the Church of Stop

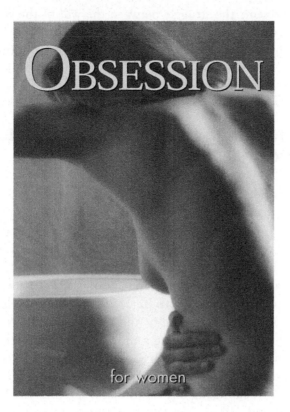

Figure 11.1   Adbusters parody of Obsession advertisement
Source: Reprinted with permission from Adbusters Media

Shopping have been turned into a play, and venues such as *The Daily Show,*
The Colbert Report, or *Last Week Tonight with John Oliver* may provide cultural
critique but are still sponsored by advertisers and promote products.

All of these examples demonstrate the difficulty of establishing authenticity
that exists apart from spectacle. As Banet-Weiser (2012, 13) argues, "Within
contemporary brand culture the separation between the authentic self and the
commodity self not only is more blurred, but this blurring is more expected
and tolerated. That is, within contemporary consumer culture, we take it for
granted that authenticity, like anything else, can be branded." What is more
important, she states, is to understand how we live our lives through brands
and how brand cultures are ambivalent, offering both possibilities of individual resistance within the parameters of consumer culture, as well as corporate
hegemony. Goldman and Papson (1996, 142) also express this tension:

"Authenticity represents the struggle between the will of the individual and the determinism of the commodity structure." Corporations that promote social causes such as environmentalism or feminism exemplify the ambivalence of brand culture, where consumers create identities through brands that position themselves as advocates for social change.

From Greenwashing to Pinkwashing: The Branding of Authenticity

Advertising constructs a social world in which "authentic" identity is expressed through consuming commodity signs (Goldman and Papson 1996, 187). These signs typically convey authenticity by "putting together a compelling tale about a product's or a brand's transparency, simplicity, or honesty" (Merrick 2014). For years, Volkswagen was "the honest car". Big brewing companies such as MillerCoors make craft beers such as Killian's Irish Red and claim its recipe comes from 1860s Ireland. Tito's Handmade Vodka brags of its founder's commitment to quality and asserts that it is "made in small batches in an old-fashioned pot, using a time honored method". Levi's Jeans provides statements of authenticity, such as an 1873 patent date, and claims to be "an American tradition, symbolizing the vitality of the West" (Patterson 2015). The Grandpa Soap Company states that its product has been "proudly made" since 1878, and that its "hardworking, simple, pure ingredients are the heart of our natural soapmaking tradition".

Authenticity is also conveyed by a brand's values as well as attributes. By "participating" in the brand, consumers take on its values. Beginning in the 1980s, as it became apparent that overconsumption was leading to environmental destruction, advertisers responded by placing the "green" consumer and the environmentally concerned corporation on the same moral ground (Goldman 1992, 193). Green products position companies as socially and environmentally responsible in order to forge positive affective relationships with consumers by differentiating "good" and "bad" consumption, and in so doing, expand market share by appealing to consumers who feel that the brand represents their values. For example, companies such as Seventh Generation sell biodegradable, vegetable-based cleaning products, as well as chlorine-free tampons and paper towels so that consumers who use these products demonstrate their concern for their environment. In this way, advertisers create sign value by differentiating their commodity from others – as "natural" or "organic" – and consumers use the sign value to construct their identities. However, green advertisers must convey authenticity in their concern for the environment, but also in the values they represent. Method, a close compet-itor to Seventh Generation, also makes "natural" environmentally friendly cleaning products that legitimate consumption by positioning it as a responsi-ble solution to environmental problems. But Method also aroused controversy when it produced an online video in support of the Household Product Labe-ling Act, which would require companies to list their ingredients. The video parodied household cleanser ads in an attempt to show the chemical residue left by typical cleaning products. The video opens as if it is a commercial for a cleanser called Shiny Suds. As we hear a lilting musical paean to the product, a woman smiles and waves at friendly animated bubble creatures that clean her bathtub. But then there is a fade to black and the ebullient tone of the ad turns sinister. The next morning when she showers, the leftover bubbles leer at her and repeatedly urge her to "use a loofah". While the intention was to communicate the need for transparency in cleaning product ingredients – and of course, to highlight that Method's ingredients were "natural" in contrast to those in other cleaning products– many people interpreted the ads as degrad-ing to women and even suggestive of sexual assault. Method responded by pulling the ad from its website and YouTube. In this case, the ad conflicted with consumers' perceptions of the company's values, though Method also claimed that 2500 letters supporting the Household Product Labeling Act were sent to Congress (Neff 2009).

In other cases, brands encourage active participation by turning consump-tion into a political act. In commodity activism, consumers act politically by choosing some brands over others. Fair Trade products, such as handicrafts, coffee, sugar, chocolate, tea, flowers, bananas, or wine, support producers from developing countries and promote sustainable development through better trading conditions and rights for marginalized producers. Companies such as Starbucks assure consumers that their products are ethically sourced, with a minimal environmental footprint; further, they boast a commitment to energy efficient stores, conservation of energy and water, renewable energy, and recycling. They also offer products such as Ethos Water, which prom-ises that a portion of the purchase price will go to the Ethos Fund to support "water, sanitation, and hygiene education programs in water-stressed coun-tries" – a strategy that also works to increase consumption. According to Ethos founder Peter Thum, "If people were willing to pay a premium for water named after its source, wouldn't they want to pay for a brand devoted to funding humanitarian water programs?" However, after revelations that Star-bucks was bottling and selling Ethos water from drought-ridden California, the company moved production to Pennsylvania (Moyer 2015). Moreover, environmental groups often protest the commercialization of any bottled water, arguing that access to water is a basic human right, and that plastic bottles have a detrimental impact on the environment.

According to Banet-Weiser (2012, 152), "Go Green is the political slogan of the 21st century; environmentalism, expressed through language and design of a brand, has become a branded product." Even a mundane product such as Tide detergent has "tips for a better life" on its website, which includes a section on how to help the environment by altering everyday actions such as washing clothes in cold water. Mark Gobe (2007) notes that consumers want products that will elevate them or connect them to history or a cause. In the contemporary milieu, "citizenship" is a fundamental emotional driver to humanize brands so that they will resonate with people. Gobe (2007, 74–75) writes, "A brand personality defined by citizenship is known mostly for its social commitment (like Starbucks, Body Shop, MAC cosmetics). Citizen brands will connect with people who aspire to love the world, who are committed to building a better environment. The emotional promise is engagement, and the consumer motivation is to create progress by doing good." Banet – Weiser (2012) discusses the rise of the citizen consumer, where individuals are encouraged to "freely choose" to participate in collective action through brands. Companies increasingly claim to stand for something besides selling, and "social responsibility" rallies consumers around a brand.

A corollary to greenwashing is "pinkwashing", where brands are associated with female empowerment. Pinkwashing was initially associated with the wearing of pink ribbons to indicate support for breast cancer research in the 1980s, but is now a moniker for various forms of cause marketing that appropriate feminist ideals. Robert Goldman (1992) refers to the early stages of pinkwashing as commodity feminism, and suggests it was a strategy in the 1980s for advertisers to overcome the "sign fatigue" of sceptical, media-savvy consumers who had grown up constantly bombarded by advertising messages, and who were also critical of the idealized images of women promoted by advertising. Banet-Weiser (2012) relates the rise of commodity feminism to niche marketing, which in the 1970s and 1980s took advantage of identity politics that both demarcated and argued for increased visibility of previously marginalized groups such as women, African Americans, or gays and lesbians. Advertisers responded to the women's movement by turning feminism into a commodity, appropriating its power while domesticating its critique of advertising. A classic case in point is the advertising campaign for Virginia Slims cigarettes from that period that associated femininity with independence, assertiveness, and choice, while simultaneously undermining its own rhetoric with the tagline "You've Come a Long Way, Baby" (as well as the use of extremely slim women to associate cigarettes with weight loss, and equating choice with an addictive drug).

Banet-Weiser (2012, 34) describes the shift from commodity feminism to commodity activism in the late twentieth century:

> Conflating individual consumption with the citizen consumer was part of advertisers' broader conflation of liberal ideals of choice and empowerment with consumption habits in the mid-twentieth century. Such conflation was less crucial in the later 20th century; the difference, however, came in what and who the citizen consumer was. Consequently, the term of the producer-consumer relationship changed too, increasingly crafted in relational terms as an exchange between marketers and consumers rather than a top-down imposition of a corporate message.

As advertisers began to focus on the creation of affective relations with consumers from the late twentieth to early twenty-first century, brands allowed individuals to both shape their identities and participate in social action through consumption. Within brand culture, supporting brands that convey positive messages about women or choosing one brand over another is presented as a political act that constitutes the "authentic" self, though within the society of the spectacle, it is a self designed and delineated by the brand. Similarly, Johnston and Taylor (2008, 167) use the term "feminist consumerism" to refer to the corporate appropriation of the ideals of the feminist movement within the broader culture and ideology of consumerism. They write that feminist themes are used to market products to women while also reinforcing the notion that individual consumption, rather than collective action, serves as "primary source of identity, affirmation, and social change" (Johnston and Taylor 2008, 177–178). Brands that employ discourses about female empowerment interpellate consumers who simultaneously create an identity and build the brand through their participation. The benchmark for contemporary "pinkwashing", or feminist consumerism, is the Dove Real Beauty campaign, considered here in detail, which illustrates the interplay of notions of authenticity, cultural resistance, and commodity activism. It demonstrates the shift in advertising that occurred from the "creative revolution" of the 1960s, where advertisers appealed to niche groups through strategies that connoted "authenticity", to the current era where consumers actively produce their identities by engaging "authentically" with brands. The relationship between brands and consumers is now a mutual transaction rather than a top-down interaction, where brands and consumers each create the other to build a "spectacular" brand culture that is the prevailing structure of social life. Yet, the construction of identity, resistance to advertising, and social action remain within this matrix. We suggest that Dove's Campaign For Real Beauty harnesses women's dissatisfaction with unattainable beauty standards and contests narrow societal definitions of beauty, but fails to critique the idea that beauty is essential to female identity and thus affirms and legitimates hegemonic beauty ideals. The Dove Campaign for Real Beauty advocates feminist consumerism as a vehicle for social change and demonstrates its limitations.

Case History: The Dove Campaign for Real Beauty

Dove Soap, made by the Unilever Corporation, was launched in the 1940s and came on the American market in 1957. It was initially developed as a result of Unilever's research to find a soap that didn't leave "scum" residue; their original product irritated the skin, but in the course of experimentation, they found that stearic acid, the same ingredient as in cold cream, would alleviate this problem. Early advertising, developed by what was then the agency Hewitt Ogilvy Benson and Mather (later Ogilvy and Mather), positioned Dove as different from other soaps because it was 25% cleansing cream and so would not dry out the skin. For example, early ads had the tagline "creams your skin as you wash" or "Dove won't dry your skin like soap can." These ads were aimed at mass (i.e. young, white, and middle-class) female consumers; as Banet-Weiser (2012, 25) asserts, they were directed to a unified subject, "one recognized as ideal in the mass-consumption, mass-production era". In an era marked by notions of abundance and conformity, and that espoused equality and equal access, even those in marginalized groups, such as the working class or people of colour, were encouraged to aspire to this ideal. Despite the fact that Dove was more expensive than other soaps, it quickly became a core brand for facial cleansing. According to Silvia Lagnado, who worked as VP at Unilever and Global Brand Director at Dove, Dove resonated "emotionally and sensorially" with women in a way that later helped them build the brand. She states, "The real success came from the shape, the promise (of beauty) the reason to believe (mildness and moisturization) and the powerful recommendation of dermatologists in the United States and Canada" (Gobe 2007, 240).

Dove's ads have always been produced by one agency, Ogilvy and Mather, which was a strong proponent of advertising that created a strong brand image. CEO David Ogilvy, author of the influential book *Confessions of an Advertising Man* (1963), had begun his career working with pollster George Gallup, and thus wrote about the importance of consumer research to identify needs and desires, and product positioning that specified both the audience and the need/desire the product promised to fulfil. For example, Dove has consistently been positioned as a "beauty bar" for women with dry skin.

While Ogilvy took a rational approach to advertising, he is often identified as a key player in the "creative revolution" in advertising in the 1960s. As we discussed in Chapter 6, the creative revolution was a response to a social and political climate marked by critiques of mass consumer culture and the emergence of identity groups, such as the youthful counterculture, women, and African Americans, who protested their exclusion from homogenous mass culture. Banet-Weiser (2012, 29) writes, "the advertising industry saw cultural and individual difference as an opportunity and reimagined its practices to capture an increasingly fragmented audience". In this way, the creative revolution marked the transition from mass to niche marketing by capitalizing on social dissent and alienation, simultaneously appealing to different identity categories and reifying them as markets. Advertisements shifted their tactics from "buy, because everyone else is" to "buy our product because it is different from everyone else's, be real, be authentic" (Banet-Weiser 2012, 32). But in order to connote authenticity, ads had to overcome criticisms of advertising as deceptive and manipulative. One strategy to overcome resistance to advertising, demonstrated by Doyle Dane Bernbach with its Volkswagen campaign, was to use humour, irony, and irreverent ads to win over "alienated" consumers (see Chapter 6). Taking a different approach, Ogilvy advocated realism in advertising, whether "slice of life" commercials or testimonials from loyal consumers. In this way, Dove's ads in the 1960s countered criticisms of deceptive advertising by relying on documentary style testimonials from "real women" who touted Dove's moisturizing benefits.

By 1986 Dove was the best-selling soap in the United States (Adbrands. net n.d.). Dove's credibility as a moisturizer was also bolstered when an independent survey conducted at the University of Pennsylvania in 1979 found that Dove irritated the skin less than other soaps, which led to a marketing campaign promoting the brand to dermatologists and allowed Dove to claim that it was recommended by doctors. But in the late 1980s, Dove shifted away from representing product attributes and began to sell self-esteem, particularly in 1990 when its patent expired and competitors, chiefly Olay, came onto the market. Use value was subsumed by sign value as "real" women stopped extolling the product's specific benefits and instead began to connect the product to feminist notions of empowerment. Rather than focusing on the product itself, Dove's key message stressed the importance of women feeling good about themselves. In the 1988 "Truth" campaign, for example, African American gospel singer Jean Rhys speaks into the camera and relates how after she began using Dove, her Reverend complimented her on her skin. This woman speaks for herself and reveals her "truth" where she is empowered by beauty products. Other ads targeted specific identity categories: "one profiled women who were 35 and older", and another focused on "brainy women, another on women with freckles" (Banet-Weiser 2012, 31).

Dove's shift from commodity feminism, where beauty products are presented as "empowering", to feminist consumption as a means to produce identities and participate in social change, occurred with the Dove Campaign for Real Beauty. In 2002, Unilever, along with its PR firm Edelman and Ogilvy and Mather, reassessed its marketing strategy in order to revitalize the brand and extend Dove from a soap to a "beauty brand" that would include shower gels, moisturizers, and shampoos. Their overall aim was to present "a powerful global message that would make Dove as iconic as Nike or Apple" (Jeffers 2005, 34). With the emergence of digital technologies, instead of a top-down interaction where consumers interpreted a predetermined meaning, the model for advertising was becoming more of a transaction that relied on the creation of an affective relationship between consumers and the brand. According to Alessandro Manfredi, Global VP for Dove, they felt that Dove's success was a result of consumers' love for the soap, but that consumers' relationships with Dove as a brand was nonexistent. They recognized, as Murray (2013, 84) writes, that "a brand needs to reach audiences' emotions by building a platform that forges an ideological alliance with a corporate identity prior to the act of material consumption". Moreover, they felt that Dove was a different product in different regions of the world, and thus wanted to create a clear global brand vision that built on the connections that Dove had already established with women. Manfredi states, "Basically, we had started this brand 55 years ago now, I think, in the U.S. with testimonials. We have a very through protocol in creating testimonials, and basically the protocol is about making sure that they are real, they are authentic, and that women really talk about their experience with the product… This has created some emotional connection with the brand in terms of people believing that this is an honest and authentic brand" (Fielding et al. 2008).

The Dove Campaign for Real Beauty thus built on Dove's previous use of testimonials from "real" women to connote authenticity. But while the "Truth" campaign had appropriated notions of female empowerment by making the pursuit of beauty a feminist act, Dove's new strategy sought to resonate emotionally with women by "jamming" the cultural representation of beauty standards that most women felt were unrealistic and unattainable. According to Olivia Johnson, strategic planner for Dove at Ogilvy and Mather in London, "We knew the way beauty brands behaved and the way they portrayed women wasn't quite right. The team's intuitive sense as human beings was that it made them feel a bit demoralized and a bit miserable. It makes you feel deflated when you see the gap between these images and your own physical reality" (cited in Jeffers 2005). The largely female agency–client team conveyed to their male colleagues the frustration women felt when confronted with beauty advertising, but they were initially unsure of how to sell beauty products by critiquing beauty. Dove worked with Strategy-One, Edelman's research and strategic consulting arm, to explore whether it was possible to talk about beauty in ways that were more "authentic, satisfying, and empowering". StrategyOne reviewed existing research and writing on beauty, appearance, and self-worth in 22 languages and 118 countries to determine current knowledge on the topic and gaps that would enable Dove to contribute to the debate in a positive way. They then commissioned feminist scholars such as Nancy Etcoff (author of *Survival of the Prettiest*), Susie Orbach (author of *Fat is a Feminist Issue*), and Naomi Wolf (author of *The Beauty Myth*) to interpret their research and prepare a white paper. Their report led to a worldwide ethnographic survey of women regarding perceptions of their bodies. The surveys asked women to assess what "beauty" meant to them and their feelings about how they were portrayed in the media. No references were made to Dove or Unilever, so that participants were unaware that a corporation sponsored the research. The study found that less than 2% of women felt beautiful; 75% wanted more diverse representations of age, shape, and size; and 76% wanted the media to portray beauty as more than physical (Murray 2013, 85). Their widespread dissatisfaction determined that there was a space for Dove to address beauty standards. It provided insight into the needs and desires of Dove's target audience – women dissatisfied with impossible-to-attain beauty standards – and helped them to determine how "beauty" could be redefined. Specifically, they found that while for the majority of women, "authentic" beauty is comprised of intangible qualities such as happiness, confidence, dignity, and humour as much as physical appearance, this concept has been replaced by a narrower, functional definition, communicated by media and assimilated into popular culture, that equates beauty with physical attractiveness. Thus, Dove's strategy was to reconfigure concepts of beauty by disconnecting sign from referent to create an alternative that would be perceived as "authentic". Notably, none of the women surveyed associated the attainment of beauty with a product, and thus Dove's strategy involved creating a positive corporate identity by positioning the brand as "the 'voice' for 'real beauty' and the vehicle for dialogue, engagement, and action" (Scott 2005). In this way, they appropriated dissatisfaction with beauty culture and rechannelled it into the Dove brand as a platform for social change. Silvia Lagnado, Unilever's brand manager for Dove, articulated the vision that emerged: "Core to our vision was widening the definition of feminine beauty and challenging the stereotypes of what beauty looks like. We wanted to position the Dove brand as a way to help women feel greater self-esteem and appreciate the diversity of beauty. We spent a lot of time and effort on research and talking with sociologists about girls' and women's body image" (Young 2006). The clearly defined market led Dove to develop the Dove Real Women print and billboard campaign, followed by the broader Campaign for Real Beauty in 2004. As Lagnado stated, the new approach enabled Dove to differentiate itself through "inspiration" rather than "aspiration" (Gobe 2007, 241) and achieve the goal of twenty-first-century advertising: to create your own space, attract your own audience, and develop a deep and long-lasting relationship with consumers (cited in Banet-Weiser 2012, 38). As Murray (2013, 84) argues from a different vantage, Dove adopted a cause-branding strategy that merged messages of corporate concern and commitment for a cause with the participation of women and girls for the same social goals, thus concealing corporate aims.

Dove initially presented its vision in a travelling art exhibit in Canada in 2004, called *Beyond Compare*, where 67 female photographers submitted photographs of everyday women that demonstrated what "real" beauty meant to them. The exhibit, which was far less expensive than a full-fledged advertising campaign, was a way to test whether Dove's approach would resonate with women. It was followed by the launch of Dove's Real Women in the United Kingdom, a print and billboard campaign for firming cream that featured a multiracial group of "ordinary" women in their twenties and thirties, none of whom fit the tall, light-skinned, thin image of women typically featured in ads. Notably, none of the women were blonde. They were recruited from newspaper ads asking for women who were not afraid to show their bodies, which were larger than those typical of models in advertisements. The same ad appeared in the United States in the summer, using women from across the country recruited from health clubs, yoga studios, on the street, and from open auditions. The women were posed together wearing only their bras and underwear; the only criterion was that "they couldn't be professional actors or models", and they had to have curves and "a certain amount of charisma" (Jeffers 2005).

The success of Real Women led to Dove's multinational, multi-tiered Campaign for Real Beauty, which launched in England in September 2004 and later appeared in Canada, the United States, and eventually 35 countries (Murray 2013). This campaign involved television, billboards, print and web advertising, interactive websites, social media, and national and grassroots outreach, all of which were adapted for different audiences around the world. The ad in the United States, for example, featured photographs of wrinkled, freckled, or full-figured women. Next to each one was a checkbox with questions such as Wrinkled? Or Wonderful? Flawed? Or Flawless? Oversized? Or Outstanding? The ads encouraged participation by directing women to Dove's website, where they could vote on the correct answer to these questions.

Dove aligned with, and appropriated, feminist critiques of oppressive beauty standards and presented itself as the spokesperson for the cause. The ad copy, as well as the website, stated, "For too long beauty has been defined by narrow, stifling stereotypes. You've told us that it's time to change all that. Dove agrees. We believe real beauty comes in many shapes, sizes, and ages. That is why Dove is launching the Campaign for Real Beauty." Dove enabled women to construct their identities through the brand, in effect "participating" in feminism by making the brand part of their everyday lives. Rather than telling women about their product and why they should buy it, Dove fosters identification with its corporate identity as voice for social change. The Campaign for Real Beauty invited women to take an oppositional stance in relation to the hegemonic beauty standards, a strategy that relied on the principles of detournement mentioned above. As Murray (2013, 86) quotes Danesi, "Alignment with co-opted subcultural signs allows consumers to think of themselves as insurgents; yet, since their rebellion occurs through consumerism, they do not 'pay the social price of true nonconformity and dissent'." Dove's messages appeared to intervene in beauty culture; they were designed "to arouse emotions against the dominant ideology of beauty and to arouse support for 'real' beauty" (Murray 2013, 92). But Dove's critique of beauty standards simultaneously directed women to its products as ways to become more beautiful. Further, Murray's (2013) analysis of *Tick Box* points out that, by tallying votes on its website and on billboards, "women become objects of approval or disapproval based on the 'real' judgment of global audiences" and so the ads have potentially disempowering consequences. Moreover, limiting responses to *yes* or *no* affirms the binary logic of the categories and leaves no room for discussion.

In 2005, Dove expanded the Campaign for Real Beauty by reaching out to young girls through television and online advertising (young girls were less likely to read print ads in women's magazines). In this phase of the campaign, Dove further developed its credibility by establishing a Self-Esteem Fund devoted to the "cause" of body image, which sought to alter the narrow societal definition of beauty by making self-esteem a component. Springer (2009) writes that much of the campaign's success "can be attributed to it being the first digital campaign to drive participants to a supportive online community that reached over 200 million people worldwide, with over 26 million people participating in the campaign online" (Celebre and Waggoner Denton

2014). Dove introduced the website with two ads designed not so much to sell the product as to create engagement with the brand, especially important among young girls in the process of establishing brand loyalty. *True Colors* was a 46-second Superbowl ad that featured young girls, aged about 10 to 13, who stare forlornly into the camera and express their anxieties as phrases such as "Wishes she was blonde" or "Thinks she is ugly" appear in a white font. Next, the "voice" of Dove interjects with comments such as "Let's tell her to be real. And brave. And true. And she'll be beautiful." The same girls are then shown dancing and smiling; the words "Dove Self-Esteem Fund" appear on screen, followed by "Because every girl deserves to be beautiful". The girls recognize their "true" beauty as Dove announces the establishment of the Self-Esteem Fund. Viewers are directed to Dove's online Movement for Self-Esteem, created as an activist site that featured workshops, projects, activities, and videos aimed at "educating" girls and women by building their self-esteem. In this way, consumers seek out the brand and participate in creating its meaning. Yet at the same time, as Johnston and Taylor (2008, 174) observe, the Dove website also included sections such as "Let's Dare to Love Our Hair" followed by shampoos, conditioners, and styling aids. They note that Dove spokespersons acknowledge their dual roles: to make women feel more beautiful and to sell products.

Dove's "Evolution" ad, which won the Cyber Grand Prix Lion Award at the Cannes International Advertising festival in 2007, is perhaps its best-known effort to "jam" cultural representations of beauty by deconstructing the way that the advertising industry digitally enhances images of women to appear flawlessly beautiful. The spot, which initially aired on YouTube, MySpace, and Google Video in 2005, features the "ordinary", imperfect face of a woman sitting in front of a mirror. In the course of 60 seconds, presented in fast motion, a team of make-up artists transform her by applying make-up to smooth her skin, remove blemishes, and accentuate her eyes. Her hair is curled and volume added. But even after this initial transformation, they use Photoshop to fill out her lips, thicken her eyelashes, and lengthen her neck, and the entire image is airbrushed. Finally, the completed image is shown on a billboard advertisement for foundation cream. The graphics read: "No wonder our perception of beauty is distorted. Take part in the Dove Real Beauty Workshop for girls." With "Evolution", Dove eschewed traditional advertising techniques and platforms through both form and content; it was calculated to become a viral ad that consumers would share with one another. Viral advertising, according to Serazio (2013), is the electronic equivalent of word-of-mouth advertising. It is appealing not only because it reduces overhead (advertisers only have to pay for production costs), but "by embedding

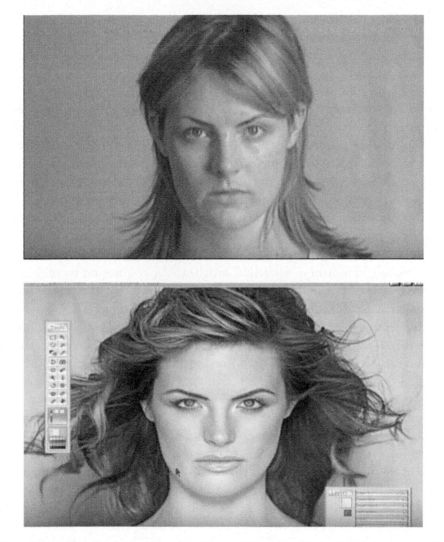

Figure 11.2 Dove's viral "Evolution" advertisement show the before and after images of a Photoshopped model

the brand in peer-to-peer flows and attaining popularity through hit counts and web traffic analytics, such marketing is thought to skirt the problem of consumer cynicism that plagues traditional advertising venues" (Wipperfurth 2005, 41). The ad embraced the transactional model of communication where consumers become active producers of meaning; it relied on consumers "freely choosing" to spread the ad whose meaning appears to be "discovered" rather than imposed. In this way, consumers are incorporated into the production process as they "work" to reproduce the ad. Viral ads such as "Evolution" work by using the productivity/agency of consumers rather than trying to control it, in effect aligning consumers with Dove in opposition to mainstream constructions of beauty (see Figure 11.2).

The Dove Real Beauty campaign is currently 11 years old. While "Evolution" was its first viral breakthough, it has continued to produce both traditional and viral ads whose purported aim is to raise self-esteem and challenge cultural definitions of beauty. For example, its "Real Beauty Sketches" ad, produced in 2013, was depicted as a "social experiment" where a forensic sketch artist drew pictures of seven women based on their self-descriptions. Prior to their session, each woman met with a stranger who also described them to the artist. The ad found that in the majority of cases, the sketches made from the strangers' points of view were most accurate and showed the women as more attractive than they described themselves. But rather than critiquing the ad industry, "Sketches" sought to evoke emotion by presenting the women's tearful reactions at the end as they realize that they judge themselves too harshly. Less than a month after "Sketches" was launched, it became the number one viral video ad of all time, with over 3,707,407 shares. It also inspired 121 print features, 484 news and lifestyle segments, and thousands of online articles with hundreds of thousands of comments (Tomalin 2013). Despite its popularity, "Sketches" was criticized for featuring primarily young, white, thin, attractive women, for perpetuating the idea that beauty was paramount in how women evaluate themselves and others, and because it took a male sketch artist to reveal women's true beauty to them (Stampler 2013).

"Patches", an ad released in 2014, presented a "research study" where a group of women were given "beauty patches" that they were told would make them more beautiful over the course of two weeks. The women all claimed that they felt more beautiful, but at the end, they were told that the patches were placebos. Instead of becoming angry at the deception, the women cried as they realized that they were beautiful all along. Johnston and Taylor (2008, 180) point out that emotions such as pain and anger are avoided in the Dove ads, so that there is a "greater focus on building positive associations that can be converted to brand loyalty, and an explicit connection between self-love and self-care through commodity consumption". Dove critiques beauty standards and at the same time encourages conformity to them by selling products such as firming and anti-ageing cream. A 2006 ad campaign for Dove Advanced Care deodorant encouraged women to "Love Your Armpits." The television ad features several women reading "an open letter to the armpit", which states, "You can be a softer, smoother, more beautiful little armpit – you deserve our best care and don't you forget that." The ad commodifies a body part by creating a problem most women did not know existed, and then offers Dove deodorant as the solution.

Notably, many of Dove's ad campaigns simultaneously work to expand markets – its Pro-Age collection of hair and skin products featured women over 50 who bared their bodies. According to Dove's marketing director, "We're encouraging them to embrace their age and inspiring women in this age group to take better care of themselves, while showing them the potential that lies within their skin and hair" (Edgar 2007). At the same time, this "challenge" to conventional beauty culture consisted of objectifying older women in the same fashion that younger women were typically presented in advertising and offered products meant to hide the "unattractive" signs of aging. Dove Men+Care, which extends body care products to men, has the tagline "Care Makes a Man S+ronger", and its website suggests "men everywhere are redefining what it means to be strong". The banner presents a suitably masculine image of NBA star Alonzo Mourning hugging his children, posing with his family, and shaking a young boy's hand at a community event. "Real" men are asked to upload photos that express what strength means to them, most of which mimic the images of Mourning on the banner. Dove attempts to expand the meaning of strength in the same way that it attempts to redefine beauty; in both cases, it fails to challenge the cultural association of men with strength or women with beauty.

Conclusion

In the 11 years since Dove began its Campaign for Real Beauty, sales increased from $2.5 billion in 2004 to $4 billion in 2014. Dove claims that its marketing strategy that links the brand to social change works; according to Nancy Volk, a member of the Ogilvy creative team, "We found out that the women and men exposed to the [Campaign for Real Beauty] became much more interested in buying anything the brand was selling... that wasn't about, 'I'm so glad they put this in the shampoo.' That was about 'I really like what the brand is doing to the world. I want to put my dollars against what they are doing.'" (Touré 2015). It is unclear whether the brand has effected social change, even it if does confirm the belief that shopping is a form of social activism. But Dove's success has clearly influenced advertising and has contributed to the growth of pinkwashing. Companies such as Nike and Gap have run ad campaigns with "real", diverse women who do not conform to traditional beauty standards. Always, a brand of feminine hygiene products, produced a viral video in 2014 that criticizes how the phrase "Like a Girl" marginalizes young women, Verizon's "Inspire Her Mind" ad addresses how girls are steered away from science and engineering, Pantene's "Not Sorry" refutes women's need to apologize and celebrates girls as smart and capable, and Under Armour's "I Will What I Want" features female athletes overcoming odds and critics. It is clear that "empowerment" – typically directed at young girls – is a popular marketing strategy.

In brand culture, companies such as Dove enable consumers to freely create "authentic" identities, though they are channelled in a particular direction. Consumers are asked to critique brand culture as part of their experience of the brand, and in so doing, they support companies who are part of beauty culture and remain within the structure of spectacle where all experience is mediated. Dove's products are designed to help women feel more beautiful – to have soft skin, firm skin, wrinkle-free skin – at the same time that its Campaign for Real Beauty claims to challenge beauty culture. The campaign not only suggests that social change – the goal of feminism – is possible through consumption of Dove products, but implies that it can be achieved through individual rather than collective action. Girls and women are "empowered" by using products rather than working to change policies or practices. Empowerment is presented as an individual choice, one that shifts attention away from societal circumstances that create girls' low self-esteem in the first place. The Campaign for Real Beauty depicts culturally diverse images of women, but there is no discourse on the disparate effects of race, class, or ethnicity on beauty standards. Dove does not seek to create awareness of how the beauty industry produces oppressive bodily ideals, nor does it critique the concept of beauty and its importance for women (rather than men). Dove markets dissent as a means to build brand loyalty and increase commodity purchases, but not to challenge the centrality of beauty in women's lives. Dove may be the voice of corporate social responsibility, but its parent company Unilever also makes Axe body spray – whose advertising is based on the objectification of women– it markets SlimFast products for weight loss, and, in Asia, Unilever sells Fair and Lovely, a skin whitening cream.

Yet, Dove and other cause marketing relies on consumers who actively participate in creating meaning. Dove developed its Campaign for Real Beauty based on women's "authentic" dissatisfactions with their cultural representations, though their critique of beauty standards encourages women to channel their dissent by engaging with brands and purchasing products. Consumers are encouraged to create identities as "activists" or as "empowered", though these are filtered through disempowering practices of consumption. As our case history has illustrated, Dove soap cannot change the world.

12

The Prosumer in Consumer Culture: YouTube and *Annoying Orange*

The twenty-first century has been marked by an exponential leap in the commercialization of culture, as brands have become increasingly embedded in the fabric of everyday life. As we have seen in previous chapters, brands have become integral resources for the construction of personal and social identities. Consumers are invited to use brands to signify who they are, and in so doing, they produce something – whether a feeling, personal relation, or experience (Arviddson 2006, 68). In this way, consumers produce and sustain the immaterial (i.e. aesthetic, emotional, or social) qualities that form the basis of a brand's sign value. Their investment produces what Maurizio Lazzarato (1997) refers to as an "ethical surplus" – a social relation, shared meaning, or sense of belonging that was not there previously. This ethical surplus that constitutes a brand's sign value is what creates a brand tribe; moreover, because brands have both sign and exchange value, the ethical surplus generated can be monetized. As a result, advertising strategies attempt to insert brands into existing structures of communication and interaction. Douglas Ruskin and Juliet Schor (2009, 410–411) use the term "ad creep", to describe the spread of advertising throughout social space and cultural institutions – indeed, into every nook and cranny of life. Brands add sign value to the multitude of products, services, places, events, and experiences that define social life. In turn, they become sustained through everyday interactions as people use brands to define their identities and relate to one another.

In this chapter we further explore prosumption (introduced in Chapter 11) as we focus on how advertising fosters participatory engagement in the digital era. We address the relationship of consumption to the production of brand value by examining YouTube as a Web 2.0 platform where the boundaries between producers and consumers, professionals and amateurs, and advertising and entertainment have become blurred. We use the YouTube web series *Annoying Orange,* one of the first examples of the monetization of YouTube, as our case study. *Annoying Orange* allows us to consider the means that both social and economic value is extracted from prosumers, so that what appears to be creative play is contained and commodified. Arvidsson (2005, 244) suggests that brands work not by imposing meanings or messages, but by "enabling or empowering the freedom of consumers so that it is likely to evolve in particular directions". We suggest that by strategically managing the ethical surplus that consumers produce when they engage with brands, brand managers control and exploit the value created by prosumers.

Consumption, Prosumption, and Digital Culture

Ritzer and Jurgenson (2010) suggest that consumer society is giving way to prosumer society, marked by an implosion of production and consumption. They give examples of people who bus their own trays at restaurants, build furniture from IKEA, or even participate on reality television programmes: these practices rely on the active participation of consumers to create meaning and value. Playing advergames, participating in online contests and quizzes based on a product, or engaging in a brand experience at Niketown are similarly examples of prosumption. In other cases, such as the sharing of viral videos, entertainment and commerce merge to engage and harness the productive activity of consumers. Even the generation of "buzz" around products is a form of prosumption that helps create brand value. These are all forms of immaterial labour that exist outside of the wage structure; theorists such as Fuchs (2011) or Andrejevic (2009) see prosumption as immaterial labour that is exploited by capital, while others such as Terranova (2004) or Arvidsson (2006) assert that immaterial labour is free in the sense of being unpaid, but also, especially in the case of Internet users, consumers, or online gamers, because it involves creative autonomy that is beyond the control of capital. However, neither see the Internet as a site of non-hierarchical, participatory culture heralded by theorists such as Jenkins (Jenkins et al. 2013)

Prosumption can be explained in terms of a transactional model of communication, which in marketing terms is referred to as "value co-creation". As Zwick et al. (2008, 163) argue, the discourse of value co-creation works "with and through the freedom of the consumer", although consumption also occurs "in ways that allow for the emergence and exploitation of valuable forms of consumer labour" (Zwick et al. 2008, 163). The co-creation economy, they argue, is based on the expropriation of immaterial cultural, technological, social, and affective labour. Crucially, in this economy, consumers do not just co-create sign value when they engage with a product, but they also produce use and exchange value. For example, brands often rely on consumers to provide creative ideas and drive their innovations.

The Internet is crucial in the development of the "means of prosumption". As Arviddson (2006, 95) writes, all the strategies of brand management work on a continuum, from the creation of *brandscapes* or branded communities that guide consumers in certain directions and product placements that insert brands into milieus, to the saturation of the life-world, paralleled by micro-surveillance techniques such as trend-scouting or data mining. These techniques, as well as the branding principle in general, are intensified on the Internet. Since 2004, Web 2.0 has described practices on the Internet where users "freely" contribute but do not control content; moreover, its emergence heralded the digital revolution that has reshaped the economy. In 2005, YouTube emerged; in 2006, Facebook became available to anyone (rather than limited to college students); in 2007, Apple launched the iPhone and initiated smartphone/app culture; in addition, Twitter emerged as an independent platform, and Hadoop launched, which helped create the storage and processing power for big data (Friedman 2016). Now, everything is digitalized, and prosumers voluntarily contribute web content such as blogs, vlogs, tweets, Facebook posts, message boards, Instagrams, wikis, Tumblrs, Vimeos, or YouTube videos. Prosumers are also those less-active contributors who enter online contests, "like" posts on Facebook, or simply watch a YouTube video and add to its "views". In all cases, the prosumers who interact and engage with Web 2.0 form what Dallas Smythe (1977) refers to as an "audience-commodity" that is sold to advertisers as an assemblage of data.

Case History: *Annoying Orange* and the Prosumer

YouTube, a prime example of Web 2.0, was founded in 2005 as a platform that enabled amateur users to share videos online. By the summer of 2006, 100 million clips were viewed daily, with an additional 65,000 new videos uploaded every 24 hours (Wasko 2009, 374). YouTube quickly became part of one of the world's largest global media companies: Google bought it for the unprecedented sum of $1.65 billion in 2006, and since 2008, it has consistently been in the top 10 visited sites globally. As van Dijck (2013, 42) notes, Google's acquisition was about bringing in communities of users, and in less than a year, YouTube became a subsidiary of a firm whose core interest was not in content but "in the vertical integration of search engines with content, social networking, and advertising". Despite its early reputation for being a youthful alternative to mainstream media, YouTube has increasingly evolved from a site where ad-free, amateur videos were posted to a site dominated by commercialized, professional videos. However, as Jean Burgess and Joshua Green (2009a) remind us, this does not mean that YouTube was ever free of commercial concerns, or that amateur and professional media content, identities, and motivations are easily distinguished.

Annoying Orange illustrates the complexity around the distinction between "amateurs" and "professionals" in a context where prosumers have access to digital technologies and platforms on which to create and distribute their work. *Annoying Orange* is a series of animated videos initially posted to YouTube by an aspiring filmmaker, Dane Boedigheimer, who posted the first video on his YouTube channel, Gagfilms, in 2009. Like most YouTube content, each episode of *Annoying Orange* is no more than a few minutes long. Its simplest episodes feature an anthropomorphized orange (see Figure 12.1) who sits on

Figure 12.1 *Annoying Orange* is a computer-generated character made by combining the eyes and mouth of a human face and an orange

a kitchen counter and directs sophomoric jokes at different fruits, vegetables, and other foodstuffs. At a time when YouTube content still largely consisted of home videos created outside of professional contexts, it had higher production values than many of the videos posted on YouTube.

In contrast to popular conceptions that users post videos to YouTube largely for social reasons, as the site gained popularity, career-driven users who aspired to professions in the technical-creative or artistic-entertainment spheres constituted a segment of YouTube prosumers along with those who were motivated to use the site for entertainment or family purposes (Li, cited in van Dijck 2009). Despite participating in the "gift economy" of the Internet, there was likely a commercial imperative behind Boedigheimer's "free" display of his animation skills. When he posted the first video, he was working as a freelance filmmaker who made short promotional videos for online businesses. The home-made *Annoying Orange* videos posted on his Gagfilms YouTube channel directed attention to his fledgling video production business. In other well-known cases of "amateur" YouTube participants with professional motivations, the supposedly "real" YouTube vlogger LonelyGirl15, who appeared from 2006 to 2008, was eventually revealed to be the creation of professional filmmakers, and in 2008 aspiring musician Ernie Rogers (aka Iamo1234) downloaded his own guitar solos 10,000 times to boost his popularity. Currently, it is possible to purchase views from YouTube view-buying sites. Or, in a twist that revealed YouTube's growing commercialization, in 2011 aspiring singer Rebecca Black paid $4000 to a professional recording studio to produce an "amateur" video that would go viral.

According to van Dijck (2013, 52), as the popularity of sites for user-generated content such as YouTube began to soar in 2006, business practices shifted to mediate between aspiring professionals and audiences, not so much to turn every amateur into a professional as to "acknowledging the growing appeal of selling home-made material to audiences and media businesses". He adds that while YouTube nurtures the concept of amateur home-made content, the myth driving this concept is the popular "rags to riches" myth (2013, 53). Boedigheimer perpetuated this myth that belied his commercial aspirations and downplayed the labour involved in creating a network of engaged viewers who would interact with his work. According to Boedigheimer, commenting on a self-promotional YouTube vlog called "Danebo Exposed", his success was fortuitous. He claims that he initially only intended to make and upload one *Annoying Orange* video, but because of the overwhelming response, he took on a writing partner, Spencer Grove, and they went on to create more, and after six months they created a YouTube channel dedicated to *Annoying Orange* (as of June 2016 there were 390 videos). Mainstream media also helped reproduce the myth of the self-made man, as indicated in the *New York Times*, "Boedigheimer got the idea for *Annoying Orange* one night in 2009 when he was lying in bed… The next day, he bought an orange at a Food For Less supermarket and went to work in his kitchen, taping a segment with a Sony camera ad using software like Final Cut Pro to make a clip for YouTube" (Barnes 2011).

As this hagiographical account implies, the ideal YouTube user is an amateur motivated by a desire for personal expression and creativity rather than financial gain. According to Nick Salvato (2009), although YouTube – and its users – privilege the professional, the presentation of amateur status and the insistence that popularity "just happens" is part of the way YouTube masks its ideological work. YouTube presents itself as a platform that can propel amateurs to fame, but not as a site where fame is manufactured. Salvato (2009, 65) writes:

> the users whom YouTube invites to "broadcast [themselves]" regularly and consistently affirm the professional, produced and defined in tandem with and at the ultimate expense of the amateur; and the potent and credible alibi of democratization is precisely what allows such an affirmation. One index of this phenomenon is the extent to which performers with commercial ambitions—and, at times, corporate sponsorship—will use the cachet of the "homegrown" and the "grassroots," predicated on their capacity to confer authenticity, to advance their budding careers.

Early YouTube achieved its cultural cache from being a platform for sharing amateur videos; according to van Dijck (2013, 110–111), Google fostered YouTube's "youthful, rebellious image" as an alternative to television and mainstream media even as it began to push professional content and to adopt conventional broadcast strategies. Boedigheimer played along, even though after he posted the fifth video he formed a partnership with *The Collective Digital Studio*, a digital distribution company that provided him with an infrastructure of support, including hiring people to help him produce content (Karpel 2012).

The Collective Digital Studio was an entertainment management and production company whose stated purpose was to locate and develop creative talent across a multitude of media platforms. It demonstrated how, as van Dijck (2013, 52) notes, "video-sharing sites have quickly become the global rodeo for talent scouts: they provide a new link in the upwardly mobile chain of the commercially driven star system". The Collective inverted the traditional media model where television and films are used to build audiences;

their innovation was to deliver an audience that already existed on the Internet to traditional media. It functioned like the Hollywood studio system: it found up-and-coming Internet stars, and produced and distributed their content for television, while they retained full ownership of the property and licensed the broadcast rights to the networks. According to CEO Michael Green, "We are at our core a management company that is focused on building audience directly between creators and the rest of the audience. And third-party distributors become our partners, but we're not dependent on them" (Levine 2012).

While The Collective managed some traditional clients, its primary relationships were with YouTube content creators such as Boedigheimer. Once they identified potentially lucrative properties, The Collective helped its clients with monetization, technology, production, and audience development, and thus complicated their "amateur" status. While The Collective helped to extend the reach of the *Annoying Orange* brand to traditional media, the YouTube infrastructure also contributed to its development. When Boedigheimer was signed by The Collective, he became a "YouTube Star" who was invited into the YouTube Partnership programme, at which point YouTube protocols helped to boost *Annoying Orange's* popularity.

YouTube and the Construction of Popularity

Initially, Boedigheimer worked without remuneration to publicize the *Annoying Orange* videos, which resulted in more than a million views in three weeks, and more than 50 million views in six months. While it is difficult to ascertain the precise mechanisms by which a video goes from zero to a million views, the rapid popularity of *Annoying Orange* was likely assisted by Boedigheimer's pre-existent following, utilization of social media, support from The Collective, and the YouTube information management system. Before Boedigheimer came to YouTube, he had made animations on other file-sharing sites such as Metacafe. In addition, Boedigheimer did not just post videos. He also had Facebook and Twitter accounts devoted to *Annoying Orange* and made sure to keep followers aware of the videos. He describes his work in the following passage:

> I made it a rule for myself that I had to have a video released every Friday, and a new post on the social media pages every day. I just made sure to keep to that schedule, as well as interact with the audience by having contests, talking to them, and really keep them involved in the brand. (Karpel n.d.)

This is the labour that is invisible in accounts of *Annoying Orange* as a "viral" success, and this circuit of interactive media is what creates community and deepens investment in the brand. It was also a key strategy for The Collective, who encouraged him to engage with social media. According to partners Reza Izad and Dan Weinstein, "In our minds the key is audience. If you can build up a large enough audience to engage online with your property, you will be able to leverage that into many opportunities, with TV being only one of them" (Humphrey 2011).

YouTube is complicit in this strategy to grow online audiences. In fact, viewership is managed through YouTube's popularity mechanisms. The site directs viewer choices through referral systems, search functions, and ranking mechanisms. van Dijck (2013, 112) writes, "YouTube's interface design and its underlying algorithms select and filter content, guiding users in finding and watching certain videos out of the millions of uploads, for instance through buttons for 'most popular'." Even more significantly, Ding et al. (2011, 363) found that 4% of YouTube's users provide 73% of the videos, and YouTube algorithms favour certain users, so that "some uploaders are more popular than others, with more users viewing their uploaded videos". Thus, YouTube's recommendation system both creates and reinforces the popularity of videos posted by prosumers such as Boedigheimer. While theoretically anyone can "Broadcast Yourself", not all content is equally visible in the YouTube attention economy.

YouTube's genre categories also help to establish popularity. *Annoying Orange* fits into what is perhaps the most popular YouTube genre, comedy. Much like traditional media, the most popular types of content on YouTube are self-perpetuating rather than random, so that content that does not fit into an established "genre" will likely not become popular. Burgess and Green (2009b, 41) write about YouTube categories, "They are not representations of reality, but technologies of re-presentation. Because they communicate to the audience what counts as popular on YouTube, these metrics also take an active role in creating the reality of what's popular on YouTube: they are not only descriptive; they are performative."

There is an advantage for YouTube to highlight certain videos, specifically because of its YouTube Partnership Program. YouTube regularly seeks to professionalize user content, both with conferences that provide tips on how to become a YouTube Star, and with its Partnership programme. Soon after Google bought YouTube, YouTube invited the most popular participants to become "partners". Boedigheimer became a partner after six months, once the *Annoying Orange* videos accumulated 50 million views. In exchange for allowing advertisements that precede each view of an *Annoying Orange* episode or appear on the *Annoying Orange* channel, partners such as Boedigheimer receive a payment. While YouTube does not reveal specific advertising revenue, and participants are contractually bound not to reveal their income from YouTube ads, YouTube says that content creators get more than half, and many make thousands of dollars a month through advertising (Fowler 2010). Currently anyone who uploads a video can go to YouTube's monetization page and open an AdSense account, which allows them to insert ads into their videos. As Andrejevic (2009, 419) notes about YouTube's appropriation of labour power, "users are offered a modicum of control over the product of their creative activity in exchange for the work they do building up online community and sociality upon privately controlled network infrastructures". Boedigheimer's creativity is the source of the ethical surplus that is of value to marketers. While Boedigheimer, The Collective, and YouTube worked to establish popularity, their purpose was to use the ethical surplus created by *Annoying Orange* to create monetary value.

Creating an Ethical Surplus

As Adam Arvidsson (2005, 237) writes, a brand's "ethical surplus" provides both economic and social value. Boedigheimer created an ethical surplus by using his *Annoying Orange* YouTube channel as a revenue-generating source while extending the brand across Web 2.0 platforms such as Facebook, Twitter, Tumblr, Google + and Formspring, in effect creating and maintaining an "affinity community" of users who connect to his brand, while also providing a resource for marketers. According to Christian Fuchs (2008, 181), YouTube is an example of a business model that is based on combining the gift, which is free, with the commodity, which is profitable. YouTube provides "free" access to prosumers; not only do they provide content for the site, but as the number of users who visit the site grows, YouTube becomes more profitable as it attracts more advertisers. More importantly, the data generated by users who visit the site helps marketers accumulate information about their habits and behaviours, and thus more effectively target them. Children are one of the groups most heavily tracked by big data (Stecklow 2010), and young males form the core audience for *Annoying Orange*. For example, *Annoying Orange's* key demographic is males aged between 13 and 34 years (Hamilton 2012; Levine 2012). Because YouTube requires users to be 13 years old to get an account, it is possible that many *Annoying Orange* fans were younger.

The benefits of targeted online advertising were still being promoted to advertisers in May 2011, as witnessed by the Digital Content Newsfronts, a two-week showcase where online video publishers and distributors gathered advertisers to educate them on online advertising. The Collective paid for a banner campaign in *Adweek* that used *Annoying Orange* as a lure to advertise online advertising to advertisers. According to Michael Green, CEO of The Collective:

> The Annoying Orange recently achieved the milestone of streaming 1,000,000,000 views on YouTube and has also surpassed the 10,000,000 fan mark on Facebook. The ads were taken out to acknowledge these achievements and to remind marketers that television is not the only medium for reaching audiences of scale.(Cohen 2012a)

Annoying Orange demonstrated that YouTube, like traditional media, could reach audiences on a large scale. It also belied the commonly held belief that one of the problems with monetizing YouTube is that advertisers were reluctant to associate themselves with content produced by "amateurs" or that advertisers were not interested in the young male demographic presumed to constitute a large part of YouTube viewership (see Andrejevic 2009, 412). According to *TubeMogul*, Boedigheimer made more than $865,000 in advertising alone in 2012 (Hamilton 2012). This figure does not account for other revenue sources such as merchandise sales, phone apps, speaker's fees, or sponsorship deals, nor does it account for revenues that he received from the television series. According to Boedigheimer's manager, "when Dane puts up a [YouTube] show on Friday, by Monday it has a million and a half views. Any cable network would take those numbers" (Fowler 2010).

While monetization explains how the economic value of *Annoying Orange* was produced, the way *Annoying Orange* engaged its audience helps to illuminate how it produced social value. While very few studies of YouTube to date have done specific content analysis of videos to account for how they create affective bonds, it is instructive to look more closely at *Annoying Orange*. Like many of the most popular YouTube videos, *Annoying Orange* relied on crass humour, parody, and play with digital form. The *Annoying Orange* character heckles and cackles in the shrill voice of an 8-year-old boy (Boedigheimer's own voice, sped up). Its source of humour is what is typically thought of as children's humour: it comes from puns or a play on a character's name or appearance, such as "Hey Apple, you look fruity," calling a pumpkin "plumpkin", or making repetitive, annoying sounds. Like much YouTube humour, it does the cultural work of mischief, which John Hartley (2009, 130) describes as "no more than experimental engagement with peer groups and places" and is what he suggests young people today turn to in their leisure time. *Annoying Orange* "makes mischief" by using its anthropomorphic animation of inanimate objects to evoke the gleeful mayhem of the classic cartoons of the thirties. According to Boedigheimer, "Watching people get annoyed by something/someone is funny… Look at cartoon characters in the past – Bugs Bunny, Woody Woodpecker, Pepe Le Pew, etc…. a lot of their humour came from being annoying. It's a fun proven device to play with" (Cohen 2010).

The appeal of *Annoying Orange* may come precisely from its evocation of "distaste" that enables its adolescent audience to differentiate itself from adults who are often disturbed by both its form and content. Felix Gillette (2013) writes, "Annoying Orange, like Woody Woodpecker before him, is the ultimate children's antihero, blissed out on bad behaviour, hammering away at everything around him, laughing in the face of the world, and flouting the rules of adult decorum with total impunity." *Annoying Orange* updated and gave new cultural value to the once familiar synchro-vox technique, which one reviewer of Clutch Cargo referred to as "the stuff of nightmares", and "the single most disturbing thing I have seen in the world of animated children's programming in my entire life" (Sexton 2008). This feeling was exaggerated at the end of every episode when Orange typically yelled "Knife!" as Boedigheimer's hand entered the frame. A giant castrating knife or churning blender or pot of boiling water obliterated the anthropomorphized food, so that an ordinary everyday action, slicing vegetables or boiling pasta, became imbued with cruelty. Like the sadistic cartoons of the 1930s, *Annoying Orange* evoked the pleasure of chaos and disruption as it simultaneously evoked distaste and disdain. Many adult viewers had strong negative responses, as judged by the comments that follow videos. But for younger viewers, *Annoying Orange* appropriated the concept of "cool" that has become a mass phenomenon of consumer society. For instance, according to Arvidsson (2006, 73), "coolness", defined as an oppositional stance, works to transform political to private and apolitical forms of resistance in the collective production of meaning. Coolness is thus produced as an ethical surplus that appropriates and tames resistance and defiance, redirecting them in the service of the brand.

As *Annoying Orange* developed, its humour became more parodic, with spoofs of popular culture icons such as Lady Gaga, Rebecca Black, and public figures such as Barack Obama and Donald Trump. In 2011, in a move initiated by NextMovie, *Annoying Orange* provided a running critical commentary over the trailer for *Mission Impossible: Ghost Protocol*, much in the parodic style of the cult show *Mystery Science Theater 3000*. As Jenkins et al. (2012)

observe, parody is a powerful way to help web content spread. It is one of the ways that "audiences transform brands into resources for their own social interactions" (Jenkins et al. 2012, 207). Parody also spread *Annoying Orange's* fan base from children to adolescents and young adults whose sensibilities were more sophisticated. Most importantly, parodies that relied on shared cultural experiences, histories, and sensibilities enabled *Annoying Orange* to create an ethical surplus that was made available to marketers.

In addition to parodies, *Annoying Orange* made use of *webrities* to "provide pleasure to audiences who enjoy mapping links between different texts and recognizing when texts are referencing each other" (Jenkins et al. 2012, 28). While the most subscribed YouTube channels cover a range of familiar genres, YouTube Stars whose brands were developed within YouTube's social network dominate the comedy category (Burgess and Green 2009b, 60). The cross-promotions practised by Boedigheimer and other YouTube Stars helped to perpetuate this rather incestuous relationship. *Annoying Orange* illustrated the mutual reinforcement of YouTube popularity, with the most well-known performers referencing one another through their videos. For example, Annoying Orange appeared in Lucas Cruikshank's web series "Fred", and Cruikshank appeared the next day in "Annoying Orange vs. Fred!!!". Evan Ferrante from Take180.com appeared in "Close Encounters of the Annoying Kind", one day after Annoying Orange appeared in Ferrante's video "Not Tom Cruise". Similarly, three of the band Weezer's members appeared in the episode "Wazzup 3: Bonsai Tree"; the episode was both a spoof of the popular "Whassup" Budweiser commercials and part of Weezer's promotion of their album *Hurley*. And James Caan became the first well-known actor to appear on the series in the episode called "Jalapeno", most probably to bring exposure to his website that promotes independent film, Openfilm.com (Cohen 2010).

Extracting Social and Economic Value from *Annoying Orange*

Viewer engagement with *Annoying Orange* was not only created internally, but was carefully cultivated across social media, and it is this cultivation that allowed marketers to extract social and economic value. By 2014, there were more than 11 million "likes" on Facebook and more than 200,000 Twitter followers, in addition to the billion YouTube views. As Lange (2009, 71) points out, attention, at a basic interactional level, is a managed achievement that requires work. If Boedigheimer could not post a weekly video, he (or some representative) organized a contest or made some effort to interact with viewers. *The Annoying Orange* website also encouraged involvement, with questions, contests, and links to the Facebook and Twitter posts, and there was a plethora of video responses and parodies of *Annoying Orange* videos on YouTube. While all consumptive activity is productive in that it generates surplus value, prosumers actively build community when they post their own parodic videos or post comments in response to *Annoying Orange*. A typical *Annoying Orange* video evoked responses or comments that numbered in the tens of thousands.

The level of viewer engagement became apparent when in September 2010, Boedigheimer ran a photo submission contest on the *Annoying Orange* Facebook page. In just over six hours there were 25,000 submissions, after which Facebook lost its capacity to hold any more photos on the page. This is the work that is done by brand managers such as Boedigheimer – they create affective communities whose tastes can be tracked by marketers. Brands are built through this investment in media culture. As Arvidsson (2005, 245) writes, brand management works "by defining the contours of what the brand *can* mean, by creating inter-textual links in media culture".

It is because of this high level of viewer involvement that corporations make deals with YouTube Stars such as Boedigheimer to pitch their products. According to Caroline Giegrich, director of innovation at Initiative, which was one of the first agencies to run a successful YouTube Stars campaign:

> What these YouTubers have proven is that they have engaged viewers – they comment, they talk on the YouTuber's Facebook page, on Twitter. The brands want millions of views, but they also want engaged viewers. If they're engaged with the stars, clearly they are engaged with the brand – it means someone is not just seeing an ad and forgetting about it. (Slutsky 2010)

Engagement marketing that encourages consumers to connect with a brand on a personal level through participation and interaction is now standard advertising practice, and *Annoying Orange* is a prime example of how this form of marketing works by developing and negotiating social networks.

With the help of The Collective, *Annoying Orange* expanded laterally across YouTube and vertically across media platforms to create a community that coalesced around it to provide both social and economic value. It became an intertextual commodity that both structured and enabled the meaning-making activity of prosumers who engage with YouTube as entertainment. Marshall (2002) examines the way that users' emotional investments are harnessed by the highly interactive intertextual commodity that has permeable bounds across media forms, so that what is marketed is not so much a product as a brand that provides a context for consumption. Nintendo was one of the first brands to engage in this form of cross-marketing, where the video game Super Mario Brothers was also sold as a T-shirt, watch, breakfast cereal, doll, magazine, snack, and lunchbox, to name a few, all of which created a structured context for kids to "freely" interact with the brand. Marshall (2002, 74) writes, "what is being played is an elaborate dance between the techniques of containing and servicing the desires of the 'audience' and the audience itself venturing into unserviced and uncommercial areas of cultural activity". Similarly, Boedigheimer opened a gaming channel on YouTube, has a Minecraft server, a series of web videos called *Danebo Exposed*, a vlog, a blog, a Danebo website, the Gagfilms website, a spin-off series, video game applications, and the *Annoying Orange* channel. In addition, there are a range of *Annoying Orange* products, such as toys, clothes, Halloween costumes, and calendars. During the 2011 Christmas season, Toys R Us promoted the toys with a dedicated brand page on its website, along with placing the first *Annoying Orange* web video on its page. The *Annoying Orange* toys were also promoted in a national multimedia advertising campaign that aired on Nickelodeon, Disney, and the Cartoon Network. By 2012, toys, clothing, and merchandise were sold at JCPenney, Toys R Us, Target, RadioShack, and Amazon, along with stickers, wallpaper and ringtones, mp3s, and podcasts on iTunes. There was even a Christmas music album released on iTunes. *Annoying Orange* was a prime example of an intertextual commodity that created a web of interconnections that organize social life around the brand and circumscribe its meaning.

Moreover, The Collective worked with Boedigheimer to produce *The Annoying Orange* as a television series that began airing on the Cartoon Network in June 2012. The Collective financed the pilot for what has become *The High Fructose Adventures of Annoying Orange* to short-circuit the long Hollywood development process that sometimes can take years to refine. Throughout the year and a half that the programme was in development, Boedigheimer used the *Annoying Orange* web series as a focus group to test new characters and ideas. The resultant television programme combined both "webrities" and celebrities. The only human character was YouTube Star Toby Turner, while the voices of well-known Hollywood names – Malcolm McDowell, Jeffrey Tambor, Jane Lynch, Billy Dee Williams, and Tim Curry – animated the characters. It was written and directed by two industry veterans, Emmy award winning writer Tom Sheppard, and producer/director Conrad Vernon. The show premiered on 11 June 2012 and had 2.6 million viewers, the highest-rated programme among viewers aged 2–11, 9–14 (a separate category), and all boys (Cohen 2012b). The programme was nominated for a Creative Arts Emmy in 2012.

YouTube has begun to expand to compete with television, both by exporting its own indigenous content to television and by mining television talent to produce its own serialized content. YouTube content can be viewed on television screens in lieu of scheduled programming, it has recruited producers, performers, and programmers from traditional media to create content for more than 100 YouTube channels, and it offers paid subscriptions to watch full-length television programmes. Moreover, mainstream media gains traction from its association with YouTube content. In addition to the studio-sanctioned critique of *Mission Impossible* mentioned above, Paramount Pictures hired Boedigheimer to produce an *Annoying Orange* video tied to the release of *Madagascar 3*, while Relativity Films employed him to produce a video that coincided with the release of *Mirror, Mirror*. Their idea was to "extend engagement with the film in a way that doesn't feel like a traditional ad" (Chemielski 2012).

The migration of content on YouTube works both ways, from professional media to YouTube, and from YouTube to mainstream media. *Annoying Orange* illustrated this permeability of media forms as it spread into popular culture, and as it transformed from a YouTube web series to a traditional television programme. *Annoying Orange*, and similar videos popular on YouTube, provide free research and development for media acquisition firms such as The Collective. Already assured of a following, these shows are less risky enterprises for ratings-wary networks. The different forms of the intertextual commodity work in tandem, together creating communities who interact with the brand. While the specific ways in which viewers interact with the brand remain indeterminate, it is their production of meaning that creates an ethical surplus in the service of the brand. In the end, though, YouTube, The Collective, and The Cartoon Network reap the benefits. In 2012, Green, CEO of The Collective, stated that *Annoying Orange* was a multimillion-dollar property but his goal was to make it one billion through a combination of YouTube, television, and merchandising (Graham 2012). As van Dijck (2009, 53) writes, "The growing role of UGC platforms as intermediaries between amateurs and professionals, volunteers and employees, anonymous users and stars, can hardly be conceived apart from 'old media' conglomerates power to select, promote and remunerate artistic content." UGC is firmly locked into the commercial dynamics of the mediascape. The dangers of this arrangement were illustrated when Boedigheimer's business relationship with The Collective broke down in 2014, after he was sued in 2013 by a North Dakota advertising agency for stealing their talking orange idea. Though the case with the advertising agency was settled, Boedigheimer initiated his own lawsuit against The Collective, arguing that he had not been paid since 2014. As a result, since then, while *Annoying Orange* still has a strong web presence, the television series went off the air. The Collective, on the other hand, in 2015 was purchased by a German media conglomerate, ProsiebenSat1and was rebranded as Studio 71 the following year. In 2016, the combined group generated 3.5 billion YouTube views per month (Spangler 2016).

Conclusion

Annoying Orange indicated the interrelationship of YouTube, broadcast television, and commercial culture, as well as the relationship between brands and prosumers in digital culture. The "success" stories of web series such as *Annoying Orange* encourage prosumers to provide content for YouTube. Those that gain significant numbers of views attract advertising and, perhaps, provide content for traditional media. They may even "partner" with firms such as *The Collective*. Yet YouTube, initially celebrated as a site for participatory culture, has developed more along the lines of traditional media that excludes participants from decision-making processes and control over practices that concern them. Christian Fuchs (2011), for one, critiques the notion of participation by noting that the lion's share of revenues garnered from online advertising on YouTube belongs to Google shareholders (in 2011, there were 18 human and corporate legal persons who owned 98.8% of the stock) rather than those who produce content. Rather, YouTube is a social factory that reproduces relations of capital and distinguishes between "the haves" – those who profit – and the "have-nots" – those who "participate" by providing free labour in exchange for creative control over content, but whose work, in the guise of play, provides access to data about users' behaviours, tastes, and preferences that in turn furthers the aims of capital.

Boedigheimer began posting videos as an ordinary user, albeit one who had some storytelling and animation skills, and he was not compensated for his work. With the help of The Collective, he became a "professional" who formed part of the commercialized media system. Yet, even as YouTube has become increasingly professionalized, both "amateurs" and "professionals" continue to coexist on YouTube, each legitimating the other. YouTube relies on perceptions that it is a democratic site for participatory culture where amateurs can share their creative practices. In so doing, it perpetuates the myth that with hard work (and a bit of luck) amateurs can be financially rewarded and propelled to fame. However, few of those who post content on YouTube make a living, and as Boedigheimer's experience illustrates, real wealth and power remains concentrated elsewhere. Overall, *Annoying Orange* reinforced the deeply embedded power structure of traditional media.

While YouTube began an as alternative to watching television, it is now a highly lucrative arm of the media industry. Increasingly it has adopted centralized strategies designed to shape and direct users' experiences. YouTube has become a tastemaker. Its structuring of taste may not be entirely conventional; it may, as in the case of *Annoying Orange*, create the affect of "distaste" to engage an adolescent audience that defines itself against notions of refinement and decorum. As with traditional media, engagement with audiences is solely for monetization by extending the reach of advertising. The problem is that, as Arvidsson (2010, 252) concludes, when an ethical surplus is filtered through a brand, "it comes to work against the productive potential of the social, on which it ultimately builds". As a result, the productive potential of prosumption becomes channelled into consumption, so that agency is circumscribed rather than augmented.

Conclusion

This book has been an investigation of advertising and consumer culture. Each chapter has provided a case history that illuminates how our cultures have operated within and have been articulated by the quite elaborate techniques of marketing and advertising. This concluding chapter is designed to identify the key insights that the various case histories have generated. These collected images and campaigns of the past structures of advertising help us see the continuities and constancies of both advertising itself and its active intervention in the shape of our contemporary culture.

What follows is a brief but vital investigation of the points of intersection that the case histories provide, with the goal of categorizing significant indices of the present and future organization of advertising and promotional culture. Advertising operates as a meaning-system for our cultures as it converts ideas and ideologies into the meaning of our objects, experiences, services, and relations. We have identified four themes that link our case histories but also help us understand how this meaning system has informed the past, the present, and the future of our worlds.

Imagining the Future

When we look in the mirror, each of us sees not our individual self but an image. That image is transformed by our own emotions, conceptions of who we are, and sometimes ideas about who we would like to be. We sometimes see a younger version of ourselves, an idealized model or celebrity version of who we might like to be, or maybe an older, tired version of our present self. And sometimes we see a face with blemishes or some other aspect that we would like to change and transform. In all these cases, advertising has likely played a role in stimulating fantasies of who we are and who we want to be. Throughout this book, our case histories have underlined how advertising provides a transformative discourse for the self and in so doing, provides pathways for the future. In Chapter 2, we described the emergence of a therapeutic ethos in the nineteenth century, a world view that legitimated the morality of personal fulfilment and gratification, and thus laid the groundwork for advertising to offer products that promised to better the self. Our case study of patent medicines illustrated how advertising presented a negating image of the self whose physical, emotional, or spiritual ailments could be remedied by a product. This self-improvement ethos of advertising articulated possible futures attainable through consumption. While our study of patent medicines focused on the United States, our case history of Nike in Chapter 8 took a global approach to describe how the concept of the individual self could be linked to products as a visible pathway to a fitter version, a new self whose ultimate reward was being in a continuous journey of self-betterment. We "just do it".

Advertising to children has also been a major way for advertisers to imagine the future through the discourse of transformation. Our case history of breakfast cereal in Chapter 5 described how its origins were connected to the therapeutic ethos: i.e., cereal was initially promoted as a product that would rejuvenate the self. Our study further indicated how advertisers used children to transform household morning rituals, originally by making cereal part of healthy family living, then moving to its later incarnation as a "fun" product that would lead to family happiness.

In the most strategic and direct way, advertising to children aims to create a viable market for a product into the future. Our Chapter 4 study of Camel cigarettes touched upon an example of how advertising to children enables advertisers to imagine their own future. Our discussion of Camel cigarettes discerned how in the 1990s, Camel was attempting to build a future market by illustrating their ads with an animated, "cool" Joe Camel character that appealed quite pointedly to young children who they hoped would become smokers. Advertising encouraged youthful consumers to collectively imagine a pathway to the future, though in this case, the association of a harmful product with "coolness" was a problematic manner of transforming the self.

Advertising and promotional culture continue to play thematically in this space of constructing future scenarios and possibilities for the individual. The expansion of self-branding via online culture explored in Chapter 10 describes the proliferation of a neo-liberal ethic of self-improvement. Branding the self perhaps expresses the way in which this imagining-the-future theme is powerfully present for both famed personalities (via endorsements of products like perfumes), star athletes (via endorsements for cigarettes or Nike products), or the micro-celebrities of YouTube that our book identifies in Chapter 12 on the marketing and promotion of *Annoying Orange*.

Imagining the future thematically is advertising's way of producing the wonder of possibility and the magic of transformation. We can see it consistently in our politics, as we developed in Chapter 11 on the successful production of Obama's online campaign of hope and the meme-like movement of the "Yes We Can" slogan. As an industry, it is perhaps advertising's main work in society to induce consumers to see the present as incomplete, but always with the possibility of being augmented by an advertised and promoted product or service.

Tribalism/Market Segmentation

The sense of belonging is a psychological, political, and cultural condition that shapes our experience of the everyday. Families, nations, gender, and ethnicity act as perhaps some of our larger and dominant belonging paradigms. These categories of belonging are nonetheless fabricated. National borders are geopolitical structures and, over time, they subsume previous borders and boundaries and these constructs became progressively real and tangible through a regular promotion of new national identities. If there is a cultural trope that can define the last 50 years in a broadly defined Western culture, it is that gender is a construct beyond biology. Gender is yet another form of positional identity that we invest with greater or lesser meaning, but which we all inhabit in a relational way. Notions of ethnicity are also convertible; and the definition of family is an equally moving identity marker that mutates in terms of inclusiveness, legal definition, and even in its extended use as a metaphor of belonging.

No matter how paradigms of belonging shift, advertising has attempted to tap into the desire for connection throughout the last two centuries. Advertising endeavours to wed the idea of belonging to something material and tangible to produce value for a product, service, or experience. In so doing, it augments that value of the collective identity itself. In the twentieth century, advertising became more adept at using differences to establish the link between products and people, a technique that could be characterized as identity resonance. From original mass-market campaigns, advertising (through its own research into psychology, demographics, psychographics and psychometrics) became better at defining how difference produced distinct markets or market segments. Consumer culture has always played on this idea of difference, and in early incarnations advertising stoked the desire to transform the self into an identity of belonging to a richer class fraction. Our case histories allowed us to identify the elaborate nuances of this simultaneous production of a desire to belong and a desire to differentiate in an identifiable way. Wealth and social status, for example, typified forms of emulative belonging that advertising images could convey. Advertising over the course of the last 150 years has blended its market-segmentation approach with the other patterns of belonging to generate a form of contemporary tribalism.

This new tribalism is at least partially built on how we attach meaning to things, but also how we feel both emboldened and empowered when our attachments are emulated and supported by others. The new tribalism that advertising and promotional culture has sanctioned has fostered equally new configurations of identity in our contemporary world.

This structure of emulative belonging and the outlines of a new tribalism can be seen in our case history of the department store in Chapter 3 where individuals were invited into various sensoria of possible reconstructions of their domestic identities, and through clothing, household décor, and other accoutrements were invited to modify their self-presentations. Similarly, cigarettes in the early twentieth century signified both masculinity and modernity, and once the market expanded to women, they provided social identities for independent modern women. One can see a similar dynamic at play in the promotional emergence of the international company IKEA, which we discuss in Chapter 7. Our case history illuminates how aspects of design similarly facilitate imaginings of social identities, through the layouts of stores themselves, the marketing of inexpensive yet aesthetically pleasing products, and a socially responsible corporate identity that appeals to a specific market segment.

Where advertising gained a level of leadership in this new tribalism can best examined in our Chapter 6 case history on the selling of Volkswagen: from an original mass production/mass belonging form of promotion in pre-war Nazi Germany, Volkswagen in the 1960s constructed an anti-consumer consumer tribe through brilliant in-the-know advertising. "Think Small" countered the large and luxury direction of car promotion and production of the 1950s and offered the Beetle a way for a counterculture to demarcate their collective identity difference beyond class.

The Nike campaigns discussed in Chapter 8 demonstrated the global nature of brand tribes that transcend cultural and national boundaries. Nike illustrates how consumers use brands to create community and express identity that goes beyond national boundaries. In Chapter 10 on self-branding, we can see how particular celebrities construct stylistically diverse identities and resell them through perfumes, a complex technique of drawing consumers in to imagine that their very individual decisions on personal comportment are somehow linked to these idealized celebrity images.

The Dove campaign detailed in Chapter 11 provided a new and different way in which a product can connect to a market segment defined by a politico-cultural agenda. Its ethics-based advertising campaign invited women to express their political predispositions by both purchasing Dove products for beauty and by connecting to a Dove-led cause that celebrated a wider conception of beauty and difference than that promulgated by mainstream media and culture.

Our case history concerning politics in Chapter 9 presented the development of some of the most elaborate techniques of connection, belonging, and differentiation. Political advertising is often all about identifying one's allegiance to a party, an individual leader or a political issue. It is a battle of differentiation at the same time as it depends on building a large enough coalition of tribes to gain a majority. Obama's campaign of 2008 and elaborated in 2012 identified how to cultivate that sense of belonging and connection via online culture and social media. If there is an insight to gain from the 2016 Presidential election it is about how political promotion has gained in sophistication related to tribalism and its advertising sister, market segmentation. Donald Trump's campaign, through its sophisticated deployment of online psychometrics, structured appeals that led people to be more emotionally invested in his candidacy. There is no question that his tribalist political campaign created a country more visibly divided into antagonistic collectives. Advertising and promotional culture are not necessarily the source for divisions of collective belonging. Nonetheless, the advertising industry has seen the economic value in constructing distinctive and visible patterns of groups, and actively built the fibres of connection that both held these groups into markets and differentiated products' images to further consolidate our now new generation of tribalism.

Participation/Prosumption

In some ways, when someone uses the incredibly common phrase "I love this [fill in name of product, programme, service or experience]", usually with an exclamation mark, they are identifying an investment of the self. It can be an overstatement and an exaggeration of this investment, but it is nonetheless a testimonial to what we see as valuable and worth sharing with others. In the most basic way, this testimonial is the beginning of how the individual is part of the chain of promotion and advertising. It demarcates the current promotional economy of online culture and social media. Our process of liking and sharing, our commenting on tweets, and our moments of visible enthusiasm through texts and emojis on Facebook or Instagram are the noticeable signs of our own forms of extending the value of meaning – the promotion – of anything else we have seen. These activities are also the source for the information economy itself and its connection to advertising as our activities are collected as data and then calibrated to intersect with various products that are then re-shared with us often as if they are part of this same stream/wall/feed of likes and shares by others. Our activity imbricates us well and truly into the advertising and promotional universe; our level of engagement and investment makes us all the new town criers of our connected online world.

This declaration of love should not be considered negative or abnormal. We, as individuals, are participating. Advertising has worked very hard over the last century to build this sense of engagement and participation, and it represents one of the central thematic structures of the industry, both in the past and into the future. When this participation is related to a product and when that endorsement can be circulated more widely through a follow-on advertisement or commercial, it has a certain authenticity that is highly prized and valued. When participation is via celebrity brand ambassadors as we detailed in our case history of self-branding in the perfume industry in Chapter 10, it articulates a connection to the individual and their appeal to a potential audience of users, but it is less participatory and more passive.

The push for participation and engagement is often a game of authenticity in the advertising industry. As we chronicled in Chapter 4, cigarette endorsements made by celebrities and sports figures associated an unhealthful product with health and vitality; similarly, the enthusiastic participation of medical doctors mixed the institutional value of a health professional with massively false claims and linked this participatory approach back to patent medicine's use of endorsements/testimonials we explored in Chapter 2. We took a different approach in Chapter 8, where we showed how Nike's use of endorsements by star athletes, particularly Michael Jordan, helped to legitimate and authenticate their product by both providing brand value to the other.

In the advertising of breakfast cereal in the twentieth century that we explored in Chapter 5, we described how promotions were used to make children more engaged in the brand: by sending box tops for toys or colouring books, they showed their investment in the product and, as in the contemporary collection of online data, gave the advertiser very valuable market information. Our case history on politics in Chapter 9 pointed to the different ways that citizens/voters could declare their support for a candidate: a poster, a bumper sticker, a lapel pin, and, in a more contemporary reconfiguration, an online sharing or declaration of support are all forms of participatory engagement. We note that by sharing advertised images of politicians and parties, potential voters extend political advertising in an effective and authentic way.

Participatory directions in advertising aim to ensure that a product is appropriated by consumers and becomes integral to their individual identities. Part of the Volkswagen moment in the 1960s explored in Chapter 6 was to make the Beetle and the VW van part of a lifestyle that helped defined the individual and/or the tribe. Advertising and promotion then were a form of interactive communication for the co-creation of the meaning of the product.

A product's identity thus became at least partly about how people used it and hopefully expressed that use to others. In many ways, this co-creative participation defines the IKEA experience: as we explored in Chapter 7, the actual building of the furniture with time and an Allen key has been a factor in how IKEA has had a closer connection to its consumers.

The expanding zenith of participation is studied in Chapter 11, which details the ways the Dove Real Beauty campaign relied on viral advertising and engagement with their website, and in Chapter 12 that explored the development of the Annoying Orange brand. Online culture has produced a generation of what is called user-generated content (UGC). YouTube has been instrumental in creating environments where individuals are simultaneously producers, consumers, and promoters. The current generation of beauty and cosmetic stars online, for instance, are these prosumers: they are individuals who simultaneously produce content, consume products, and provide advice on how to use the products that they are advertising. Prosumption blends promotion, production, and consumption in a highly obvious display of complicity in promotional culture.

The process of products becoming extensions of the meaning of ourselves is not new. These kinds of intimate connections are as ancient as craft knowledge and how our identities have always been linked to the objects we make, the tools we use, and the food we create. Advertising and promotional culture have simply become better able to produce a form of communicative link to how we use objects to make our lives meaningful and how we like to express that meaningfulness and connection to others.

Blurring Advertising and Entertainment – Leading the Attention Economy

When something changes in our environment, we are distracted and look at the new event. If we hear a plane or see it in the sky, we are drawn away from what we had been doing and observe this new event. This general notion of distraction is a key theme that our book has identified through its case histories. In other words, advertising could be defined as fundamentally a very heuristic yet still refined technique for drawing our attention. Our work in this book is a nuanced exploration of the leading edge of the attention economy. Advertising identifies our continuous struggle over meaning, significance, and value: we are challenged through advertising to recalibrate the value of things, the significance of a service, and the actual meaning of all the various commodities that come alive partially through advertising in our lives.

Part of the reason we have difficulty assigning meaning in the attention economy is that advertising, which often leads the struggle for our attention, is by its very practices very successful at blurring the lines of identification. Any advertisement, quite obviously, is not the object or the service: it is text and/or image; it ranges from voice-over and explanation to simply an activity or experience. Many types of advertising resemble storytelling: they generally replicate the forms of narrative, or provide dramatic and entertaining communication that we have been drawn to through popular culture. An advertisement in the most condensed form tries to entertain by making us laugh or cry or, at the very least, participate in an experience.

What is evident in our case histories is that this objective of blurring advertising with entertainment and other cultural forms is endemic to the history of advertising. As we noted in Chapter 2, patent medicines were often peddled in travelling medicine shows, and Lydia Pinkham even had a song that advertised her product. In Chapter 3, we saw that department stores – the twentieth-century dens of consumer culture – from their beginnings have regularly produced show-piece windows that merged art and commerce, while in-store entertainment events turned stores into centres of social life. Shopping remains one of the top recreational activities in many countries, and part of this phenomenon is related to the sophisticated way in which ambient forms of promotion and advertising both distract and entertain. In a similar fashion, our Chapter 5 case history explored ambient advertising campaigns for cereal that were aimed at children. We noted that hundreds of radio and television programmes were wholly sponsored and owned by the cereal companies themselves. In that case, the line between advertising and entertainment was completely blurred for more than 50 years. With the limited regulation in much of online culture, a similar pattern of blurring and ambient promotion occurs in children-related videogames and other forms of entertainment. Indeed, our Chapter 12 case history works through this divide between advertising and entertainment that is a regular feature of YouTube. Products are part of the programme, as YouTube Stars often sell a panoply of products under the guise of being an authentic individual expressing their creativity in the service of their loyal fan community.

It is a common phenomenon that when we watch our news or get our entertainment on mobile phones and other online devices, or when we click on something that has attracted us, it is predated by an advertisement. As with television and radio, we have now naturalized and normalized the symbiotic relationship of advertising, news, and entertainment. In many cases, we find it difficult to discern the difference between the promotional information and the supposed news or entertainment content. Stylistically, they often resemble each other and in terms of quality, the advertisement often far exceeds the shared content. Equally interesting, the organization of our content online often resembles the brevity that advertising messages have perfected over the last century as we have chronicled in the case histories of this book: we now click and migrate our minds from one short-attention-span piece of news or entertainment to the next as we navigate our social media–generated "news" feed.

The implications of this breakdown and blurring of content and the insinuation of promotional content into the melange has become increasingly serious in contemporary culture. The attention economy operates under this wider promotional aesthetic across genres, and perhaps the biggest implication of this content blur occurs in our relationship to news and politics. In the 2016 Brexit referendum campaign in the United Kingdom (where Britons voted to leave the European Union) and in the 2016 Presidential election where Donald Trump was elected President of the United States, the blurring of fact and fiction became endemic to our politics. Promotional aesthetics' migration to online culture matched the overwhelming way people depend on social media for their information. Fake news, in its production of techniques of directed promotional persuasion, is one of the outcomes of these rounds of unpredictable politics and the now normal blurring in the attention economy of fact, fiction, persuasion, promotion, and advertising. The blur of fact and fiction, which has had its natural and nurturing home in advertising and promotion, has at minimum been an influence on producing a new political tribalism internationally. The exchange and movement of promotionally stylized fictionalized information distances individuals from each other and is leading to unpredictable, if not dangerous, political and cultural consequences.

Final Thoughts

This book and its case histories hopefully provide a valuable map for understanding how these four themes that have been generated by advertising and promotional culture operate in our everyday, highly mediatized lives. Advertising has produced a prevalent and powerful discourse around *imagining the future* and it has been massively influential in how we imagine and value ourselves. Advertising identifies possibility and transformation, and this communication of potential has dovetailed into our desires for self-improvement, if not social and political improvement. As we have discussed in our Conclusion, there is a new *tribalism* that is emerging that is at least connected to the advertising industry's very sophisticated techniques of increasingly targeting and segmenting our cultures into distinct markets and ensuring that differentiated promotional messages reach only those identified individuals. Over its long arc in the production and communicating of meaning, advertising and promotional culture has cultivated a distinctly developed and nuanced form of ***prosumption/participation*** in our everyday worlds. From the co-creating online personality to the way in which individuals extend and promote – essentially do the advertising work – through their liking and sharing of content and stories related to products, services, and experiences, we are expanding the way in which we actively inhabit a hybridized and connected world to these promoted products. In a sense, each of these themes is a component in how advertising and promotion have become the avant-garde of the ***attention economy blur*** – both historically, as we have seen in our case histories, and increasingly in its new iteration and formations in online and social media sites.

Advertising distracts, but it also attracts and allures. Our book has explored this fascinating connecting communicative juggernaut. The four themes we have listed in our Conclusion perhaps even acknowledge our imbrication in advertising and promotional culture: along with the title of our book, they are our efforts at **branding** our message in the hopes that our readers will take these ideas and their implications for even further and deeper analytical inquiry.

References

Aaker, J. 2010. "Obama and the Power of Social Media and Technology". *The European Business Review*, May–June 2010. Online at: http://faculty-gsb.stanford. edu/aaker/pages/documents/TEBRMay-June-Obama.pdf

Aaker, D.A. and Joachimsthaler, E. 2000. *Brand Leadership: Building Assets in an Information Economy*. New York: Simon and Schuster.

Abelson, Elaine. 1989. *When Ladies Go A-Thieving: Middle Class Shoplifters in the Victorian Department Store*. Oxford: Oxford University Press.

Ackerman, Frank. 1997. "Overview Essay: History of Consumer Society". In *The Consumer Society*, edited by Neva Goodwin, Frank Ackerman and David Kiron. New York: Island Press.

Adbrands.net. n.d. *Dove*. Online at: http://www.adbrands.net/us/dove_us.htm

Advertising Age. 1999. "Ad Age Advertising Century: Top Ten Slogans", 29 March. Online at: http://adage.com/article/special-report-the-advertising-century/ad-age-advertising-century-top-10-slogans/140156/

Advertising Age Encyclopedia of Advertising. 2003. "RJ Reynolds". Online at: http:// adage.com/article/adage-encyclopedia/r-j-reynolds-tobacco-reynolds-american/

AdSlogans. 2016. "Advertising Slogan Hall of Fame". Online at: http://www.adslogans.co.uk/site/pages/gallery/id-walk-a-mile-for-a-camel.8372.php

Althusser, Louis. 1970. *On Ideology* [translated by Ben Brewster]. New York: Verso Books.

Andrejevic, M. 2009. "Exploiting YouTube: Contradictions of User-Generated Labor". In *The YouTube Reader*, edited by Pelle Snickars and Patrick Vonderau. Stockholm: National Library of Sweden, 406–423.

Anderson, A. 2000. *Snake Oil, Hustlers, and Hambones: The American Medical Show*. Jefferson, NC: McFarland & Company.

Anonymous. 1950. "Wayne for Camels". *The Pop History Dig*. Online at: http://www. pophistorydig.com/?p=5369

Applegate, E. 1998. *Personalities and Products: A Historical Perspective on Advertising in America*. Westport, CT: Greenwood Press.

Arndt Anderson, H. 2013. *Breakfast: A History*. Lanham, MD: Rowman & Littlefield.

Arvidsson, A. 2005. "Brands: A Critical Perspective". *Journal of Consumer Culture* 5 (2): 235–258.

Arviddson, Adam. 2006. *Brands: Meaning and Value in Media Culture*. New York: Routledge.

Associated Press. 2013. "Number of Active Users at Facebook Over the Years", 1 May. Online at: http://news.yahoo.com/number-active-users-facebook-over-230449748.html

Banet-Weiser, S. 2012. *Authentic: The Politics of Ambivalence in Brand Culture*. New York: New York University Press.

Barnes, B. 2011. "Animated Fruit with Ambition". *New York Times*, 2 October. Online at: http://www.nytimes.com/2011/10/03/business/media/annoying-orange-tries-for-a-tv-career.html?pagewanted=all

Barnes-Brus, Tori. 2014. "Advertising Motherhood with the Lydia E. Pinkham Medicine Company". *Radcliffe Institute for Advanced Study* at Harvard University.

Bartholomew, A. and O'Donohoe, S. 2003. "Everything under Control: A Child's Eye View of Advertising". *Journal of Marketing Management* 19 (4): 433–457.

Baudrillard, Jean. 1970. *The Consumer Society: Myths and Structures* [translated by Sage Publications]. London: Sage.

Baudrillard, Jean. 1995. *Simulacra and Simulation* [translated By Sheila Faria Glaser]. Ann Arbor, MI: University of Michigan Press.

Baumann, Zygmont, quoted in Sparke, Penny. 2013. *An Introduction to Design and Culture 1900 to the Present*. New York: Routledge, 112.

Bell, Daniel. 1976. *The Cultural Contradictions of Capitalism*. New York: Basic Books.

Benson, Susan Porter. 1979. "Palace of Consumption and Machine for Selling: The American Department Store, 1880–1940". *Radical History Review* 21: 199–221.

Beschloss, M. 2016. "The Ad that Helped Reagan Sell Good Times to an Uncertain Nation". *New York Times*, 7 May.

Bingham, A. Walker. 1994. *The Snake Oil Syndrome: Patent Medicine Advertising*. Hanover, MA: Christopher Publishing House.

Birk, Lisa. 2014. *Dead Darlings: Everything Novel*. Blog. 14 May. Online at: http://deaddarlings.com/author/lisa-birk/

Bomey, Nathan. 2016. "FTC Sues Volkswagen Over 'Deceptive' Diesel Claims". *USA Today*, 19 March.

Borio, G. 2001. "Tobacco Timeline". Online at: http://archive.tobacco.org/History/Tobacco_History.html

Boerner, Kathy. 2016. "IKEA Launches Pilot Virtual Reality (VR) Kitchen Experience for HTC Vive on Steam". *IKEA Corporate* News, 4 April. IKEA.com.

Bredin, M., Henderson, S. and Matheson, S.A. 2011. *Canadian Television: Text and Context, Film and Media Studies Series*. Waterloo, ON: Wilfrid Laurier University Press.

Buckingham, D. 2011. *The Material Child: Growing Up in Consumer Culture*. Malden, MA: Polity.

Burgess, J. and Green, J. 2009a. "The Entrepreneurial Vlogger: Participatory Culture Beyond the Professional-Amateur Divide". In *The YouTube Reader*, edited by Pelle Snickars and Patrick Vonderau. Stockholm: National Library of Sweden, 89–107.

Burgess, J. and Green, J. 2009b. *YouTube: Online Video and Participatory Culture*. Malden, MA: Polity Press.

Burns, Sarah. 1996. *Inventing the Modern Artist: Art and Culture in Gilded Age America*. New Haven, CT: Yale University Press.

Callahan, S. 2012. "My Yard, My Candidate: The Social Psychology of Lawn Signs". *The Conversation*, 24 September. Online at: http://theconversation.com/my-yard-my-candidate-the-social-psychology-of-lawn-signs-8976

Campbell, Horace. 2010. *Barack Obama and Twenty-first Century Politics: A Revolutionary Moment in the USA*. New York: Pluto Press.

Carell, Kerry. 2005. IKEA. *Bloomberg Business*, 13 November.

Carnegie, D. 1984. *How to Win Friends & Influence People*, Revised edition. London and Sydney: Angus & Robertson.

Carpenter, C. A. 2010. "The Obamachine: Technopolitics 2.0". *Journal of Information Technology & Politics* 7 (2–3): 216–225.

Celebre, A. and Waggoner-Denton, A. 2014. "The Good, the Bad, and the Ugly of the Dove Campaign for Real Beauty". *The Inquisitive Mind* 2 (19). Online at: http://www.in-mind.org/article/the-good-the-bad-and-the-ugly-of-the-dove-campaign-for-real-beauty

Chemielski, D. 2012. "Studios Draft YouTube Stars to Promote Films". *LA Times*, 22 June. Online at: http://articles.latimes.com/2012/jun/22/business/la-fi-ct-abraham-lincoln-20120623

Clark, Eric. 1988. *The Want Makers: The World of Advertising: How they Make You Buy*. New York: Viking.

Clausager, A.D. 2000. Ivan Hurst Obituary. *The Guardian*, 17 March. Online at: http://www.theguardian.com/news/2000/mar/18/guardianobituaries

Cohen, J. 2010. "Academy Award Nominee James Caan Meets the Annoying Orange". *Tubefilter*, 18 December. Online at: http://www.tubefilter.com/2010/12/18/james-caan-meets-the-annoying-orange/

Cohen, J. 2012a. "The Annoying Orange Advertises Advertising to Advertisers". *Tubefilter*, 11 May. Online at: http://www.tubefilter.com/2012/05/11/annoying-orange-advertising/

Cohen, J. 2012b. "Annoying Orange' TV Premiere Gets 2.6 Million Viewers". *Tubefilter*, 15 June. Online at: http://www.tubefilter.com/2012/06/15/annoying-orange-tv-premiere-viewers/

Collins, Lauren. 2011. "House Perfect: Is the IKEA Ethos Comfy or Creepy?". *New Yorker*, 3 October. Online at: http://www.newyorker.com/magazine/2011/10/03/house-perfect.

Connolly-Ahern, Colleen and Herror, Julio César Herrero. 2006. "Political Advertising in Spain and Portugal". In *The Sage Handbook of Political Advertising*, edited by Lynda Lee Kaid and Christina Holtz-Bacha. Thousand Oaks, CA: Sage, 97–108.

Conrad, Peter and Valerie Leiter 2009. "From Lydia Pinkham to Queen Levitra: Direct-to-Consumer Advertising and Medicalization". In *Pharmaceuticals and Society: Critical Discourses and Debates*, edited by Simon J. Williams, Jonathan Gabe, and Peter Davis. New York: Wiley Blackwell.

Crawford, Elizabeth Crisp. 2014. *Tobacco Goes to College: Cigarette Advertising in Student Media, 1920–1980*. Jefferson, NC: McFarland & Company.

Creamer, M. 2008. "Obama Wins! Ad Age's Marketer of the Year". *Advertising Age*, 17 October. Online at: http://adage.com/article/moy-2008/obama-wins-ad-age-s-marketer-year/131810/

Cremer, Andrea. 2015. "Insight: 'Das Auto' No More: VW Plans Image Offensive". *Reuters*, 15 December.

Cross, Gary. 2013. "Origins of Modern Consumption: Advertising, New Goods, and A New Generation, 1890–1930". In *Routledge Companion to Advertising and Promotional Culture*, edited by Matthew McAllister and Emily West. New York: Routledge, 11–23.

Cummings, M., Brown, A. and Steger, J. 2005. "Youth Marketing". In *Tobacco in History and Culture: An Encyclopedia*, edited by Jordan Goodman. New York: Granite Hill Publishers, 689–693.

Currid-Halkett, E. 2010. *Starstruck: The Business of Celebrity*, 1st edition. New York: Faber and Faber.

Dalecki, L. 2008. "Hollywood Media Synergy as IMC". *Journal of Integrated Marketing Communication*, 47–52.

Dary, David. 2008. *Frontier Medicine: From the Atlantic to the Pacific 1492–1941.* New York: Knopf.

DeBord, G. 1995. *The Society of the Spectacle* [translated by Donald-Nicholson Smith]. New York: Zone Books.

Delany, C. 2013. "The Nuts and Bolts of Obama's Data-Driven Campaign". *Campaigns and Elections*, January–February: 16–17.

Devlin, L.P. 1981. "Reagan's and Carter's Ad Men Review the 1980 Television Campaigns". *Communication Quarterly* 30 (1): 3–12.

Ding, Y., Du, Y., Hu, Y., Liu, Z., Wang, L., Ross, K.M. and Ghose, A. 2011. "Broadcast Yourself: Understanding YouTube Uploaders". *ACM SIGCOMM Internet Measurement Conference* (IMC Digital Library), 361–370.

Dobrow, Larry. 1984. *When Advertising Tried Harder. The Sixties: The Golden Age of American Advertising.* New York: Friendly Press, Inc.

Dyhouse, C. 2010. *Glamour: Women, History, Feminism.* London and New York: Zed Books.

Edgar, M. 2007. "Pro-Age Takes Dove's 'Real Beauty' to Next Level". *Women's Wear Daily*, 12 January.

Edvardson, Bo and Enquist, Bo. 2009. *Values-Based Service for Sustainable Business: Lessons From IKEA.* New York: Routledge.

Elliot, Stuart. 1991. "The Media Business: Advertising; Camel's Success and Controversy". *New York Times*, 12 December. Online at: http://www.nytimes.com/1991/12/12/business/the-media-business-advertising-camel-s-success-and-controversy.html

Elliot, Stuart. 1998. "The Media Business: Advertising; Volkswagen and Arnold Communications Pitch a Beetle with 'More Power' and 'Less Flower'". *New York Times*, 13 March.

Elliot, Stuart. 2012. "IKEA to Unveil Catalog with Interactive Features". *New York Times*, 11 November. Online at: http://mediadecoder.blogs.nytimes.com/2012/11/11/ikea-to-unveil- catalog-with-interactive-features/?_r=0

Ewen, Stuart, and Ewen, Elizabeth. 1988. *All Consuming Images: The Politics of Style in Contemporary Culture.* New York: Basic Books.

Ewen, Stuart, and Ewen Elizabeth. 1992. *Channels of Desire: Mass Images and the Shaping of American Consciousness.* Minneapolis, MN: University of Minnesota Press.

Fyborsdottir, K. 2011. "The Story of Scandinavian Design: Combining Function and Aesthetics". *Smashing Magazine*, 13 June. Online at: http://www.smashingmagazine. com/2011/06/13/the-story-of-scandinavian-design-combining-function-and-aesthetics/

Featherstone, Mike. 1991. *Consumer Culture and Postmodernism*. London: Sage.

Featherstone, Mike. 2007. *Consumer Culture and Postmodernism*, 2nd edition. New York: Sage.

Fielding, Daryl, Lewis, Dennis, White, Mel, Manfredi, Alessandro, and Scott, Linda. 2008. "Dove Campaign Roundtable". *Advertising and Society Review* 9.4. Online at: https://muse-jhu-edu.ezproxy.neu.edu/article/257392

Fischer, P.M., Schwartz, M.P., Richards Jnr, J.W., Goldstein, A.O., and Rojas, T.H. 1991. "Brand Logo Recognition by Children Aged 3 to 6 years. Mickey Mouse and Old Joe the Camel". *Department of Family Medicine*. Online at: http://www. ncbi.nlm.nih.gov/pubmed/1956101

Forbes. 2013. "Roger Federer – Celebrity 100". *Forbes*. Online at: http://www.forbes. com/profile/roger-federer/

Fordyce, T. 2013. "Rory McIlroy, Nike and the 250 million, 10-Year Sponsorship Deal". *BBC Sport*, 14 January. Online at: http://www.bbc.com/sport/0/golf/21018786

Forty, Adrian. 1986. *Objects of Desire: Design and Society Since 1750*. New York: Pantheon Books.

Fowler, G. 2010. "Now Playing on a Computer Near You: A Fruit with an Obnoxious Streak". *Wall Street Journal*, 26 April. Online at: http://online.wsj.com/article/SB1 0001424052748703404004575198410669579950.html

Fox, S. 1997. *The Mirror Makers: A History of American Advertising and Its Creators*. Chicago, IL: University of Chicago Press.

Frank, Thomas. 1998. *The Conquest of Cool: Business Culture, Counterculture, and the Rise of Hip Consumerism*. Chicago, IL: University of Chicago Press.

Friedman, T. 2016. "Trump and the Lord's Work". *New York Times*, 3 May.

Frith, K. and Mueller, B. 2003. *Advertising and Societies: Global Issues*. New York: Peter Lang.

Frith, K.T. and Mueller, B. 2010. *Advertising and Societies: Global issues, Digital Formations*. New York: P. Lang.

Fuchs, Christian. 2008. *Internet and Society: Social Theory in the Information Age*. New York: Routledge.

Fuchs, C. 2011. *Foundations of Critical Media and Information Studies*. New York: Routledge.

Gagnier, Regenia. 2000. *Economics and Aesthetics in a Market Society*. Chicago, IL: University of Chicago Press.

Gardner, M.N. and Brandt, A.M. 2006. "'The Doctors' Choice is America's Choice': The Physician in US Cigarette Advertisements, 1930–1953". *American Journal of Public Health* 96 (2): 222–232.

Garfield, Simon. 2011. *Just My Type: A Book About Fonts*. New York: Gotham Books.

Gauntlett, David. 2015. *Making Media Studies: The Creativity Turn in Media and Communications Studies*. New York: Peter Lang.

Gillette, F. 2013. "The Popularity Issue: Web Series: The Annoying Orange". *Bloomberg Businessweek*. Online at: http://images.businessweek.com/ss/10/08/0812_popularity_index/27.html

Giroux, G. 2012. "Voters Throw Bums in While Holding Congress in Disdain". *Bloomberg News*, 13 December. Online at: http://www.bloomberg.com/news/2012–12-13/voters-throw-bums-in-while-disdaining-congress-bgov-barometer.html

Gobe, Marc. 2001. *Emotional Branding: The New Paradigm for Connecting Brands to People*. New York: Allsworth Press.

Gobe, M. 2007. *Brandjam: Humanizing Brands Through Emotional Design*. New York: Allworth Press.

Goldhaber, Michael 2006. "The Value of Openness in an Attention Economy". *First Monday* 11 (6). Online at: http://firstmonday.org/ojs/index.php/fm/article/view/1334

Goldman, R. 1992. *Reading Ads Socially*. New York: Routledge.

Goldman, R. and Papson, S. 1996. *Sign Wars: The Cluttered Landscape of Advertising*. New York: Guilford Press.

Goldman, R. and Papson, S. 1998. *Nike Culture: The Sign of the Swoosh, Core Cultural Icons*. London: Sage.

Goodrum, Charles and Dalrymple, Helen. 1990. *Advertising in America: The First 200 Years*. New York: Henry N. Abrams.

Graham, J. 2012. " YouTube Hit 'Annoying Orange' Now Set for TV". *Chicago Suntimes*, 12 August. Online at: http://www.suntimes.com/entertainment/television/10224793–421/youtube-hit-annoying-orange-now-set-for-tv.html

Gratton, C., Liu, D., Ramchandani, G. and Wilson, D. 2012. *The Global Economics of Sport*. Milton Park, GA, and Abingdon, Oxon: Routledge.

Gundle, Stephen. 2008. *Glamour: A History*. Oxford and New York: Oxford University Press.

Gunter, Barrie, Oates, Caroline and Blades, Mark. 2005. *Advertising to Children on TV: Content, Impact, and Regulation*. Mahwah, NJ: Lawrence Erlbaum.

Halberstam, D. 2001. *Playing For Keeps: Michael Jordan and the World He Made*. London: Yellow Jersey Press.

Hamilton, A. 2012. "From YouTube to Boob Tube: Dane Boedigheimers's Annoying Orange TV Show Has Kids Hooked". *Time*, 3 December. Online at: http://business.time.com/2012/12/03/youtube-to-boob-tube-dane-boedigheimers-annoying-orange-tv-show-has-kids-hooked/

Hansegard, Jen. 2013. "The Long, Slow Process of IKEA Design". *Wall Street Journal*, 14 October. Online at: http://www.wsj.com/articles/SB10001424052702303376904579134743769761378

Harold, C. 2009. "Pranking Rhetoric: 'Culture-Jamming' as Media Activism". In *The Advertising and Consumer Culture Reader*, edited by Joseph Turow and Matthew P. Mcallister. New York: Routledge, 348–368.

Hartley, J. 2009. "Uses of YouTube: Digital Literacy and the Growth of Knowledge". In *Youtube: Online Video and Participatory Culture*, edited by Jean Burgess and Joshua Green. Malden, MA: Polity Press, 126–143.

Haug, Wolfgang Fritz. 1986. *Critique of Commodity Aesthetics: Appearance, Sexuality, and Advertising in Capitalist Society*. Minneapolis, MN: University of Minnesota Press.

Hautala, Heidi. 2011. "The Glamorous Life of Chanel No. 5 – A Contribution to the Theory of Glamour". Master's Thesis, Department of Journalism, Media and Communication, Stockholm University. Online at: http://www.diva-portal.org/smash/get/diva2:425240/FULLTEXT04

Haynes, A.A. and Rhine, S.L. 1998. "Attack Politics in Presidential Nomination Campaigns: An Examination of the Frequency and Determinants of Intermediated Negative Messages against Opponents". *Political Research Quarterly* 51 (3): 691–721.

Hebdige, D. (1981). "Object as Image: The Italian Scooter Cycle" Reprinted in The Consumer Society Reader, edited by Martyn J. Lee. Oxford: Blackwell, 2000.

Hine, Thomas. 1986. *Populuxe*. New York: Knopf.

Hiott, Andrea. 2012. *Thinking Small: The Long, Strange Trip of the Volkswagen Beetle*. New York: Ballantine Books.

Holtz-Bacha, Christina and Kaid, Lynda Lee. 2006. "Political Advertising in International Comparison". In *The Sage Handbook of Political Advertising*, edited by Lynda Lee Kaid and Christina Holtz-Bacha. Thousand Oaks, CA: Sage, 3–14.

Hotten, Russell. 2015. "Volkswagen: The Scandal Explained". *The Guardian*, 10 December.

Howard, Teresa. 2004. "IKEA Builds Brands on Furnishings Success". *USA Today*, 29 December.

Howard, Vicki. 2006. *Brides, Inc. American Weddings and the Business of Tradition*. Philadelphia, PA: University of Pennsylvania Press.

"How Marketers Target Kids". 2016. *Media Smarts: Canada's Centre for Digital and Media Literacy*. Online at: http://mediasmarts.ca/marketing-consumerism/how-marketers-target-kids

Humphrey, M. 2011. "YouTube PrimeTime: The Collective Explains How a Digital Studio Works". *Forbes.com*, 17 October. Online at: http://www.forbes.com/sites/michaelhumphrey/2012/10/17/youtube-primetime-the-collective-explains-how-a-digital-studio-works/

IKEA. 1999–2012. "The IKEA Way". Online at: http://www.ikea.com/ms/en_GB/about_ikea/the_ikea_way/

IKEA. 2016. "Facts and Figures". Online at: http://www.ikea.com/ms/en_GB/about_ikea/facts_and_figures/facts_figures.html

Interbrand. 2014. "Interbrand Releases 14th Annual Best Global Brands Report", updated 30 September 2013. Online at: http://www.interbrand.com/en/newsroom/press-releases/2013-09-30-d355afc.aspx

Jamieson, K.H. 1996. *Packaging the Presidency: A History and Criticism of Presidential Campaign Advertising*. New York: Oxford University Press.

Jeffers, M. 2005. "Behind Dove's "Real Beauty". *Adweek*, 12 September.

Jenkins, H., Ford, S. and Green, J. 2013. *Spreadable Media: Creating Value and Meaning in a Networked Culture*. New York: New York University Press.

Jessop, A. 2012. "The Final Four and Nike". *The Business of College Sports*, 20 March. Online at: http://businessofcollegesports.com/2012/03/30/the-final-four-and-nike/

Johnstone, Richard. 2011. "Decluttering with IKEA". *Inside Story*, 1 April. Online at: http://insidestory.org.au/decluttering-with-ikea

Johnston, J. and Taylor, J. 2008. "Feminist Consumerism and Fat Activists: A Comparative Study of Grassroots Activism and the Dove Real Beauty Campaign. Signs". *Journal of Women in Culture and Society* 33 (4): 941–966.

Johnson, T. and Perlmutter, D.D. 2011. *New Media, Campaigning and the 2008 Facebook Election*. London and New York: Routledge.

Julin, Suzanne. 2006. "Tobacco and Cigarette Smoking". In *Historical Dictionary of the 1940s*, edited by Ryan, J.G. and Schlup, L.C. Armonk, New York: M.E. Sharpe, 375.

Kable, Greg. 2016. "VW Plans Radical New Electric Vehicle for 2019". *Autocar*. 29 February.

Karpel, A. 2012. "Turning a YouTube Hit into a TV Show: The Annoying Story of a Multi-Platform Orange". *Fast Company*, 4 June. Online at: http://www.fastcocreate.com/1680862/turning-a-youtube-hit-into-a-tv-show-the-annoying-story-of-a-multi-platform-orange

Kakutani, Michiko. 1986. "Books of the Times: Populuxe" [Book Review]. *New York Times*, 29 October. Online at: http://www.nytimes.com/1986/10/29/books/books-of-the-times-547986.html

Keller, Alexandra. 1995. "Disseminations of Modernity: Representation and Consumer Desire in Early Mail Order Catalogs". In *Cinema and the Invention of Modern Life*, edited by Leo Charney and Vanessa Schwartz. Berkeley, CA: University of California Press.

Kellogg Co. 2016. "An Historical Overview". Online at: http://www.kellogghistory.com/history.html

Klein, N. 2000. *No Logo: Taking Aim at the Brand Bullies*. London: Flamingo.

Klingman, Anna. 2007. *Brandscapes: Architecture in the Experience Economy*. Cambridge, MA: MIT Press.

Komprad, Ingmar. 1976–2013. *Testament of a Furniture Dealer*. Online at: http://www.ikea.com/ms/en_AU/pdf/reports-downloads/the-testament-of-a-furniture-dealer.pdf

Kremer, William. 2012. "James Buchanan Duke: Father of the Modern Cigarette". *BBC News Magazine*. Online at: http://www.bbc.com/news/magazine-20042217

Kristofferson, Sara. 2014. *Design by Ikea: A Cultural History*. London: Bloomsbury Academic.

Laermans, Rudi. 1993. "Learning to Consume: Early Department Stores and the Shaping of the Modern Consumer Culture (1860–1914)". *Theory, Culture and Society*, 10: 79–102.

Laird, Pamela Walker. 1998. *Advertising Progress: American Business and the Rise of Consumer Marketing*. Baltimore, MD: John Hopkins University Press.

Lange, P.G. 2009. "Videos of Affinity on YouTube". In *The YouTube Reader*, edited by Pelle Snickars and Patrick Vonderau. Stockholm: National Library of Sweden, 70–88.

Larrabee, D. 2013. "Beyonce Releasing New Fragrance 'RISE' In February 2014". *Hollywood Life*. Online at: http://hollywoodlife.com/2013/12/20/beyonce-rise-new-perfume-february-2014-fragrance-announcement/

Lasn, K. 1999. *Culture Jam: How to Reverse America's Suicidal Consumer Binge – And Why We Must*. New York: Harper Collins.

Lawrence, F. 2010. "Drop that Spoon! The Truth about Breakfast Cereals". *The Guardian*, 23 November. Online at: http://www.theguardian.com/business/2010/nov/23/food-book-extract-felicity-lawrence

Lazzarato, M. 1997. *Lavoro Immateriale*. Verona: Ombre Corte.

Leach, William R. 1993. *Land of Desire: Merchants, Power, and the Rise of a New American Culture*. New York: Vintage Books.

Lears, T. J. Jackson. 1981. *No Place of Grace: Anti-Modernism and the Transformation of American Culture, 1880–1920*. Chicago, IL: University of Chicago Press.

Lears, T.J. Jackson. 1983. "From Salvation to Self-Realization: Advertising and the Therapeutic Roots of Consumer Culture, 1880–1930". In *The Culture of Consumption: Critical Essays in American History 1880–1980*, edited by Richard Wightman Fox and T. J. Jackson Lears. New York: Pantheon, 3–38.

Lears, T.J. Jackson. 1994. *Fables of Abundance: A Cultural History of Advertising in America*. New York: Basic Books.

Lee, N. 2001. *Childhood and Society: Growing Up in the Age of Uncertainty*. Buckingham: Open University Press.

Leiss, W., Kline, S. Jhally,. 1990. *Social Communication in Advertising: Consumption in the Marketplace*, 2nd edition. New York: Routledge.

Leiss, W., Kline, S., Jhally, S. and Botterill, J. 2005. *Social Communication in Advertising: Consumption in the Marketplace*, 3rd edition. New York: Routledge.

Levine, D.M. 2012. "The Surprising Rise of 'Annoying Orange:' How The Collective Brings Internet Stars to TV". *Adweek*, 27 January. Online at: http://www.adweek.com/topic/annoying-orange

Liljenwall, R. (ed.). 2004. *The Power of Point of Purchase Advertising: Marketing at Retail*. Washington, DC: Point-of-Purchase Advertising International.

Lindqvist, Ursula. 2009. "The Cultural Archive of the IKEA Store". *Space and Culture* 12 (1): 43–62.

Lipovetsky, Gilles, 1994. *The Empire of Fashion: Dressing Modern Democracy* [translated by L. Porter]. Princeton, NJ: Princeton University Press.

Lipsitz, George. 2001. *Time Passages: Collective Memory and American Popular Culture*. Minneapolis, MN: University of Minnesota Press.

Lum, K.L, Polansky, J.R., Jackler, R.K. and Glantz, S.A. 2008. "Signed, Sealed and Delivered: Big Tobacco in Hollywood: 1927–51". *Tobacco Control* 17: 313–323.

Mack, J. 1992. *Without Walls: Heil Herbie* [Documentary film].

Marchand, Roland. 1985. *Advertising the American Dream: Making Way for Modernity 1920–1940*. Berkeley, CA: University of California Press.

Marcial, Gene. 2014 "Quietly, Nike Is Winning From Global Hoopla Over Fiery World Cup Games". *Forbes*, 1 July. Online: http://www.forbes.com/sites/genemarcial/2014/07/01/quietly-nike-is-winning-from-global-hoopla-over-fiery-world-cup-games/

Marshall, P. David. 2014. "Persona Studies: Mapping the Proliferation of the Public Self". *Journalism* 15 (2): 153–170.

Marshall, P. David. 2002. "The New Intertextual Commodity". In *The New Media Book*, edited by Dan Harries. London: British Film Institute, 69–82.

Marshall, P. David. 2014 (1997). *Celebrity and Power: Fame in Contemporary Culture*, 2nd edition. Minneapolis, MN: University of Minnesota Press.

Marshall, P. David 2016. "Exposure". In *Companion to Celebrity Studies*, edited by P. David Marshall and Sean Redmond. Boston, MA: Wiley, 497–517.

Martineau, Pierre. 1957. *Motivation in Advertising: Motives that Make People Buy*. New York: McGraw Hill.

McGee, M. 2005. *Self-Help, Inc.: Makeover Culture in American Life*. Oxford and New York: Oxford University Press.

McNamara, Kim. 2015. *Paparazzi: Media Practices and Celebrity Culture*. Cambridge, UK and Malden, MA: Polity Press.

McKendrick, Neil, Brewer, John and Plumb, J.H. 1982. *The Birth of a Consumer Society: The Commercialization of Eighteenth Century England*. Bloomington, IN: Indiana University Press.

Mekemson, C. and Glantz, S.A. 2002. "How the Tobacco Industry Built its Relationship with Hollywood". *Tobacco Control* 11 (1): i81–i91. Online at: http://tobaccocontrol.bmj.com/content/11/suppl_1/i81

Merrick, A. 2014. "Marketing 'Real' Bodies". *New Yorker*, 1 April. Online at: http://www.newyorker.com/business/currency/marketing-real-bodies

Michman, Ronald D., EMazze, Edward M. and Greco, Alan James. 2003. *Lifestyle Marketing: Reaching the New American Consumer*. Westport, CT: Greenwood Publishing Group.

Merrin, William 2014. *Media Studies 2.0*. New York: Routledge.

Moltoch, Harvey. 2005. *Where Stuff Comes From: How Toasters, Toilets, Cars, Computers, and Many Other Things Came to Be As They Are*. New York: Routledge.

Moor, L. 2007. *The Rise of Brands*. Oxford and New York: Berg.

Morozov, Evgeny. 2014. "Making It: Pick Up a Spot Welder and Join the Revolution". *New Yorker*, 13 January. Online at: http://www.newyorker.com/magazine/2014/01/13/making-it-2

Moyer, J. 2015. "Starbucks Moves Ethos Water from California after Droughtshaming". *The Washington Post*, 12 May. Online at: https://www.washingtonpost.com/news/morning-mix/wp/2015/05/12/starbucks-moves-ethos-water-from-california-after-droughtshaming/

Moynihan, Ray and Cassels, Allan 2005. "A Disease for Every Pill". *Nation*, 29 September. Online at: http://www.thenation.com/article/disease-every-pill

Mukerji, C. 1983. *From Graven Images: Patterns of Modern Materialism*. New York: Columbia University Press. Cited in Roberta Sassatelli. 2007. *Consumer Culture: History, Theory, and Politics*. New York: Sage.

Murray, D.P. 2013. "Branding 'Real' Social Change in Dove Campaign for Real Beauty". *Feminist Media Studies* 13 (1): 83–101.

Museum of Moving Images. 2012. "The Living Room Candidate: Presidential Campaign Commercials, 1952–2012". Online at: http://www.livingroomcandidate.org/commercials/1952/never-had-it-so-good

Myers, Kathy. 1986. *Understains: The Sense and Seduction of Advertising*. London: Comedia.

Neff, J. (2009) "Method Pulls 'Shiny Suds' Commercial After Sexism Complaints". *Advertising Age*, 2 December.

Newell, J., Salmon, C.T. and Chang, S. 2006. "The Hidden History of Product Placement". *Journal of Broadcasting and Electronic Media*, 575–594.

Nike. 2013. *Annual Report 2013*. Online at: http://s1.q4cdn.com/806093406/files/doc_financials/2013/docs/nike-2013-form-10K.pdf

Nike. 2014. *Annual Report 2014*. Online at: http://s1.q4cdn.com/806093406/files/doc_financials/2014/docs/nike-2014-form-10K.pdf

Ogilvy, D. 1963. *Confessions of an Advertising Man*. London: Southbank Publications.

Palahniuk, Chuck. 1996. *Fight Club*. New York: Norton.

Pardee, T. 2010. "Media-Savvy Gen Y Finds Smart and Funny is New 'Rock N' Roll". *Advertising Age*, 11 October. Online at: http://adage.com/article/news/marketing-media-savvy-gen-y-transparency-authenticity/146388/

Patterson, T. 2015. "Who Gets to Wear Shredded Jeans?". *New York Times*, 25 April. Online at: http://www.nytimes.com/2015/05/03/magazine/who-gets-to-wear-shredded-jeans.html?_r=0

Patton. P. 2002. *Bug: The Strange Mutations of the World's Most Famous Automobile*. Cambridge, MA: Da Capo Press. Kindle AZW file.

Penn, Alan. 2011. "Who Enjoys Shopping in IKEA". *YouTube*, 18 January. Online at: https://www.youtube.com/watch?v=NkePRXxH9D4

Phillips, N. 2012. "How was 91 percent of Congress Re-elected Despite a 10 percent Approval Rating?". *Huffington Post*, 13 November. Online at: http://www.huffingtonpost.com/todd-phillips/congress-election-results_b_2114947.html.

Pike, A. 2011. *Brands and Branding Geographies*. Cheltenham: Edward Elgar.

Presbey, Frank. 1929. *History and Development of Advertising*. New York: Doubleday, Doran and Co.

Ragas, M. and Kiousis, S. 2011. "Intermedia Agenda-Setting and Political Activism: MoveOn.org and the 2008 Presidential Election". In *New Media Campaigning and the 2008 Facebook Election*, edited by David D. Perlmutter and Thomas Johnson. New York: Routledge, 18–36.

Rantanen, T. 2006. *The Media and Globalization*. London: Sage.

Rieger, Peter. 2013. *The People's Car: A Global History of the Volkswagen Beetle.* Cambridge, MA: Harvard University Press.

Ries, Al. 2009. "Advertising Could Do with Bernbach's Genius". *Advertising Age*, 6 July.

Ritzer, G. and Jurgenson, N. 2010. "Production, Consumption, Prosumption: The Nature of Capitalism in the Age of the Digital Prosumer". *Journal of Consumer Culture* 10 (1): 13–36.

Rojek, C. 2001. *Celebrity.* London: Reaktion.

Rosenberg, Chaim M. 2007. *Goods for Sale: Products and Advertising in the Massachusetts Industrial Age.* Amherst and Boston, MA: University Press.

Rospars, J. 2014. "How Howard Dean's Scream Helped Obama Land the Presidency". *Time*, 1 July. Online at: http://time.com/2946448/howard-dean-scream-obama-president/

Ross, M. 2014. "Facebook Turns 10: The World's Largest Social Network in Numbers". *ABC News*, 4 February. Online at: http://www.abc.net.au/news/2014–02-04/facebook-turns-10-the-social-network-in-numbers/5237128

Ruskin, G. and J. Schor. 2009. "Every Nook and Cranny: The Dangerous Spread of Commercialized Culture". In *The Advertising and Consumer Culture Reader*, edited by Joseph Turow and Matthew P. McAllister. New York: Routledge.

Rutenberg, J. 2008. "Nearing Record, Obama's Ad Effort Swamps McCain". *New York Times*, 17 October.

Salvato, N. 2009. "Out of Hand: YouTube Amateurs and Professionals". *TDR: The Drama Review*, Fall: 67–83.

Samuel, Lawrence. 2012. "Thinking Smaller: Bill Bernbach and the Creative Revolution in Advertising of the 1950s". *Advertising and Society Review* 13 (3). Online at: https://muse-jhu-edu.ezproxy.neu.edu/article/491080

Scammell, Margaret and Langer, Ana Ines. 2006. "Political Advertising in the United Kingdom". In *The Sage Handbook of Political Advertising*, edited by Lynda Lee Kaid and Christina Holtz-Bacha. Thousand Oaks, CA: Sage, 65–82.

Schifferes, S. 2008. "Obama Rules the TV Ad Airwaves". *BBC News*, 29 October. Online at: http://news.bbc.co.uk/2/hi/americas/us_elections_2008/7694856.stm

Schor, J. 2004. *Born to Buy: The Commercialized Child and the New Consumer Culture.* New York: Scribner.

Schudson, Michael. 1984. *Advertising: The Uneasy Persuasion: Its Dubious Impact on American Society.* New York: Basic Books.

Schultz, E.J. 2016. "FTC Charges Volkswagen with Deceptive Advertising". *Advertising Age*, 29 March.

Schwartz, Tony. 1974. *The Responsive Chord.* Garden City and New York: Anchor Books, Anchor Press/Doubleday.

Scott, J. 2005. "The Beauty Myth". *Research*, 1 July. Online at: http://www.research-live.com/features/the-beauty-myth/2001483.articl

Sennett, Richard. 1976. *The Fall of Public Man.* New York: W.W. Norton.

Serazio, M. 2013. *Your Ad Here: The Cool Sell of Guerilla Marketing*. New York: University Press.

Sexton, T. 2008. "Clutch Cargo: The Cartoon Designed Specifically to Ignite Nightmares". *Yahoo Associated Content*, 13 August. Online at: http://voices.yahoo.com/clutch-cargo-cartoon-designed-specifically-to-1769141.html

Sharkey, Tina. 2012. "What's Your Tribe? Tap into Your Core Consumer's Aspirations Like Nike, Gatorade, BabyCenter and REI Do". *Forbes*, 25 January.

Sivulka, Juliann. 1998. *Soap, Sex, and Cigarettes: A Cultural History of American Advertising*. New York: Wadsworth.

Slutsky, Irina. 2010. "Meet YouTube's Most in Demand Brand Stars". *Advertising Age*, 13 September. Online at: http://adage.com/article/digital/meet-youtube-s-demand-brand-stars/145844/

Smart, Barry. 2005. *The Sport Star: Modern Sport and the Cultural Economy of Sporting Celebrity, Theory, Culture & Society*. London: Sage Publications.

Smythe, D. 1977. "Communications: Blindspot of Western Marxism". *Canadian Journal of Political and Social Theory* 1 (3): 1–28.

Spangler, Todd. 2016. "Collective Digital Studio Changes Name to Studio71". *Variety*, 27 January.

Sparke, Penny. 2013. *An Introduction to Design and Culture 1900 to the Present*. New York: Routledge.

Springer, P. 2009. *Ads to Icons: How Advertising Succeeds in a Multimedia Age*, 2nd edition. Philadelphia, PA: Kogan Publishing.

Stage, Sarah. 1979. *Female Complaints: Lydia Pinkham and the Business of Women's Medicine*. New York: Norton.

Stampler, L. 2013. "Why People Hate Dove's 'Real Beauty Sketches' Video". *Business Insider*, 22 April.

Starr, Paul. 1982. *The Social Transformation of American Medicine*. New York: Basic Books.

Stecklow, S. 2010. "On the Web, Children Face Intensive Tracking". *Wall Street Journal*, 17 September. Online at: http://online.wsj.com/article/SB10001424052748703904304575497903523187146.html

Stenbo, John. 2009. *The Truth About Ikea: The Secret Behind the Words. Fifth Richest Man and the Success of the Swedish Flatpack Giant*. Ondon: Gibson Square Books.

Stelter, B. 2008. "The Facebooker Who Friended Obama". *New York Times*, 7 July. Online at: http://www.nytimes.com/2008/07/07/technology/07hughes.html?pagewanted=all&_r=0

Stewart, Julianne. 2006. "Political Advertising in Australia and New Zealand". In *The Sage Handbook of Political Advertising*, edited by Lynda Lee Kaid, and Christina Holtz-Bacha. Thousand Oaks, CA: Sage, 269–284.

Story, M. and French, S. 2004. "Food Advertising and Marketing Directed at Children and Adolescents in the US". *International Journal of Behavioural Nutrition and Physical Activity*, 1–3.

Strasser, S. 2009. "The Alien Past: Consumer Culture in Historical Perspective". In *The Advertising and Consumer Culture Reader*, edited by Joseph Turow and Matthew P. MacAllister. New York: Routledge, 25–37. Reprinted from Strasser, S. 2003. "The Alien Past: Consumer Culture in Historical Perspective". *Journal of Consumer Policy* 26 (4), 375–393.

Sturken, M. and Cartwright, L. 2001. *Practices of Looking: An Introduction to Visual Culture*. Oxford: Oxford University Press.

Sutherland, A. and Thompson, B. 2001. *Kidfluence: Why Kids Today Mean Business*. Toronto: McGraw-Hill Ryerson.

Sweeney, M. 2009. "Barack Obama Campaign Claims Two Top Prizes at Cannes Lion Ad Awards". *The Guardian*, 29 June.

Tate, Cassandra. 1999. *Cigarette Wars: The Triumph of "The Little White Slaver"*. New York: Oxford University Press.

Tedlow, Richard S. 1996. *New and Improved: The Story of Mass Marketing in America*. Boston, MA: Harvard Business School Press.

Terrace, V. 2004. *The Television Crime Fighters Factbook: Over 9,800 Details from 301 Programs from 1937–2003*. Jefferson, NC: McFarland & Company.

Terranova, T. 2004. *Network Culture: Politics for the Information Age*. London: Pluto.

The Center for Responsive Politics. 2009. "Barack Obama (D): Donor Demographics, 2008 Cycle". *Opensecrets.org*. Online at: http://www.opensecrets.org/pres08/donordemCID.php?cycle=2008&cid=n00009638)

The Center for Responsive Politics. 2013. "2012 Presidential Race". *Opensecrets.org*. Online at: https://www.opensecrets.org/pres12

Thomson, P. 2005. "Celebrity and Rivalry: David [Garrick] and Goliath (Quin)". In *Theatre and Celebrity in Britain, 1660–2000*, edited by Mary Luckhurst and Jane Moody. New York: Palgrave Macmillan, 127–147.

Thrift, N. 2010. "Understanding the Material Practices of Glamour". In *The Affect Theory Reader*, edited by Melissa Gregg and Gregory J. Siegworth. Durham, NC: Duke University Press, 289–308.

Toland Frith, K. and Mueller, B. 2010. *Advertising and Societies: Global Issues*, 2nd edition. New York: Peter Lang.

Tomalin, E. 2013. "Dove Real Beauty Sketches Becomes the Most Views Online Video Ad of All Time". *Unruly Media*. Online at: http://unruly.co/news/article/2013/05/20/dove-real-beauty-sketches-becomes-viewed-online-video-ad-time/

Topher. 2015. "Topher's Breakfast Cereal Character Guide". Online at: http://www.lavasurfer.com/cereal-kelloggs.html

Touré, M. 2015. "Top Ad Campaigns of the 21st Century: 1. Dove: Campaign for Real Beauty". *Advertising Age*, 12 January: 16–17.

Trentman, Frank. 2016. *Empire of Things: How We Became a World of Consumers, from the Fifteenth Century to the Twenty-first*. London: Allen Lane.

Turner, Graeme 2015. *Reinventing the Media*. London: Routledge.

Turner, W.S. 1965. *The Shocking History of Advertising*. New York: Penguin Books.

Turow, J. 2011. *The Daily You: How the New Advertising Industry is Defining Your Identity and Your Worth*. New Haven, CT: Yale University Press.

Twitchell, James B. 2000. *Twenty Ads that Shook the World*. New York: Three Rivers Press.

Twitchell, James B. 2009. "Reflections and Reviews: An English Teacher Looks at Branding". In *The Consumer Culture Reader*, edited by Joseph Turow and Matthew P. McAllister. New York: Routledge.

van Dijck, J. 2013. *The Culture of Connectivity: A Critical History of Social Media*. New York: Oxford University Press.

Veblen, Thorstein. 1970. *The Theory of the Leisure Class: An Economic Study of Institutions* [Reprinted]. London: Allen and Unwin.

Wagner, K.M. and Gainous, J. 2009. "Electronic Grassroots: Does Online Campaigning Work?" *The Journal of Legislative Studies* 15 (4): 502–520.

Warner, J. 2007. "Political Culture Jamming: The Dissident Humor of The Daily Show with Jon Stewart". *Popular Communication*, 17–36.

Wasko, J. 2009. "The Political Economy of YouTube". In *The YouTube Reader*, edited by Pelle Snickars and Patrick Vonderau. Stockholm: National Library of Sweden, 372–386.

Wayne, Leslie. 1985. "How a Popular Beer Fell Out of Favor". *New York Times*, 3 March 3s.

Webley, K. 2010. "A Brief History of the Happy Meal". *Time*, 30 April. Online at: http://content.time.com/time/nation/article/0,8599,1986073,00.html

West, S. 2005. "Siddons, Celebrity and Regality: Portraiture and the Body of the Ageing Actress". In *Theatre and Celebrity in Britain, 1660–2000*, edited by Mary Luckhurst and Jane Moody. New York: Palgrave Macmillan, 191–213.

WGBH. 2012. "Tupperware! Plastics and American Culture after World War II". *PBS: American Experience*. Online at: http://www.pbs.org/wgbh/americanexperience/features/general-article/tupperware-plastics/?flavour=mobile

Whitaker, Jan. 2006. *Service and Style: How the American Department Store Fashioned the Middle Class*. New York: St. Martin's Press.

Williams, R. 1980. "Advertising: The Magic System". In *Problems in Materialism and Culture*. London: Verso, 170–195.

Williamson, Judith. 1978. *Decoding Advertisements: Ideology and Meaning in Advertising, Ideas in Progress*. London: Boyars.

Wipperfurth, A. 2005. *Brand Hijack: Marketing Without Marketing*. New York: Portfolio Trade.

Wischhover, C. 2013. "10 New Designer Perfumes and Their Runway Doppelgangers". *Fashionista*. Online at: http://fashionista.com/2013/04/10-new-designer-perfumes-and-their-runway-doppelgangers/odlr-5/

Wolfe, C. 1991. "The Return of Jimmy Stewart: The Publicity Photograph as Text". In *Stardom: Industry of Desire*, edited by Christine Gledhill. London and New York: Routledge, 92–106.

Woodham, Jonathan. 1999. *Twentieth-Century Design*. Oxford: Oxford University Press.

World History Project. n.d. "Kellogg's Offers First Cereal Premium Prize". Online at: https://worldhistoryproject.org/1910/kelloggs-offers-first-cereal-premium-prize

Wrigley, Neil and Michelle Lowe. 2002. *Reading Retail: A Geographical Perspective on Retailing and Consumption Spaces*. London: Harper Press.

Yohn, Denise Lee. 2015. "How IKEA Designs Its Brand Success". *Forbes*, 10 June. Online at: http://www.forbes.com/sites/deniselyohn/2015/06/10/how-ikea-designs-its-brand-success/

Young, J.H. 1960. "Patent Medicines: An Early Example of Competitive Marketing". *Journal of Economic Medicine* 20 (4): 648–656.

Young, James Harvey. 1961. *The Toadstool Millionaires: A History of Patent Medicines in America Before Federal Regulation*. Princeton, NJ: Princeton University Press.

Young, R. 2006. "Profile of a Marketing Champion: Unilever's Sylvia Lagnado". *Marketing Profs*, 31 October. Online at: http://www.marketingprofs.com/6/young35.asp

Zwick, D., Bonsu, S. and Darmody, A. 2008. "Putting Consumers to Work: Co-Creation and New Marketing Govern-Mentality". *Journal of Consumer Culture* 8(2): 163–196.

Index

Printed by Printforce, the Netherlands